Critical Resistance

From Poststructuralism
to Post-Critique

David Couzens Hoy

The MIT Press
Cambridge, Massachusetts
London, England

First MIT Press paperback edition, 2005

© 2004 Massachusetts Institute of Technology

MIT Press books may be purchased at special quantity discounts for business or sales promotional use. For information, please email <special_sales@mitpress.mit.edu> or write to Special Sales Department, The MIT Press, 55 Hayward Street, Cambridge, MA 02142.

Set in Palatino by Binghamton Valley Composition. Printed and bound in the United States of America.

Library of Congress Cataloging-in-Publication Data

Hoy, David Couzens.
Critical resistance : from poststructuralism to post-critique / David Couzens Hoy.
p. cm.
Includes bibliographical references and index.
ISBN-13: 978-0-262-08330-0 (hc. : alk. paper) — 978-0-262-58263-6 (pbk. : alk. paper)
ISBN-10: 0-262-08330-2 (hc. : alk. paper) — 0-262-58263-5 (pbk. : alk. paper)
1. Critical theory. 2. Opposition, Theory of. I. Title.

HM585.H698 2004
301'.01—dc22   2003060177

10 9 8 7 6 5 4

for Jocelyn, my most irresistible critic

Contents

Acknowledgments ix

Introduction   1
Resistance and Freedom   1
Why "Resistance" Now?   6
The Plan of the Book   12

1 Nietzsche: "Who Interprets?"   19
Deleuze: The Beginnings of Poststructuralism   21
The Poststructuralist Nietzsche   31
Pluralism and the Possibility of Critique   41
The Body as Multiple Interpretations   46
Post-Critique: Different Stories   53

2 Foucault: "Essays in Refusal"   57
The Body as Resistance   59
Normalization   64
The Historicity of Ethics   69
The Life-and-Death Struggle in Bio-Power   72
Foucault's Social Ontology of Resistance   81
Critique as Desubjectivation   87
Post-Critique: Judith Butler   93

3 **Bourdieu: "Agents, Not Subjects"   101**
   Merleau-Ponty's Phenomenology   102
   Bourdieu: Habitus and Field   105
   Agents vs. Subjects   114
   Bourdieu vs. Derrida   123
   Bourdieu's Social Ontology of Resistance   131
   Post-Critique: Philosophy and Race   139

4 **Levinas and Derrida: "Ethical Resistance"   149**
   Levinas: Intersubjectivity and the Face   149
   Levinas: "Guiltless Responsibility"   159
   Derrida and the Deconstruction of 'Death'   163
   Heidegger on Being-toward-Death   168
   Levinas's Critique of Heidegger   171
   Derrida's Rejoinders   173
   Ethics without Foundations?   178
   Post-Critique: Derrida and the Messianic   185

5 **Post-Marxism: "Who Is Speaking?"   191**
   Resisting "False Consciousness"   191
   Critical Theory   197
   Hegemony Theory: Laclau and Mouffe   201
   Critical Debates   205
   Deconstructing the Future   207
   Post-Critique: Slavoj Žižek   214

   Postscript: On Deconstructive Genealogy   227
   The Limits of Pluralism   231
   Why It Matters   234

   Notes   241
   Bibliography   257
   Index   263

Acknowledgments

Although this book is produced with the present waves of resistance in mind, I have been thinking about these issues for a long time. Bits and pieces of the material here are revised from earlier publications. In particular, portions of lectures that I gave at an NEH Summer Institute appeared as "Critical Resistance: Foucault and Bourdieu" in a Routledge volume edited by Honi Haber and Gail Weiss, *Perspectives on Embodiment: The Intersections of Nature and Culture* (1999). Other ideas were explored in *Philosophy and Literature* (volume 18) and in *New York Literary Forum* (volume 8/9).

I received generous support from the National Endowment for the Humanities and from the University of California at Santa Cruz. The students in my graduate seminar in the winter of 2002 helped me to think through the material. Most of all, Jocelyn and Meredith Hoy have been invaluable interlocutors during the writing of this book, and I appreciate their support, patience, and critical resistance.

Critical Resistance

Introduction

Resistance and Freedom

"How is freedom measured in individuals and peoples?" asks Friedrich Nietzsche. "According to the resistance which must be overcome," he answers, "according to the exertion required, to remain on top."[1] Resistance and freedom on this view are linked both conceptually and practically. To the extent that attempts to build freedom into the social structure miscarry, resistance will arise. The motivation for resistance comes from encountering constraints on freedom. These constraints cannot be absolute, however, and resistance would not be possible unless some degree of freedom remained.

Nietzsche's pithy analysis may provide an answer to the question of what freedom is by showing the conceptual linkage of freedom and resistance. But then the question becomes "What is resistance?" While this question is not a canonical one in the Anglophone tradition, resistance has been a central theme in the political and social theory of a group of French philosophers whose work became influential during the political disturbances of the 1960s and the 1970s. North Americans were quick to label these philosophers 'poststructuralists'—a word that, for reasons that will become apparent, is problematic and finally inadequate in the present-day context. This book is intended as a historical and topical guide through the different ways in which these French philosophers have asked about what resistance is and how it is possible. Nietzsche's deceptively clear answer to these questions will in the end prove to be cogent; however, before his answer can be seen as a prefiguration of poststructuralism, the history of Nietzsche's influence on and reception by Gilles Deleuze, Michel Foucault, and Jacques Derrida must be explained. Note, for instance, that resistance as Nietzsche understands it can go in two directions. The resistance can be to domination, and in the name of emancipation. But it can also be domination's resistance to emancipatory efforts. In the quotation above, Nietzsche uses 'resistance' to refer to the opposition that emancipation meets. In this book, in contrast, I will be using 'resistance' in the sense that is heard most often in connection with poststructural social theory: as the emancipatory resistance to domination. The word 'resistance' does not of itself distinguish between emancipation and domination. That is why I speak of *critical* resistance. Critique is what makes it possible to distinguish emancipatory resistance from resistance that has been co-opted by the oppressive forces.

The critical dimension of poststructuralism is achieved by using the technique that Nietzsche calls *genealogy*. Inherited from Hume,[2] Nietzsche's genealogical analyses are critical in that they identify resistance and analyze the background practices that lead to it. Genealogy is also critical insofar as it suspects that consciousness's sense of freedom hides deeper motivations that call this sense of freedom into question. What seems like freedom at the level of self-consciousness may in effect be a self-denial that grows out of *ressentiment*, a resentment of oneself that arises because one is not powerful enough, and thus not free enough, to generate one's own values. Genealogy does not deny that there is a level of conscious agency, but it doubts the efficacy and autonomy that self-consciousness attributes to itself. For instance, for Nietzsche early Christianity may think of itself as founded on love for the other, whereas genealogy sees it as growing out of weakness and hate, to the point where it turns on itself in ascetic self-abnegation.

Resistance to power and domination may thus be more complex than it appears on the surface. The social features that are being resisted may produce the shape that resistance takes. Two examples suggested by the political theorist Wendy Brown are workers who dream of a world without work and teenagers who long for a world without parents. These initial imaginings of freedom still presuppose and may even be constrained by the social categories and social identities ("workers," "teenagers") they are trying to resist.[3] Thus, the teenager who imagines a world without parents is in fact still presupposing the subject identity "teenager," and therefore the same social organization that is resented. The general point is that utopian imaginings of freedom may not be aware of the extent to which they presuppose the patterns of oppression that they are resisting. This is not to say that resistance is inevitably ineffectual or hopeless, but it does suggest that resistance is contextually bound to the social and psychological structures that are being resisted. Indeed, drawing a distinction between resistance and compliance would not be possible outside of a given power regime. The particular social structure provides the grid of intelligibility for making sense of the actions as conforming to or dissenting from the given power configuration.

Of course, resistance may try to legitimate itself by appeal to context-transcendent or even to context-independent principles. Abstract universals by themselves, however, do not explain how the situation gives rise to resistance, and they do not address such questions as how the identities (e.g., "worker" or "teenager") that are being resisted were produced in the first place. Abstract principles tend to assume that power can always be distinguished from freedom, and that it makes sense to think of a world of freedom without power. In contrast, from the genealogical perspective domination and resistance are intimately related to each other. The perception of social constraints is itself produced by social constraints, and thus is just as likely to perpetuate these constraints as to escape them.

It is not an accident, therefore, that the theorists I will be examining are not primarily concerned with the specification of universal principles or with the articulation of a theory of justice in the abstract. They are interested in the concrete background from which resistance grows, but they do not necessarily reject universal principles. Nevertheless, the grounds for debate are beginning to be clear. From the poststructural perspective, whatever the theory's aspirations for universality are, principles gain such universality through abstraction and therefore by themselves may seem too thin to be applied concretely. In criticizing the limitations of abstract principles, poststructuralism need not be read as making a complete break with the philosophical tradition. Instead, it can be seen as connecting to a different branch of the tradition, one that is less impressed by the emphasis on formal principles in Plato and Kant than by the focus on concrete phronesis or practical knowledge in Aristotle and Vico.[4] Resistance makes more sense for an approach that starts from the concrete universality of an actual social group than for one that starts from the abstract universality of formal principles as determined through a thought experiment. Plato's imaginary Republic, Kant's Kingdom of Ends, Rawls's veil of ignorance, and Habermas's ideal speech situation are examples of the rationalist approach. Poststructuralism prefers a genealogical critique that wrestles with the emancipatory potential of the concrete social situation.

In contrast, from the perspective of rationalist theorists who aspire either to global accounts of the end of history or to abstract, universal principles for any and every society, resistance will seem to be too limited a notion. If resistance is itself an effect of the social structure it deplores, these theorists infer, it then lacks the normative content that will guide political action. Such theorists want to know "in the name of what" resistance is justified. Without such a transcendent principle, they fear that practical resistance would degenerate into directionless flailing and childish whining. Not all resistance will strike everyone as justified or emancipatory, so some will feel that more needs to be said about how to distinguish resistance that is emancipatory from other forms, such as resistance that is reactionary. Even those who are sympathetic to poststructuralism may worry that to equate resistance with what is progressive and good is to buy into the standard way of thinking of power as bad and freedom as good, when this dichotomy is part of what is in question.

Hesitations about the normative usefulness of the notion of resistance arise, in short, if resistance is simply reactive. In reacting to domination, resistance may appear to be the act of taking a purely negative position against something, without any substantive vision of what it is for. Resistance can take place without a particular political program, and it may deny or ignore its own desire for power. Those who are disappointed with resistance as a political activity may feel that, insofar as it is strictly reactive, it lacks a positive vision of what is to be achieved by social change. They feel that resistance stands against, not for. To put the point in Nietzschean language, they fear that resistance knows only how to say "no," not how to say "yes" to a different view of society that would change the status quo.

The challenge in this book is to see whether the various theorists can explain *critical* resistance, and whether their accounts point toward the possibility of resistance that is not merely reactive. The theories and the phenomena that I address here are not infantile outbursts or unthinking reactions. To be critical, resistance must be able to identify its injuries and to articulate its grievances. At the same time, critique that does not lead to engagement in resistant practices seems pointless. To echo Kant, the guiding idea of this book is that critique without resistance is empty and resistance without critique is blind.

Why "Resistance" Now?

Why write a book on resistance at this particular moment? Let me give some examples to show the current need for thinking about resistance in its various dimensions. These examples involve political, social, and ethical resistance. On the overtly political scale, the desire to articulate the nature and possibility of resistance is increasing with the growing dissension nationally and internationally over the policies of the United States in the Middle East and in Asia. There is also the international resistance to the phenomenon known as globalization. Insofar as the globalization is perceived as the expansion of American interests, it is stirring up fears of exploitation and feelings of resentment among less well off people and nations. These resistance movements call for a better understanding of how resistance is possible.

From a more theoretical standpoint, the collapse of the Berlin Wall and the dissolution of the Soviet Union have also led to a need to rethink the rhetoric of resistance. With doubts about a philosophy of universal history and its rhetoric of total revolution, ideas such as social class, class struggle, classless society, class consciousness, and ideology are being called into question. In this general sea change, if 'resistance' begins to be heard more often than 'revolution', then its connotations must be clarified.

Another form of resistance involves social movements. Movements that have focused attention on race or on gender and sexuality and movements on behalf of prisoners are examples of a different type of resistance that problematizes social norms and aims at social change. (There is, for instance, a group that works with and for women prisoners and that calls itself, appropriately in my view, "Critical Resistance.") Social resistance may manifest itself in opposition to the ways that institutions shape individuals, but it may also reflect opposition to social policies that shape populations. Examples of the latter would be medical practices and health care. This difference between social forces that shape individuals and social forces that shape populations is the difference between what Foucault calls "disciplinary power" and "bio-power." A major issue here is that one wants to be able to say not only that resistance to different forms of social power has been more effective in some areas than in others, but also that some social movements have led to greater social improvement than others. Poststructural social theory is assumed to have some difficulty in explaining what counts as "improvement" insofar as it denies that there is a totalizing standpoint from which to judge overall social progress.

Closely related to social resistance yet significantly different is another type of resistance to norms: ethical resistance. Ethical resistance involves the individual more than the institution or the population. It may be the basis for an individual's choice of engaging in social or political resistance. Yet it requires a different kind of explanation. For Emmanuel Levinas, ethical resistance is not the attempt to use power against itself, or to mobilize sectors of the population to exert their political power; the ethical resistance is instead the resistance of the powerless.

Levinas influences Jacques Derrida, who maintains that the paradigm for ethical resistance is such that ethical resistance will inevitably fail. The ultimate resistance is in the face of death. Life can even be defined as the resistance to death. To find examples of ethical resistance, one need not look to experiences of limit situations, as Sartre did in imagining what it was like to be a resistance hero in wartime. A more mundane, less dramatic, but not less heroic example is the day-to-day resistance to decline and death of someone with a serious physical disability or illness, such as polio. This resistance is better described as ethical than as moral, for it shows up in the person's *ethos*, which in this case is the person's perseverance, despite infirmity, in meaningful activities. However, no matter what form ethical resistance takes, it should be thoroughly honest with itself. The ethical resistance must live with its embodied limitations, and in limit situations it may have to acknowledge its powerlessness vis-à-vis that which ultimately cannot be resisted.

Looking ahead to a future that may not come, the analyses in this book anticipate the increasing need to know more exactly what is meant by 'resistance' and how it is possible.

These different kinds of resistance—political, social, and ethical—require different types of explanation. This book is not intended to be a practical guide that will show people how to resist. It does not attempt to tell people what to do. In fact, it is based on the assumption that such a how-to book could not be written. Instead, the book is more concerned with different explanations of the phenomena of resistance. On some critics' constructions, for instance, poststructuralism theorizes power as being so pervasive and insidious that resistance seems to be pointless. Thus, Fredric Jameson warns that Foucault is trapped in a "winner loses" logic.[5] Jameson notes that the more Foucault wins by portraying society as carceral, the more he loses insofar as his critical voice of refusal becomes increasingly paralyzed. This line of criticism was pressed against Foucault's theory of disciplinary power from many sides right at the start. As a result, Foucault immediately began to develop a social ontology to explain how resistance is possible even if there is no "outside" to power that could check power. Pierre Bourdieu offers another sociological model to explain resistance, but it too encounters the criticism that his social ontology makes resistance seem pointless. Bourdieu's notion of the habitus, that is, the set of social dispositions that make us who we are, initially seems to be so constraining that social change would be unlikely or even impossible. Resistance thus becomes a phenomenon that theories emphasizing the social construction of subjects ought to explain. Resistance is both an activity and an attitude. It is the activity of refusal. It is also an attitude that refuses to give in to resignation. Daniel Bensaïd points out in *Résistances* that Gilles Deleuze admired the absolute disobedience of Herman Melville's character Bartleby, who continually responds "I would prefer not to."[6] Bartleby's employer becomes obsessed with this passive resistance. As Melville explains, an earnest person who prefers an attitude of resignation and submission, will find such passivity at once incomprehensible and aggravating. Whereas resignation abandons possibilities and takes the current social configuration as inevitable, resistance is disconcerting because it challenges standard patterns of behavior. In Melville's story, one side of Bartleby's passive resistance is that it represents a critique of slavish daily subordination. Unlike resignation, resistance can lead to hope—that is, to an openness to the indefinite possibility that things could be different, even if one does not know exactly how.

Derrida also admires Melville's story. In his essay "Resistances," Derrida attests to the special significance that both Bartleby and 'resistance' have for him. The word *'résistance'* is untranslatable, Derrida quips, even into French. "Ever since I can remember," he says, "I have always loved this word."[7] Derrida finds Bartleby to be emblematic not only of resistance generally but, more specifically, of *ethical* resistance, the nonresistance of the powerless even in the face of death.

Resistance can range from the polite demurral of Bartleby's "I would prefer not to" to the in-your-face refusal exemplified by the 1968 slogan "Soyons réalistes, demandons l'impossible!" Slavoj Žižek reasserts this motto at the conclusion of his debate with Judith Butler and Ernesto Laclau.[8] In the present context, to be realist and to demand the impossible means, for Žižek, not to take the globalization of capitalism as the only possibility, but to resist it even when one does not have a better alternative to offer. Daniel Bensaïd, drawing on the work of Françoise Proust, expresses most sharply the issue that I think Deleuze, Derrida, and Žižek are signaling.[9] Their view is that, although resistance should not be blind, agents need not know explicitly all their reasons and principles in advance. Resistance itself may be required to make explicit through the resulting situation what the motives and grounds for that act of refusal are. On this account, the engaged agents will find out what is possible by seeing what their resistance opens up.

This sequence will undoubtedly appear backward to the more rationalistically inclined social theorists who believe in the primacy of universal principles. These theorists want the agent to articulate the principles that would legitimate the envisioned social change before actually taking social or political action. On their model, the ideal of a society without resistance makes perfectly good sense. In contrast, from the poststructuralist perspective, a society without resistance would be either a harmless daydream or a terrifying nightmare. Dreaming of a society without resistance is harmless as long as the theorist does not have the power to enforce the dream. However, the poststructuralist concern is that, when backed by force, the dream could become a nightmare.

The poststructuralist inability to imagine a society without relations of power has made it the target of Michael Walzer[10] and other critics who view poststructuralism as an expression of the "infantile leftism" that was common in the 1960s. The assumption is that, because the poststructuralists could not imagine a society without power, the poststructuralist attitude is one of resignation and of despair about the possibility of social improvement. However, it is less often noticed that Foucault could not imagine a society without resistance. Insofar as resistance harbors hopes for social amelioration, poststructuralism therefore is mischaracterized by the charge that it is resigned to the status quo.

In all fairness to the universalist, however, it must be acknowledged that resistance, if it starts from the situation, should not limit itself to tactical assessment or to merely instrumental reasoning about how best to achieve the social goals. In addition to tactical assessment, there should be critical assessment of the goals. In this kind of critical assessment, there may even be a need to reflect on and to posit universal principles. Thus, even if the universalist mischaracterizes the poststructuralist position, it does not follow that the universalist is misguided. Which position is better and what 'better' could even mean are questions that can be raised once the different theoretical stances are properly characterized. In this book, my aim is to present a balanced characterization of the poststructuralist position. The debate with the universalist is worked out at length in *Critical Theory*, which I co-authored with Thomas McCarthy.[11] The present book is a "prequel" to *Critical Theory*.

The Plan of the Book

I realize that the concern for the problem of resistance may seem like a strange French import. However, a premise of this book is that resistance is a recognizable topic that deserves systematic attention. To introduce the perhaps unfamiliar idea of theorizing resistance, the book is organized as follows.

The first three chapters develop and consider attempts to construct a "social ontology" that will explain how resistance is possible. By this I mean a theoretical model of the salient features of the social configuration. Different theorists will offer differing models, and these models are not to be taken as having metaphysical or foundationalist necessity. One especially Nietzschean feature that is found in some of these social ontologies is an interest in the body rather than in self-consciousness as the source of resistance.

I label this interest in the body "Nietzschean" because it represents a departure from the Kantian and Hegelian identification of freedom and rational self-consciousness. In contrast to Kantians and Hegelians, who believe that freedom and autonomy require rational self-transparency, Nietzscheans think that much of what we do is conditioned by embodied social background practices that we do not and perhaps cannot bring fully to consciousness. Theorists subscribing to embodiment differ, however, on the degree of the opacity of these background practices. There will be room for disagreement in the following pages about just how opaque we are to ourselves and as to what this opacity implies for our capabilities as ethical, political, and social agents. Thus, in addition to laying out these differing theories and methodologies, I will also be exploring the normative application of these social ontologies.

For this investigation of the social ontology of resistance, I have chosen as paradigms Foucault and Bourdieu in addition to Nietzsche. That these three should be grouped together is not obvious, and indeed there are some strong tensions that result from trying to relate them. However, the Nietzsche that I am presenting first is a "French Nietzsche"—that is, an interpretation of Nietzsche that sees him as offering a philosophy of interpretation. His genealogical strategy is not only an interpretive approach to cultural and social practices; it also offers an explanation of the basis and effects of interpretation itself. A theory that defends the interpretive character of understanding will be pluralist. By this I mean that the monistic ideal of the one right understanding that explains all the data and observations will be displaced by an openness to the possibility of plural understandings.

Chapter 1 reconstructs the history of Nietzsche's influence on and reception by French poststructuralism. The change

in French philosophy that takes place in the 1960s and the
1970s as the poststructuralist paradigm replaces the phenomenological paradigm is charted by exploring a series of
readings of Nietzsche by Gilles Deleuze, Michel Foucault,
Jacques Derrida, Sarah Kofman, and Eric Blondel. On these
French readings of Nietzsche that see him as a pluralist, the
body is seen precisely as the locus of the competing alternative interpretations. These readings of Nietzsche are shown
to go hand in hand with the development of the poststructuralist paradigm of philosophy that emerged during that
period. The chapter pays particular attention to Nietzsche's
aphoristic style and genealogical approach as well as to his
central ideas, such as the will to power.

Displacing the Cartesian metaphors of consciousness
with a pluralist understanding of the body begins the dis-
mantling of Cartesian assumptions that is required if one is
to think in terms of Foucault's social ontology. Foucault
turns Nietzschean genealogy into a strategy for reading the
history of the social and cultural practices of embodiment
and the changes in subjectivity that take place over time.
Chapter 2 investigates how Foucault's analyses of disciplinary power and bio-power allow for the possibility of critical resistance. For Foucault, all domination is power, but not

all power is domination. Therefore, Foucault can be critical
of domination without abandoning his theory that power
relations are inevitable. If subjects are socially constructed
through what Foucault calls governmentality, critique
works by a process that he calls desubjectification or desubjugation. Critique does not tell people who they really are
and what they ought to do. Instead, in Foucault's hands, critique challenges their understanding of who they are, and it
leads them to resist their attachment to their social identities
and ideals. This chapter also explains some frequently over-

looked differences between disciplinary power and bio-power, and it discusses Judith Butler's informative answer to the Foucaultian question "Why resist?"

One difficulty that arises with the Nietzschean emphasis on the historical malleability of subjectivity and embodiment is that pluralism seems to turn into sheer, unconstrained pro-liferation. The task then becomes to explain why a thousand possibilities are not simply actualized, and why instead soci-eties manage to be fairly stable. Pierre Bourdieu's notion of the stabilizing habitus is the focus of chapter 3. Bourdieu's notions of the habitus and the field are shown to follow from the phenomenology of Maurice Merleau-Ponty, as do Bourdieu's views that (contrary to Sartre) there is no radical freedom and that Merleau-Ponty is right that freedom is always situated. Bourdieu distinguishes agents from subjects and theorizes the practical sense of the former. He thinks that language is not autonomous from power, and he thus criti-cizes both Jacques Derrida and J. L. Austin for playing down the role of social power. At the same time, Bourdieu rejects Jürgen Habermas's search for universally legitimating prin-ciples in the ideal speech situation. For both Foucault and Bourdieu, power works best when it is invisible. When power becomes visible precisely as domination, it provokes resistance. Bourdieu argues that his method of reflexive socio-analysis reveals the arbitrariness of social relations scientifically, and thus that it makes resistance genuinely critical.

Another tool for critical resistance is deconstruction. Derrida himself sometimes calls his enterprise a decon- structive genealogy. In chapter 4, questions come up about the foundations of ethics—more precisely, about whether ethics requires a foundation. I use 'ethics' broadly to refer to obligations that present themselves as necessarily to be fulfilled but that are neither forced on one nor enforceable. In particular, I investigate the *ethical* resistance that comes not from power but from lack of power. The resistance of the completely powerless Other is perhaps paradoxically the most powerful form that resistance can take. Levinas's writings on the face of the Other and Derrida's meditations on the relevance of death to ethics are signs of the ethical turn in Continental philosophy that occurs in the 1980s and the 1990s. This ethical turn may well have been a result of criticisms of poststructuralism for being at least inattentive to and at worst unable to explain normative issues. If there is to be a deconstructive genealogy, it must provide at least some examples of how it understands itself in relation to ethics.

Chapter 5 explores poststructuralism's abstention from critical theory's use of both the method of *Ideologiekritik* and the idea of ideology as false consciousness. Foucault and Bourdieu both shun the notion of ideology because of its association with false consciousness, and Derrida thinks that the word 'ideology' has been used up, like a coin on which the faces have been worn smooth. Although the post-Marxists Ernesto Laclau and Chantal Mouffe retain the concept of ideology, they do so by challenging the idea of society. On their account, the belief in fixed social structures is what is illusory or ideological, and society is really an infinite play of differences. The chapter then shows how Slavoj Žižek's first major book in English radically altered the terrain of the debate. For Žižek ideology is not a mask that conceals social reality. Indeed, to continue to speak of 'ideology' is possible only if the term can be freed from the representationalism that depends on the epistemological contrast between ideological illusion and reality or the true state of affairs. The book ends by considering the claim that a combination of deconstruction and genealogy is a valid and effective tool for critical resistance, and that it may well be the best tool that is currently available.

At the end of each chapter I include reflections that transcend poststructuralism and that therefore require another label. I propose 'post-critique' as the label not only for what comes after poststructuralism, but also as a substitute for 'poststructuralism.' To explain this substitution, let me emphasize again that poststructuralism is only a term of convenience for classifying French philosophers whose work became important as the influence of the structuralist human sciences declined. However, as soon as structuralism is no longer a contender, the designator 'poststructuralism' also loses its contrast class and ceases to have a point. Historically, only the period from about 1962 to about 1984, the year of Foucault's death, could be identified as poststructuralist. However, the philosophers classified as poststructuralists would not have accepted that label, just as most of them did not want to be identified as postmodernists. Their predecessors, the philosophers who were doing phenomenology, did have an explicit investment in that recognizable research program. Even so, in addition to phenomenology, other philosophical programs, including hermeneutics and critical theory, were live options at the time. Perhaps no single term can be expected to cover all the disparate styles of philosophizing in a particular period. But at least 'post-critique' is flexible enough to cover a wide range of work in Continental philosophy since 1984, and even since 1962.

Though post-critique may appear to be a short form for 'post-critical theory,' post-critique need not think of itself as the legacy of Frankfurt School critical theory exclusively. For instance, the social theorists Judith Butler, Slavoj Žižek, and Ernesto Laclau have shown that they can engage one another in productive discussion even if they diverge in their intellectual provenance and their theoretical commitments. Therefore, a flexible label is required to show that they share enough of a paradigm to interact with one another. 'Post-critique' is sufficiently flexible to include them, and also to include, for example, other current social theorists who are investigating race and gender.

Labels come and go, however, and this book may turn out to be the only exemplar of the genre of post-critical social theory. At least, that is the rubric under which I turn to the specific philosophers who best exemplify it. Let me caution in advance, however, that the accounts of resistance offered by these divergent theorists cannot be synthesized in some super-theory of what resistance really is. At best, each account can be tested against itself and its immediate neighbors to see whether it explains how resistance can be critical. Moreover, there is the further question of how critical resistance can be socially and ethically effective in particular situations. Whether philosophy should even hope to be able to answer this question is debatable. Foucault would have urged people to find their own practical answers to it, but not to expect philosophy to legislate *the* answer. Though some will bemoan this attitude as an impoverishment of philosophy, others will share Foucault's view that philosophy should not presume "to dictate 'what is to be done.' "[12] However far these questions about critical resistance are taken, I hope to have shown that discussion should include, and could well begin from, the theories I investigate here.

1   Nietzsche: "Who Interprets?"

The movement called French poststructuralism is unimaginable without the influence of Friedrich Nietzsche. Whether the poststructuralist reading of Nietzsche is correct or not is, of course, a contested question. The French readings of Nietzsche that appeared since the 1960s may in turn be unimaginable apart from the philosophical interests of the poststructuralists. Why does so much hang on reading Nietzsche? The most straightforward answer is that Nietzsche is the antidote to the Cartesian conception of the subject that infects Kant, Hegel, Husserl, and Sartre despite their efforts to criticize or even to reject the cogito. Thus, Nietzsche is important to the poststructuralists because he shows a way out of the traditional epistemological and metaphysical conceptions of subjectivity and selfhood. But his writings on moral psychology are equally important, and his sharp criticisms of moral traditions avoid appeal to universal ethical principles or a Kantian categorical imperative. If the epistemological and metaphysical picture of the autonomous cogito or noumenal self is challenged, then the picture of the moral agent as acting reflectively on the basis of abstract principles must also be revised. Nietzsche's moral psychology, particularly his emphasis on the body rather than on consciousness, provides an alternative account of human understanding and comportment.

In this chapter I consider some French readings of Nietzsche that see the Nietzschean conception of the body as a valid corrective of the Cartesian-Kantian conception of the conscious self. My purpose in starting with Nietzsche is that I doubt that Foucault, Derrida, Deleuze, and perhaps even Levinas and Bourdieu will be understood unless the Nietzschean alternative to Cartesianism is also understood. The issue is not so much the body versus the mind, but whether a human being is a single atomistic unit or a multiplicity of competing and perhaps irreconcilable forces. If the Nietzschean position seems to prize complexity above coherence, it also recognizes the situatedness of the agent and the challenge of creating integrity in the face of conflicting demands and perspectives.

To summarize this Nietzschean position, which will often seem counterintuitive from the Cartesian standpoint, I will elaborate four points in this chapter. First, Nietzsche emphasizes the body because insofar as the body is always located somewhere, it is what makes intelligibility possible. As the French phenomenologist Maurice Merleau-Ponty also realized, the body locates perspectives and focuses interpretations. Second, although the Nietzschean criticizes the Cartesian for ignoring the philosophical significance of the body, the Nietzschean is not a reductionist. Despite Nietzsche's emphasis on physiology and his use of biological metaphors such as digestion, his position is best understood as not trying to reduce all other levels to the biological body. Third, methodologically the Nietzschean (unlike the Cartesian) does not aspire to philosophical foundationalism. Although Nietzsche seems to replace the mind with the body, the body is itself just another interpretation, not something given prior to interpretation and certainly not the set of uninterpreted universals that phenomenologists such as Husserl hoped to describe. The fourth point to bring out, then, is the extent to which, unlike for philosophers who follow Kant's account of the unity of consciousness (i.e., the "transcendental unity of apperception"), for Nietzscheans the body is not a presupposed unity, but a plurality or multiplicity. The alleged unity is not a given, but is only ever to be achieved (and inevitably only incompletely, as a fictional or imaginary unity). The subject is therefore never at one with itself, but always involves a plurality of bodily forces.

Deleuze: The Beginnings of Poststructuralism

If pressed to say when poststructuralism began, I would probably respond, after expressing my doubts that there is a single movement, that its beginnings could be traced back to Gilles Deleuze's *Nietzsche and Philosophy* (1962).[1] Although this book is not yet in the more radical style of Deleuze's later collaborations with Félix Guattari, it does mark the beginning of a new style of reading Nietzsche. At the same time it also stands at the opening of a new way of doing philosophy, one that marks its departure not only from Heidegger's fundamental ontology but also from Hegelian dialectics. The break from Heidegger and Hegel in the conception of philosophical methodology is accompanied by another break a few years later with Marxism and Freudianism. In this section I will first discuss Deleuze's critique of Hegelian approaches to philosophy before turning to the question of Nietzsche's relation to Marxism and psychoanalysis.

In the early 1960s French philosophy wrestled with the Hegelian method of dialectic, as typified in the famous story from *The Phenomenology of Spirit* of the struggle to the death that Alexandre Kojève called the master-slave relation. Deleuze makes a major break possible by arguing that Nietzsche's genealogical investigations represent an entirely different way of doing philosophy. Although Nietzsche does not always write in aphorisms, Deleuze picks out this feature of his style and shows how it breaks with the spirit of seriousness that is inevitably exuded by didactic prose (even in Deleuze's own book, which is not aphoristic). "A Nietzschean 'aphorism,' " Deleuze says, "is not a mere fragment, a morsel of thought: it is a proposition which only makes sense in relation to the state of forces that it expresses, and which changes sense, which must change sense, according to the new forces which it is 'capable' (has the power) of attracting."[2] The importance of aphorism, and its relation to the fragment, becomes a major theme for subsequent poststructuralism. Deleuze's inspiration depends on recognizing that although the aphorism seems like a quasi-fragment, in fact there is a difference between the aphorism and the fragment. A fragment implies the idea of a larger macrocosm, of which the fragment is but a piece and from which it takes its significance. An aphorism, in contrast, is a self-contained microcosm of meaning. An aphorism can be explicated indefinitely, and its significance will vary along with changes in the context in which it is interpreted. In contrast to most philosophers, who want their texts always to mean the same thing (namely, what they intend them to say), Nietzsche's aphoristic style manages to mean something different with each reading.

Nietzsche's style thus exemplifies what I am calling critical resistance. Resistance is critical in that it does not insist on truths that are true forever, no matter what the context or circumstances are. Instead, Nietzsche's style is attuned to the situation in which it is read. The insistence that Nietzsche's

Not disputing truth but value of truth

texts are able to change their meaning (for instance, as readers become less concerned with Hegelian and Heideggerian
theses and more with Marxian and Freudian approaches)
need not imply any disrespect for truth or for truthfulness.
On Deleuze's account, Nietzsche realizes that the problem is
not truth but stupidity. 'Stupidity' is, of course, a technical
term meaning *a lack of a sense for what is important.* Deleuze
underscores the point: "Stupidity is not error or a tissue of
errors. There are imbecile thoughts, imbecile discourses, that
are made up entirely of truth."[3] As I read Deleuze, he could
agree with Bernard Williams, who argues in *Truth and Truthfulness* that Nietzsche should be read not as disputing the
idea of truth per se but as attempting to revalue the value of
truth and truthfulness.[4] Nietzsche's genealogical criticisms
of the Platonic tradition dig underneath utterances that are
taken to be true or false to identify the conditions that make
it possible for these utterances even to count as potentially
true or false. As the conditions change, what truths are
worth pointing out will also change. Deleuze is suggesting
that stupidity is the failure to be attuned to what should be
said under the changed circumstances.

   The issue is therefore not truth or falsity, but the interpretation and evaluation of what should be said and why. As
interpretive, and particularly as evaluative, Nietzsche's
genealogical mode of inquiry is therefore *critical.* Critique is
not simply negative or reactive. Unlike revenge, grudge, or
ressentiment, critique is, according to Deleuze's reading of
Ecce Homo, "the active expression of an active mode of existence, attack and not revenge, the natural aggression of a
way of being, the divine wickedness without which perfec-
tion could not be imagined."[5]

   In addition to being critical in a positive sense, genealogy
is a form of *resistance* insofar as Nietzsche's evaluations are

understood to be affirmative. Connecting resistance and affirmation may seem to confuse the negative and the positive. However, one must understand Deleuze's account of "affirmation," which influences the understanding of just about everything that Nietzsche wrote. In particular, Deleuze's idea is that "affirmation" does not imply "acceptance." For Deleuze's Nietzsche, to affirm is not simply to put up with, bear, or accept; it is to create, "to release, to set free what lives."[6]

Deleuze runs risks when he says more strongly that "to affirm is not to take responsibility for, to take on the burden of what is."[7] This claim leads to the charge that Deleuze applauds irresponsibility. Vincent Descombes says, for instance, that a neo-Nietzschean philosophy such as Deleuze's "that chooses to understand autonomy as irresponsibility ends up in an apology of tyranny."[8] Even if Deleuze's countercultural enthusiasms suggest such a conclusion, I think that his philosophical point is different. The object of his critique here may be the psychological attitude of *taking* responsibility for something, as if responsibility were entirely up to oneself to decide. Deleuze follows Nietzsche in the second essay of *The Genealogy of Morals* and distinguishes between responsibility in terms of debt, which is a feature of the objective social situation, and responsibility in terms of guilt, which is a subjective state whereby one suffers from the objective debt and takes on the suffering internally as guilt.[9] Deleuze claims that the point is a genealogical and not a psychological one. That is, Deleuze is not merely criticizing a form of self-deception, but he is instead making a point about the meaning of 'responsibility'. One can perfectly well criticize responsibility in the sense of psychological guilt without rejecting the objective situational responsibility. After all, if someone is in debt to you (and not just financially), you do not want them merely to take that responsibility on themselves and *feel* guilty. Instead, you want them actively to *do* something to discharge the debt. Taking concrete steps to discharge the debt is an appropriate sign of responsibility, one that is preferable to psychologically taking responsibility for being in debt without doing anything to discharge it objectively.

But responsibility is just one part of the larger issue about affirmation. For Deleuze affirmation does not mean compliance (for instance, by the victims), or conformism. Affirmation is not merely saying "yes." There is a difference between saying "yes" when one is habitually unable to say "no" and saying "yes" even though in the past one has resisted going along with particular propositions or practices. Furthermore, I would like to add to Deleuze's account by maintaining that resistance itself as an activity is not simply saying "no." An activity must work itself out in practice, and practice necessarily involves commitments or affirmations. The critical aspect of the activity is what works to prevent the affirmative moment from being a moment simply of complicity or conformism.

Anticipating both Foucault's account of the disciplinary training that produces docile bodies and Bourdieu's account of the habitus that leads people to "misrecognize" power relations as "natural" and "universal," Deleuze's Nietzsche (in the second essay of *The Genealogy of Morals*) sees culture as employing "training procedures" that turn people into a species of "gregarious, docile and domesticated animal."[10] Anticipating Derrida on "the play of difference," Deleuze argues that affirmation cannot be opposed to negation, as the dialecticians would have it, for otherwise affirmation would be making opposition essential to itself. Deleuze then characterizes affirmation not through opposition to negation, but through the play of difference: "Affirmation is the enjoyment and play of its own difference.... But what is this play of difference in affirmation? Affirmation is posited for the first time as multiplicity, becoming and chance. For multiplicity is the difference of one thing from another, becoming is difference from self and chance is difference 'between all' or distributive difference."[11] This characterization allows Deleuze to read the will to power as "the differential element that produces and develops difference in affirmation, that reflects difference in the affirmation of affirmation and makes it return in the affirmation that is itself affirmed."[12] Deleuze goes on to infer from the logical claim that "difference is pure affirmation" to the psychological assessment that "difference is happy" and that "multiplicity, becoming and chance are adequate objects of joy by themselves and that only joy returns."[13] What enables Deleuze to make this apparent leap from logical affirmation to psychological joy? On my reading, this cheerful affirmation of affirmation is possible because of its *liberating* effect. The genealogical project unveils the self-destructiveness of what Hegel calls "unhappy consciousness." Exposing the negativity in the corresponding states that Nietzsche calls "bad conscience," "ressentiment," and asceticism has, in Deleuze's mind, "liberation as its object."[14] Bad conscience, ressentiment, and asceticism happen when what Nietzsche calls "active forces" become reactive. Active force is defined by Deleuze as "plastic, dominant, and subjugating force" that "goes to the limit of what it can do" and which "affirms its difference, which makes its difference an object of enjoyment and affirmation." Reactive force separates itself from what it can do and "denies or turns against itself."[15] The body is the relation between dominant and dominated forces. As a plurality of these forces, the body is a multiplicity that is unified only insofar as some of these forces dominate others.

Even if this reading of Nietzsche is disputable, it is still an intriguing interpretation of the multiplicity of the body and its relation to consciousness. This way of expressing the relation of active and reactive forces may make it sound as if the reactive forces are weaker than the active forces. However, if it is true that for Nietzsche the reactive forces give rise to the fictions or lies of the ascetic slaves, that does not mean that the reactive forces are weaker or less forceful than the active forces. The active forces are in fact deceived by the reactive forces insofar as the active forces become separated from what they can do. Again anticipating Foucault's point that from a fictitious normalization real power relations are formed, Deleuze remarks, "while it is true that active force is fictitiously separated from what it can do, it is also true that something real happens to it as a result of this fiction."[16] This transformation of fiction into reality goes in two directions, inward and outward. When directed outward, ressentiment takes on the form of a hatred of others and is based on the fiction that "it is your fault!"[17] When directed inward, the result is bad conscience and the invention of sin insofar as one says "It is my fault!"[18] The important point is that if these are traits of the slave rather than the master, they are not weaker traits. Contrary to the Kojève-Hegel story, on the Deleuze-Nietzsche story the reactive forces of the slave who hates not only all others, but also himself, become the dominating forces in a regime of reactive forces.[19] Contrary to the dialectician, the struggle is not where the strong prevail over the weak,[20] but instead where "the weak triumph."[21] Deleuze says that one of Nietzsche's finest insights is that "the strong always have to be defended against the weak."[22]

In a regime of reactive forces, the world thus becomes inverted, and the weak rule the strong. But this inverted regime is not in the best interests of anyone, because people do not see themselves as they could potentially be. Instead, the fiction of the real as it is in itself is formed, and the slaves fashion a corresponding sense of their own reality. They then try to become the principle of reality as it is in itself by "taking responsibility for" this reality, as if reality depended on their willingness to bear its burden.

Philosophy has thus arrived at the idealism that is epitomized in both Kant and Hegel, insofar as for both of them "being is affirmed in man at the same time that man affirms being."[23] Affirmation is here conceived reactively as acceptance (and in particular as the acceptance of responsibility for reality). But it overlooks the fact that if there were such a thing as reality, it would not be dependent on people's acceptance in this way. That is, I believe, why Deleuze infers that there is not just a fiction, but a lie involved here: "Being, truth, and reality," he writes "are themselves only valid as evaluations, that is to say as lies."[24] The lie comes in when humans tell themselves not just that there is a reality in itself, for this would be simply a fiction. The lie comes insofar as humans believe first that reality depends on their acceptance of it, and then hide from themselves that this is an evaluation, a decision that they have made about the normative status of the sensible world. Deleuze thinks that Nietzsche's transformative affirmation, his revaluation of valuation, involves seeing that "there is no truth of the world as it is thought, no reality of the sensible world, [and that] all is evaluation, even and above all the sensible and the real."[25]

The question that Deleuze's account leaves for subsequent Nietzsche interpretation is whether this apparent denial of reality is any less idealistic than the Kantian and Hegelian tradition that Deleuze is trying to escape. The issue changes its character when the relation of Nietzsche to Marxism and psychoanalysis becomes pertinent. If Deleuze is right that Nietzsche's style makes him more sensitive to context than most philosophers, then Deleuze himself must confront the change in the intellectual climate that takes place between the early 1960s and the early 1970s. What happens is that the predominant philosophical interest in Husserl, Heidegger, and Hegel is replaced by a concern for Marx, Freud, and Nietzsche. Indeed, Deleuze's Nietzsche book is probably an important factor in this climatological change. Therefore, when the dialectical method is no longer so influential, it becomes important to explain the genealogical method in relation to other forms of thought, such as those of Marx and Freud, with which genealogy has a greater affinity.

Methodologically Nietzsche is usually aligned with Marx and Freud as a philosopher of suspicion because they all find that human subjectivity has deeper roots than the subjects themselves can access consciously. On Deleuze's reading, however, Nietzsche is different from what Marxism and Freudianism have come to stand for (which Deleuze does not assume to be identical with a more careful reading of Marx and Freud directly). The Nietzschean notion of will to power does not function causally from below like Marx's account of economic power and Freud's theory of unconscious desire. In a 1973 article titled "Nomad Thought,"[26] Deleuze suggests that if Marx and Freud mark "the dawn of our culture," Nietzsche is the "dawn of counterculture." Whereas Marx has been institutionalized or in Deleuze's terms "recodified" as the doctrines of Marxism in the public domain of the state and Freud has been recodified in the form of the psychoanalytic theory of the private romance of the family, Nietzsche resists being recodified at all. To a great extent this resistance is due to Nietzsche's style, and particularly his penchant for writing aphorisms. For Deleuze, "an aphorism means nothing, signifies nothing, and is no more a signifier than a signified."[27] As a result Nietzsche escapes recodification by expressing what cannot be codified, and indeed, he confounds all codes. Nietzsche's effect on philosophy or theory is thus one of *perpetual decodification,* a phrase that is reminiscent of the call for perpetual revolution. This constant displacement that is represented by Nietzsche's style of writing and thinking is what Deleuze calls "nomadism." Nomads "begin to decodify instead of allowing themselves to become overcodified."[28] Among the means that they use are both schizophrenic laughter and revolutionary joy. By making us laugh at their laughter, nomads such as Nietzsche and Kafka confound the codes and promote tomorrow's health. Of course, Deleuze recognizes that society will try to internalize and integrate (i.e., co-opt) the nomadic unit, and the reason is that it is easier to deal with an intrinsic despotic unit than with an uncodifiable extrinsic nomadic unit.

Deleuze ends the essay by asking "Who are our nomads today, our real Nietzscheans?"[29] Certainly part of the answer to that question would be those theorists like Deleuze himself who are classified as poststructuralists because of their affinity with Nietzsche. These neo-Nietzscheans then inherit the standard accusations that are leveled against Nietzsche: that they are unable to account for agency, responsibility, rationality, human nature, community, and ethical and political values.[30] If the sweeping character of these charges makes them risible, the situation is tricky because answering these charges requires one to adopt the spirit of seriousness. This attitude will make the answers seem readily recodifiable. They will be instantly assimilated to familiar debates such as those between universalists and pluralists, or between communitarians and libertarians. The difficulty of Deleuze's later writings is certainly due in part to his acute awareness of this danger of recodification.

There is no way around this danger, however, so there is no reason not to try to deal with these problems directly. The Nietzschean picture of the interpreting body is a powerful alternative to the Cartesian picture of the cogito. However, while the Nietzschean model avoids certain problems that the Cartesian model encounters, it confronts us with some different and difficult questions. One of the most important of these is, how is critical resistance possible? Specifically, how much multiplicity is healthy? Another question that then follows is whether the Nietzschean body can even be resistant. If the body is so malleable, how could it resist forces that try to form it? How would it sense that it was being not just formed, but deformed? Subsequent French commentators on Nietzsche wrestle with these questions, and I now turn to their efforts to work out coherent interpretations that supply cogent answers.

The Poststructuralist Nietzsche

Nietzsche's influence on poststructuralism was reciprocated in poststructuralism's influence on the reading of Nietzsche. Deleuze's book on Nietzsche was followed by essays by the early Foucault and Derrida that led to a general rethinking of both Nietzsche and the nature of philosophy.[31] In particular, poststructural theory in its early days radicalized the hermeneutical conception of philosophy as interpretation. Both hermeneutics and poststructuralism are informed by Nietzsche's project of displacing the Platonic, Cartesian, and Kantian privilege given to knowledge and explanation over understanding and interpretation. The hermeneutical view that philosophy itself should be understood as interpretation rather than explanation is consistent with Nietzsche's metaphilosophical claim that there are only interpretations.

As one might expect, the relationship between hermeneutics and poststructuralism is an uncomfortable one. The later Deleuze, for instance, strongly resists the idea of interpretation, and Foucault and Derrida also have reservations about the conservative metaphysical and epistemological implications of commentary and exegesis. However, as Sarah Kofman and some other French Nietzsche scholars realized, Nietzsche's thought that there are only interpretations is not an attempt to supply an alternative metaphysics or epistemology. "There are only interpretations" is neither a metaphysical claim about what there is nor an epistemological assertion about what can be known; it is a pragmatic hypothesis. As a philosophy of interpretation, then, poststructuralism can be considered a development of hermeneutical philosophy, conceived in opposition to Cartesian and Kantian epistemology and metaphysics.[32]

The reason why interpretation is so important to a discussion of critical resistance is that critique is an interpretive enterprise. Critique cannot rest its case simply on an appeal to the facts if what counts as factual is a function of the interpretive purposes and goals that determine which features of the situation are selected as salient. In the hermeneutic tradition understanding is therefore described as a circle. The hermeneutic circle is often stated in terms of the relation between part and whole: the whole cannot be understood without an understanding of its parts, but the parts cannot be understood without an understanding of the whole. This circle could also be stated in terms of the relation between text and context, between observation and theory, or between fact and significance. The apparent circularity is that in these pairings each item cannot be determined independent of the other. However, although that circularity is not vicious or self-refuting, it is problematic. The idea that there is no uninterpreted bedrock to anchor interpretation raises the specter of relativism. If critique is a matter of interpretation, and if, interpretation goes "all the way down," then hermeneutics would not appear to be a sufficient basis for critical resistance. If there are no limits to what interpretations can say, critique becomes vacuous and resistance becomes directionless.

Both hermeneutics and poststructuralism have wrestled with this difficulty. But just as 'interpretation' can mean different things, so too can there be different philosophies of interpretation, and different hermeneutics. In one early essay, "Nietzsche, Freud, Marx," Foucault comes close to identifying with Nietzsche's hermeneutical views (although in other places he tends to be critical of hermeneutics in its traditional conception as the recovery of meaning).[33] One respondent to Foucault in the ensuing discussion even infers that for Foucault traditional philosophical questions are to be replaced by questions about techniques of interpretation. Foucault implies as much by calling attention to Nietzsche's view of philosophy as a "philologie sans terme" (philology without end).[34] For Nietzsche there is no end to interpretation because there is no beginning. Foucault glosses this idea by saying that "if interpretation can never be completed, that is quite simply because there is nothing to interpret."[35] What he means by this apparent paradox is that there is nothing absolutely first, nothing given independent of our way of taking it: "There is never, if you like, an *interpretandum* that is not already *interpretans*, so that it is as much a relationship of violence as of elucidation that is established in interpretation."[36]

Nietzsche's famous interest in the claim that there are no facts but only interpretations and in the claim that words or concepts originate as metaphors thus leads Foucault to maintain that it would be the death of interpretation if there were something primary that an interpretation could eventually recapture. But is Foucault correct in his claim that it is not the "death" but the "life" of interpretation "to believe that there are only interpretations"?[37] The traditional epistemologist would maintain instead that the very concept of interpretation entails that what is being interpreted cannot be merely another interpretation. To believe that interpretation is *only* of other interpretations would seem to make interpretation pointlessly regressive and potentially nihilistic. The claim that there is nothing to interpret but interpretations raises the danger not only of relativism but also of nihilism—relativism if any interpretation is as valid as any other; nihilism because, if anything at all can be said, then there is nothing worth saying.

Neither Nietzsche nor Foucault would have to draw this nihilistic conclusion from the belief in the inevitability of interpretation. If Nietzsche accepted this reasoning about the life of interpretation, he would not conclude from it that there is nothing worth saying; rather, he would conclude that only then is it worthwhile to say anything. This transformation depends on Nietzsche's ethical affirmation: we become what we actually say and do. Our interpretations of the world do have value for us insofar as they make us who we are. The further question of whether an interpretation has value "in itself," and not merely "for us," does not make sense, for there is no such thing as "value in itself." Because the "for us" is *always* implicit, it would be redundant and pointless even to add it as a qualifier. How we interpret ourselves in the world is thus not meaningless; on the contrary, only in the context of interpretation is meaningfulness at all possible.

Foucault's essay "Nietzsche, Freud, Marx" was written early in his career when he was developing his methodology as a historian of science. As a historian, Foucault is wrestling with the problem of the apparent discontinuity or incommensurability of scientific and philosophical theories. In the manner of the hermeneutic historian of science Thomas Kuhn, Foucault is asking us to bracket our contemporary scientific and philosophical views in order to make earlier views intelligible. The issue turns on trying to understand the relation between older scientific or philosophical theories and newer ones. For example, the statements made by Paracelsus in the sixteenth century would today not even count as candidates for appropriate scientific things to say about the world. Now imagine a Nietzschean or a poststructuralist philosopher who is trying to think in an entirely new way (and Nietzsche is certainly questioning what the conditions would be for the very possibility of thinking in a new way). The difficulty is that from the present standpoint the projection of an entirely new standpoint would seem as incomprehensible as the most gnomic sayings from the sixteenth century. If poststructuralism could succeed in its attempt to be a radically new way of thinking about the nature of thought, then it poses a dilemma for those who are still trying to think in the earlier manner insofar as the poststructuralist innovations would be unintelligible from the superseded standpoint.

Derrida's strategy of deconstruction also confronts this problem. Derrida realizes that the only resources for intelligibility are the categories and the vocabulary of the earlier tradition. Nietzsche's aphorisms are a case in point. If they work, they do so by using the old metaphysical or onto-theological terms in the very act of revealing their inadequacy. Derrida sees that this incommensurability problem occurs only if the distinction can be drawn not simply between different scientific theories but between different conceptual schemes. Kant's table of categories, including the most basic notions of thought (for instance, substance, causation, and necessity), raises the disturbing possibility of the same content's being construed radically differently by different categorical schemes. Derrida enters the discussion by challenging the very distinction between scheme and content that generates the problem of incommensurability. Derrida sees that the Kantian scheme/content distinction is disrupted by the incompleteness of Nietzsche's style. Nietzsche's aphorisms force thought to move off in multiple directions, and the interpretive process of connecting the texts to one another is part of this movement. As read by Derrida, Nietzsche's style thus makes it difficult to say that there is even one conceptual scheme, let alone two (or more).

Derrida's interpretive procedure of deconstruction has affinities with Nietzsche's genealogical mode of inquiry, and Derrida has applied deconstruction to Nietzsche's texts in several places. A good example of his reception of Nietzsche is *Spurs: Nietzsche's Styles* (1978). Particularly illuminating is Derrida's apparently casual discussion of a scrap of paper found in Nietzsche's desk on which is written "I have forgotten my umbrella." This example from Nietzsche's *Nachlass* quickly becomes a paradigm for Derrida for precisely the reasons that would have caused most interpreters to ignore it. The line, says Derrida, has "no decidable meaning."[38] There is no way even to determine whether the fragment is at all significant. Its fragmentary character and the fact that it is written with quotation marks make it contextless and indecipherable. For Derrida, this example frustrates the traditional hermeneutic interpreter who searches for the "hidden meaning," the underlying totality of texts, but who in this case could not decide whether the text is hiding some-

Read or article on "texts"

thing, or whether it is in fact even a "text" (that is, a candidate for philological study). Derrida plays with the possibility of elevating this "text" to the status of a paradigm, suggesting that the same conditions hold for all Nietzsche's (and Derrida's) texts, and perhaps for all writing as such.

Clearly, however, Derrida's reading of the fragment operates by finding significance in its very insignificance. The interest of this reading is heightened, furthermore, by the fact that any text, by being a text, inheres in an intertextual network. An example of intertextuality is provided by any interpretation, which is just the conjunction of two texts, the interpreting and the interpreted ones. Derrida's discussion of this fragment occurs in the context of criticizing Heidegger and rescuing Nietzsche's texts from Heidegger's readings of them. This particular fragment is especially interesting because of another text in which Heidegger, in explicating his central concept of the forgetting of Being, mentions and dismisses as an example a philosophy professor's forgetting his umbrella. Nietzsche could not have read Heidegger's text, and Heidegger did not know about Nietzsche's sentence, but "forgetting" for Nietzsche is a concept with a special use that Heidegger also takes over. Once the fragment is "read" in this intertextual network, its fragmentary character is not dissolved, but its "readability" is increased.

Derrida's discovery of how to read across the barrier of incommensurability is reflected in new French approaches to Nietzsche scholarship in the late 1960s and early 1970s. Jean Granier's *Le problème de la vérité dans la philosophie de Nietzsche* (Seuil, 1966) and Sarah Kofman's *Nietzsche et la métaphore* (Payot, 1972) represent two competing methodologies. The short period of time between the appearances of these books belies a significant methodological difference, produced by a marked change in the intellectual

climate in Europe. This difference is nicely observable in
Kofman's review of Granier's book in *Critique* (April 1970). I
focus on that particular piece to bring out the specific concerns of these fascinating transitional years when a new
philosophical paradigm emerged in French thought.[39]

What occurs during this time is a paradigm shift in how
to read Nietzsche, particularly in relation to Heidegger. Is
Nietzsche the last of the metaphysicians, as Heidegger reads
him, or do Heidegger's own metaphysical tendencies blind
him to Nietzsche's emergence as the first non-metaphysical
thinker? Behind this latter question is the implication that
Nietzsche, at least as read by Deleuze, is the first proto-
poststructuralist. In any case, a significantly different
Nietzsche emerges when his texts are read through
Deleuze's or Derrida's eyes than when they are read
through Heidegger's eyes.

Despite the fact that Granier adds to his book an appendix
criticizing Heidegger's reading of Nietzsche, Kofman thinks
Granier is too caught up in the Heideggerian problematic. As
a result, she concludes, he makes a crucial mistake in interpreting Nietzsche's theory of interpretation. The question is:
What is the goal of rigorous philology as Nietzsche sees it?
Granier traces a potential antinomy in Nietzsche's various
statements about the interpretive character of genealogy. On
Granier's reading, Nietzsche seems to swing from a perspec-
tivistic phenomenalism, according to which there is only a
multiplicity of interpretations, to the notion of rigorous philology whereby the task is to read through to "*the* text of nature."
This task implies an original and single truth about the text.

Kofman objects to Granier's view that the will to power
transcends itself toward the "text" of Being by means of rigorous philology (that is, genealogy). The goal is not an
"unveiling of Being in its truth," and it is not possible to sep-

arate the text from its interpretations. Granier tries to solve
the antinomy between dogmatism and relativism by arguing
that although there can be no exact interpretation and no
verification of any given interpretation, interpretations can
nevertheless be falsified. But on Kofman's account Granier is
still thinking metaphysically in maintaining that the text of
Being constitutes the interpretations. Kofman suggests the
reverse—that the interpretations constitute the text, and thus
constitute Being as text (by making chaos intelligible): "It is
interpretations which constitute [Being] as a text and as intelligible; it is they that are multiple, confused, and contradictory, and they that a good philology must disentangle."[40]
   On Kofman's reading, for Nietzsche the goal of rigorous
philology is not to sort out the original, uninterpreted text
from its interpretations. But then the problem of relativism
arises: if it is true that "a text without interpretation is no
longer a text,"[41] how can the good philologists prefer certain
interpretations (including their own) to others? As I understand Kofman's response, it depends on distinguishing the
conditions that hold for first-order interpretations from those
of higher-order interpretations. The first-order interpretations
are the immediate result of the instinctual need to make life
intelligible. The higher-order interpretations often mask the
interpretive character of the first-order ones. A strict philology should thus be honest with itself. It should present its
own interpretation not only as an interpretation but also as an
interpretation of an interpretation. Given Kofman's critique of
Granier, the "spirit of justice" that pervades this new philology has nothing to do with an open but passive reception of
"Being." The mood of the Nietzschean genealogist is not
Heideggerian *Gelassenheit,* the laid-back attitude of "letting
Being be," but rather an active "multiplying of perspectives"
in order to enrich and embellish life.[42]

As I understand Kofman, this clever solution has the advantage of showing that Nietzsche's conception of genealogy as rigorous philology does not necessarily re-admit the metaphysical notion of a unique and univocal "text of Being." Genealogy cannot be accused of smuggling in the dream of the philosophical method which, as rigorous science, aspires to the ideal of the one right interpretation. But does it avoid the complete relativism that Husserl and other proponents of philosophy as rigorous science fear? Whereas Granier could see no middle ground between dog-matism and relativism, Kofman identifies what she thinks is a satisfactory one: the pluralism that can discriminate between healthy and sick, between life-affirming and life-abnegating, interpretations.

However, my own worry about Kofman's solution is that her pluralism compounds the basic difficulty. For to say that the life-affirming interpretations are those that multiply rather than inhibit the formation of other perspectives or interpretations is simply to prefer pluralistic interpretations of interpretation to monistic ones. "Multiplying perspec-tives" is only a criterion for discriminating among higher-order interpretations, and it does not serve the philologist in the critical evaluation of first-order interpretations.

Kofman's Nietzsche would appear to be advocating a view that goes well beyond the practical hermeneutical advice of Thomas Kuhn to give the implausible statements of early "science" the benefit of the doubt. Kofman's plural-ism approximates the more radical methodological anar-chism that Paul Feyerabend (in *Against Method*, for instance) calls the principle of proliferation: "the more theories the better."[43] Feyerabend also expresses his methodological anarchism with the slogan "anything goes." For Kofman to explain rigorous philology as "permitting an indefinite interrogation and an indefinite multiplicity of hypotheses" has the advantage of saving Nietzsche from the paradox that would result if his new philosophy were a new metaphysics.[44] If Nietzsche's project is to undercut metaphysical notions by showing their hypothetical character, genealogy cannot be claiming that the idea of the will to power is the "essence of Being" or the fundamental reality behind all appearances. Kofman points out that several of Nietzsche's texts indicate that the will to power should be taken not as a dogmatic truth but only as an interpretive hypothesis.[45] Hypotheses must be testable, however, and they must have a determinate utility.

But saying "anything goes" could not be what Nietzsche had in mind. Although Kofman's analysis in this review captures clearly what Nietzsche means by an *honest* philology, it does little to explain how philology can be rigorous or how genealogy can be the critical ground for resistance. To prefer proliferation to truth as a criterion for discriminating among theories of interpretation does not clarify but in fact makes problematic the effectiveness of Nietzsche's genealogical, deconstructive criticisms of such phenomena as slave morality and Christianity. Sheer proliferation cannot serve as the basis for critique and it does not appear to give resistance any direction. I will now consider whether a hypothesis having only the effect of "permitting an indefinite interrogation and an indefinite multiplicity" of further hypotheses should be abandoned for that very reason.

Pluralism and the Possibility of Critique

The poststructuralist readings of Nietzsche continually run up against the problem of delimiting proliferation, a problem that also troubles attempts to implement the Nietzschean and Derridean notion of infinite play. Of course, Nietzsche's remarks about interpretation have been noticed before because they are closely connected with his much-discussed perspectivism. But my view is that Nietzsche's remarks about rigorous philology, and his projection of what is essentially a new hermeneutics, offer an *alternative* to his talk about perspectivism. This alternative language has the advantage not only of avoiding the epistemological paradoxes accompanying the image of multiple perspectives but also of enabling resistance to be critical, at least in principle.

Given the emergence of a hermeneutical philosophy emphasizing the interpretive character of all understanding and taking the understanding of written texts as a basic philosophical model, Nietzsche's analogy between his genealogical philosophy and rigorous philology becomes interesting in its own right, without any need to tie it to perspectivism. To think that thought's relation to reality is more like that of an interpretation to a text has an important advantage over perspectivism. My intuition is that there is less likely to be a "fact of the matter" or a "thing-in-itself" in the interpretation-text relation than in the perspective-thing relation. The standard epistemological or realist intuitions commonly associated with perspectivism lead to saying that there is a true state of affairs because there is a thing that is independent of the various perspectives. These realist intuitions need not come into play in thinking about interpretation rather than perception. Of course, a text also consists of black marks on pages, but I think it will be granted that in reading a text one does not first see black marks and then reconstruct them into a meaning component. Instead, from the outset one is already conscious of meaning components in ways that will vary from reading to reading.

There are problems with the concept of interpretation, but they are not the same as the problems with the concept of perspective. The question about how I can know that I am seeing the same table as you are if it looks different to both of us calls for philosophical clarification of, for instance, what "same" or "know" could mean here. Yet when I play a recording of a Mozart horn concerto, I know that I am playing the same disk, and the same performance of the same concerto. It also makes sense to say that I hear the concerto differently each time. This claim that I hear the piece differently is not incompatible with the prior claim that I am listening to the same piece, but in fact requires it. No philosophical clarification is required, for these claims are not metaphysical ones and involve no special epistemological commitments.

The matter is not radically different when the question is whether you are reading the same text as the one I am reading (or writing). Presumably the fact that you are reading on a printed page at a later time what I read in manuscript at an earlier time is irrelevant. A text is not a given in the same respects that a physical object is. It would be awkward to say that a text (as distinct from the printed page) has properties independent of possible readings, or interpretive understandings of it, whereas the philosophical literature indicates that many philosophers find it more natural to speak of the physical object's having certain (primary) qualities whether or not the object is seen.

Derrida's example of Nietzsche's "I have forgotten my umbrella" serves to show that, although the words here can be recognized as a sentence (more precisely, as the name of a sentence, because the sentence is in quotation marks), whether it is recognized as a *text* depends on giving it an interpretation. This is, at least, the Nietzschean thought that Kofman expresses when she says that "a text without interpretation is no longer a text." Nothing like idealism is entailed by this way of speaking, and it shows that Nietzsche's notion of rigorous philology is a way of avoiding the paradoxes he encounters in expressing his theory as perspectivism. It must also be noted that Derrida's example of the umbrella fragment questions the intelligibility of its own suggestion of treating every text as a fragment of a lost or incomplete context. In parentheses he adds this thought: "The concept of fragment, however, since its fracturedness is itself an appeal to some totalizing complement, is no longer sufficient here."[47] The suggestion that Nietzsche's books and his oeuvre may not form a coherent, unified totality is, of course, a reasonable interpretive hypothesis. More troublesome is the suggestion of eliminating any "appeal to some totalizing complement."

Is the "drive towards totality" a necessary moment of reading? Is it a prerequisite for resistance? A positive answer to these questions suggests the rationalist intuition that, unless one fully comprehends the text or the situation, a reading or an action is unwarranted and directionless. In contrast, the hermeneutical notion of *phronesis* supports a more qualified response. One has to start from where one is, and the ideal of a complete comprehension of anything may be unintelligible. The moderate hermeneutical answer is thus to say that any reading must involve both the attempt to construct a comprehensive totality and a healthy skepticism about the possibility of complete success in doing so. Reading would thus be the interplay between construction (or rational reconstruction) and deconstruction. The latter moment would be necessary to guard against reading familiar expectations into the text, and would have the benefit of allowing the strangeness of the text to appear.

Deconstruction's notion of the infinite play of differences, which is the heart of deconstruction, suggests the more radical response of rejecting the questions. The idea that a sign takes its meaning from all the other signs that are not expressed may not be a convincing analysis of language, but it does suggest that the ideal of a closure to understanding represents an unachievable telos. Deconstruction explores the periphery of a text's self-understanding in order to bring out the elements of uncertainty, the unsaid that decenters a discourse. The discourse that tries to be coherent and complete can be so only by ignoring what it does not want to see. Deconstruction makes this process of repression evident, and it calls attention to the "marginal" things that the discourse makes crucially inessential.

The traditional champion of epistemology could respond that a moment of construction is necessarily involved in any deconstructive reading. Any text must be read as part of a larger system. This system would be formed both by the exclusions of the text itself and by the text's inherence in an intertextual web (insofar as any text is itself only an interpretation). Construction would then be implicit in any successful act of reading, as reading could occur only insofar as it identified the text as part of a whole.

The poststructuralist metaphor of the infinite play of differences, when pushed to its limit, would imply more radically that it is neither necessary nor possible to understand the whole before understanding the parts. Reading would not be a part-whole relation, and there would be no hermeneutic circle. Any text would be only a fragment, and a fragment of a disseminated system. This system is not thought of as an organic whole, with beginning and end, but rather as the interplay of generative differences, open-ended in all directions. As the system can continue to generate new sentences, even the genealogical deconstruction will never reach an ultimate ground, not even in postulating will to power.

Coming back to Nietzsche, it should now be evident that the poststructuralist conception of texts and interpretations as the play of differences in multiple, disseminated systems can claim to be healthy and life affirming if the proliferation of interpretations is indeed the life and not the death of interpretation. But is it? Interpretations conflict and compete, and some must be preferred to others. The principle of proliferation, however, is too thin by itself to account for this feature. It cannot be used to decide which interpretations are better, but at most only to reject a specific higher-order interpretation of interpretation, namely the dogmatic theory that asserts the necessity of being able to grasp any text that is a comprehensible work in a single correct reading. The principle of proliferation cannot even be used to reject dogmatic first-order interpretations that assert of any given text that it must be read in just this way. In fact, the principle seems forced to controvert its intention by saying "the more of these dogmatic readings the better." Proliferation thus appears to lack survival value, and it cannot by itself be the basic principle of either critique or resistance. This outcome supplies a Nietzschean reason for looking further for an account of the conditions of intelligibility.

The Body as Multiple Interpretations

The problem of interpreting Nietzsche at this point is to retain his account of multiplicity without letting it devolve into sheer proliferation. One approach that French commentators have taken is to emphasize the body as the locus of limitations on what is possible. Centering on the body has the result of decentering the subject. Nietzsche's critique of subjectivity follows from his view that consciousness is not the causal initiator of experience but instead, more of an experiential by-product. As he quips in *Beyond Good and Evil*, "L'effet c'est moi."[48] But if the observable I is an effect, not a cause, of what is it an effect? A natural answer is, the body. As Zarathustra says in book 1 to the "Despisers of the Body," "there is more reason in your body than in your best wisdom"; moreover, "the awakened and knowing say: body am I entirely, and nothing else; and soul is only a word for something about the body."[49]

Does this assertion substitute a foundationalism of the body for the Cartesian foundationalism of the mind? Moreover, what exactly does Nietzsche mean by the body? Nietzsche believes that everything begins through the body, but on his view, the "body" is itself not a single thing. The body is nothing but the effect of the many various drives that coexist in it. In §19 of *Beyond Good and Evil* he says twice that the body is "but a social structure composed of many 'souls.'"[50] I take 'souls' to mean *modules* that process different parts of the experiential stream. The idea of modules seems particularly appropriate in that Nietzsche also speaks of "under-wills" or "under-souls." More pertinently, the idea of the body as a "social structure" suggests that these modules are competing with one another to become dominant parts of the picture. The sense that this process is a function of one central ego is just the result of the success of some victorious modules in coming together in a coherent way that also meshes smoothly with the environment.

One should note that by "social structure" Nietzsche here is not referring to what is now spoken of as the social construction of subjectivity, since his point is more of a psychological than a sociological one. He is asserting that the body (or at least the embodied mind) is itself like a society in that it is nothing but the nexus of forces that are often competing with one another. The illusion of the unity of consciousness is thus the effect that results from the fortuitous triumph of some of these competitors. But of course the source of these competing forces is often social, so Nietzsche could accept the general idea of social construction as long as that notion is not understood voluntaristically as a product of conscious choice.

Another way to think about the body as a plurality of drives is to think of the body as nothing but the nexus of different drafts or interpretations.[51] The body is itself only an interpretation of how the various drafts are to be reconciled. What is to be eschewed is the assumption that there is an interpreter who is doing the interpreting. In *The Will to Power*, Nietzsche asks "Who interprets?" and then answers: our "affects."[52] That is, affective modules that come into play before consciousness are already at work in configuring how we will experience the world. Significance is contributed by affective processes prior to conceptual or cognitive processes. The data flow that is being processed is not a given that carries its meaning on its face, but how significant it is and how it is to be construed is always already interpretive. To the positivists' assertion that there are only facts, Nietzsche responds "No, facts is precisely what there is not, only interpretations."[53] What he means is that for there to be data that count as factual there must be an interpretation in which the factual claims make sense. An interpretation is not simply a collection of data, but it involves a background understanding of what counts as significant and what does not.

Consciousness is not what it takes itself to be, namely the origin of experience and action. Instead, it is the outcome of an interpretive process that finally emerges explicitly and that can be articulated in language. In *The Will to Power* Nietzsche asks whether it is necessary to posit an interpreter behind the interpretation. He concludes that to do so is only an invention or hypothesis: "The 'subject' is not something given, it is something added and invented and projected behind what there is."[54] In *The Gay Science* Nietzsche accepts the phenomenon of consciousness, but attributes much less importance to it than the Cartesian does: "Man, like every living being, thinks continually without knowing it; the thinking that rises to *consciousness* is only the smallest part of all this—the most superficial and worst part—for only this conscious thinking *takes the form of words, which is to say signs of communication, and this fact uncovers the origin of consciousness*."[55] The issue may appear to be about the distinction between what is conscious and what is unconscious, but that is not the central point. The body is like a plurality of intellects, or modules, and the Cartesian hypothesis of a central, conscious supra-module that controls these sub-modules is one that we can do without.

If the Nietzscheans can plausibly give consciousness a less central place, should they be challenged for giving the body an apparently foundational role? At first glance there are passages where Nietzsche indeed seems to be arguing for a reductionist position whereby physiology is the bottom line. However, the appeal to the body actually plays a different role. If Nietzsche were a reductionist, he could not also be a perspectivist, since the very idea of perspectivism is that there is no single standpoint that tells the whole story. The body will therefore play a different role in perspectivism than it plays in reductionism.

The best account of Nietzsche's approach to this problem has been advanced, in my opinion, by the French philosopher and Nietzsche scholar Eric Blondel. Although Blondel is not a poststructuralist, I am drawing him into the discussion because of his textual care in explaining both Nietzsche's interpretive pluralism and Nietzsche's theory of the body. The point of insisting on the body is that it is always located somewhere, and thus it serves to limit and singularize perspective. Blondel makes this point by saying that "to interpret is to have a *body*, and to be a perspective."[56] A perspective is always a perspective from some point or other, and the body serves as the situated locus. But given that what the body itself is at any particular moment is only one possible draft or interpretation, the Nietzschean conception of the body cannot function as the bottom line of the reductionist explanation. As Blondel reads Nietzsche, the body is "the place in which different perspectives confront one another."[57] The body is thus less like the final bottom line of the best causal explanation of who we are, and more like an arena of gladiators in which various self-understandings compete with one another.

In sum, the Nietzschean body is an interpretive plurality. Blondel draws our attention to places where Nietzsche stresses this pluralism. In *Zarathustra* the body is said to be "a great reason, a plurality with one sense, a war and a peace, a herd and a shepherd."[58] *Ecce Homo* speaks of it as a "tremendous variety that is nevertheless the opposite of chaos."[59] In *The Genealogy of Morals*, the body is described as "a thousandfold process."[60] Nietzsche wants to get back to the level of the body, but not for reductionist or foundationalist purposes. Instead of explanation, Nietzsche emphasizes interpretation. Moreover, the Nietzschean theory of interpretation is such that there is not a single, final interpretation that serves as the end of inquiry. Instead, for Blondel, "Nietzsche's apparently biologizing texts, far from reducing the ideal to the body, are merely attempts to bring culture (conceived of *as* a body) back to the fundamental interpretation, the physiological body being one case of interpretation among others."[61]

Nietzsche's account of the body as a plurality depends on understanding it as interpretation, and thus as analogous to a text. On Blondel's reading, Nietzsche transforms the ideas of both body and culture by understanding them as like a text, which has "an infinitely plural outside which prohibits the text from turning in on itself."[62] Blondel finds evidence for this analogy to textuality in places such as *Daybreak* §119, where Nietzsche says that "all our so-called consciousness is a more or less fantastic commentary on an unknown, perhaps unknowable, but felt text."[63] *The Will to Power* adds famously that subjectivity is not what does the interpreting, but is instead itself a result of interpretation: "One may not ask: 'who then interprets?' for the interpretation itself is a form of the will to power, exists (but not as a 'being,' but as a process and a becoming) as an affect."[64]

Thinking of the body in terms of the process of interpreting a text leads toward a hermeneutical position whereby the important question is not "What is the body?" but instead "What is interpretation?" "Asking what the body is," Blondel argues, "means asking what interpretation is."[65] When pushed to the limit, for Blondel this question leads Nietzsche to think that "the ultimate principle is not the body, but interpretation, the 'body' being merely the metaphor of interpretation, the human means of interpreting it."[66]

Nietzsche's metaphors often play with the imagery that he in fact wants to reject. Thus, Nietzsche might sound like a foundationalist in his use of archaeological metaphors for his genealogical method of digging down through sedimented layers of ressentiment before getting to the deeper

explanations of human motives and actions. But finally, says
Blondel, Nietzsche only plays with the archaeological analogy to show that there is no philosophical ground [*Grund*].
Instead, in *Daybreak* 5 (44), for instance, he speaks of the
Unergründlichkeit, the impenetrability of action, and insists
that "the motives for our actions remain in the dark."[67] A
more elaborate play on the root word *Grund* comes from the
playful suggestion that Nietzsche digs deeper, not to get to
the real grounds, but to go *underground* [*untergründlich*] and
to get underneath the alleged grounds for action and belief,
"undermining them from beneath."[68] Blondel cites *Daybreak*'s preface (§2), where Nietzsche says, "I descended into
the depths, I tunneled into the foundations, I commenced an
investigation and digging out of an ancient *faith*, one upon
which we philosophers have for a couple of millennia been
accustomed to build as if on the firmest of foundations."[69]
Of course, one further implication of the archaeological
metaphor is that what Nietzsche is investigating, which
includes many current beliefs, is in fact in ruins.

In these digs, a central pillar that Nietzsche wants to
undermine is the idea of a single constituting subjectivity.
Blondel argues that Nietzsche's novelty is to construe the
body as like a political organization of unstable forces and
of frictions that can be regulated only temporarily. The
Cartesian picture assumes that selfhood implies the absence
of conflict because of the apparently smooth flow of the
stream of consciousness. This apparent concord gives rise to
the further illusion that moral thought directs action. For
Nietzsche, however, the reverse is true: moral thought follows conduct. The apparent unity of the self implied by the
illusion of moral agency is only an imaginary result of a
temporary political victory. Blondel stresses the middle
term in the idea of the will *to* power ("Wille ZUR Macht")

and maintains that "life is the instability of power-relations, there is no domination, only a struggle *for* domination."[70] No *single* meaning can therefore emerge from this conflict of interpretations. Even the notion of the will to power is misleading in the singular, and Blondel finds Nietzsche correcting himself by saying that "man is 'a plurality of' wills to power."[71] Therefore, even the political metaphor has to be qualified, for selfhood is not the result of an internal monarchy. A close look at Nietzsche's political metaphors shows that hierarchies are constantly changed, and there is no single monarch. Instead, Nietzsche invokes such notions as "regency councils," or at most *eine regierende Vielheit* (a reigning collectivity), an "aristocracy within the body, the plurality of masters."[72]

Blondel's fine-honed readings thus show that even at the level of Nietzsche's metaphors, one can find the insistence on the body as a multiplicity of interpretations. For Nietzsche, "it is not necessary to admit that there is *only a single subject*"; instead, Nietzsche's view is that "we are a multiplicity *that has constructed an imaginary unity for itself.*"[73] The unity of apperception that Kant posited is replaced by a self that is constructed from competing sources and forces. This imagined unity can be turned into an accomplishment of unity, but only if there is sufficient strength to turn the fiction into a true story.

Post-Critique: Different Stories

The analysis up to now leads to the following pressing question for post-critical reflection: Does this Nietzschean insistence on multiplicity fracture and fragment human action to such an extent that unity disappears altogether? Daniel Dennett's idea of consciousness as "multiple drafts" rather than as a Cartesian theater is a useful image in dealing with this issue in Nietzsche. The theory that consciousness is not a single, sequential story, but that it is always the simultaneous possibility of multiple drafts, can free us from the idea of consciousness as a central and constant point in the stream of the contents of consciousness. For Dennett, "at any point in time there are multiple 'drafts' of narrative fragments at various stages of editing in various places in the brain."[74] There is no single final draft that is the correct account, and no final unity of consciousness, although the drafts compete with one another for dominance. However, although *multiple* drafts struggle with one another, it should not be forgotten that these are *drafts* and *interpretations*. The struggle is between different ways of telling the story so as to link the impulses and actions together. Each draft tells a single story. That is, there is a particular way of arranging the disparate elements into a coherent configuration. But there are different stories, and many can be true. A true story is itself only a particular way to tell such a story, never the only story. Other drafts are always possible.

With this account of multiple interpretations, then, we can see how the Nietzschean could reconcile plurality and singularity, both of which are crucial to one's sense of oneself. However, this solution comes up abruptly against another question: Are all drafts equally good? Nietzsche himself obviously prefers some stories to others. Moreover, he criticizes the "motley" [*bunt*] herd for its eclectic combination of incongruous elements and its failure to bring about an artistic synthesis. He prefers a strong will over a weak will, but because of his critique of the Cartesian conception of the will, he must offer a different account of this distinction. In his view, the difference between a weak will and a strong will is that the former shows the incoherence of impulses whereas the latter shows some of these impulses mastering the others and producing a sense of unity. The strong will is the result of an *interpretation*. But again, an interpretation is not something imposed by a subject on the needs and drives; rather, the needs are themselves interpretations.[75]

If this reading is plausible, there is also a close connection between interpretation and the will to power. In fact, §643 of *The Will to Power* identifies the will to power itself as what interprets, and interpretation in turn is seen as an attempt at mastery: "Interpretation is itself a means of becoming master of something." Multiplicity is thus a more primordial feature than the Cartesian singularity, but as finite beings we cannot live with sheer multiplicity. We must delimit and narrow down our possibilities, and this happens through the projection of a coherent interpretation. The point of "becoming master" is thus that the plurality of meanings limits itself.

In recognizing the need to delimit multiplicity, Nietzsche is not returning to the Cartesian ideal of singularity. Insofar as Nietzsche takes the text as the paradigm and not the psychological subject, interpretation becomes the two-sided task of balancing multiplicity and unity. Because humans are finite beings, interpretations are necessarily limited, and cannot include all the multiplicity that is in fact possible. Hence, there is a necessary emphasis on coherence and delimitation in the process of interpretation, and interpretation goes in the direction of reducing plurality in favor of unity. At the same time, however, interpretation must also seek plurality at the expense of unity. Interpretation can pluralize the text by addressing questions that push the text in new and unforeseen directions. Interpretation is an ongoing process of balancing coherence and complexity. For the sake of coherence interpretation will sometimes have to pay less attention to complexity, but at other times it may have to admit to complexities that challenge the assumption of coherence. For the French Nietzschean there is no final state of equilibrium to this balancing act, and no single, correct interpretation at the end of inquiry.

The poststructural Nietzschean does not construe interpretation as if it were the attempt to come closer to being the final draft that is reached at the end of inquiry. Instead, the value of an interpretation will depend on its *plasticity*. Plasticity involves both transposability and innovation. Transposability is the capacity of the interpretation to survive when transposed into new and unforeseen contexts. This is the conservative dimension of interpretation insofar as interpretation resists change and seeks to maintain its epistemic and normative assumptions. However, survival also depends on being innovative and being able to open up new possibilities. Janus-faced, the process of interpretation must look both backward and forward. At the same time, to be able to make this distinction between backward and forward, there must be a standpoint and a perspective. For the Nietzschean this distinction would be possible only for embodied beings who find themselves already occupying a delimited standpoint.

These French readings of Nietzsche have unearthed in Nietzsche's writings a novel understanding of human embodiment that places a high value on difference rather than identity, on particularity rather than generality, on specifics rather than universals, and on concreteness rather than abstraction. Now it is time to turn from the French readings of Nietzsche to the French theorists in their own right. I start with the most Nietzschean of all, Michel Foucault.

Foucault: "Essays in Refusal"

Is the body invariant across history and culture, or is it the product of social constitution? If the phenomenologists prefer the first alternative, later French social theorists such as Michel Foucault and Pierre Bourdieu see subjectivity as extensively constructed by social and historical factors that are below the level of consciousness and thus less transparent to phenomenological introspection. Foucault and Bourdieu want to show to an even greater extent than the earlier movement of phenomenology did how most of our comportment is already built into our bodies in ways that we do not and perhaps cannot attend to explicitly.

In contrast to his phenomenological predecessors, then, Foucault takes up Nietzsche's hypothesis that over the course of history the body may be entirely malleable. Foucault says of what Nietzsche calls "effective history" or genealogy that it

places within a process of development everything considered immortal in humanity. We believe that feelings are immutable, but every sentiment, particularly the noblest and most disinterested, has a history. . . . We believe, in any event, that the body obeys the exclusive laws of physiology and that it escapes the influence of history, but this too is false. The body is molded by a great many distinct regimes; it is broken down by the rhythms of work, rest, and holidays; it is poisoned by food or values, through eating habits or moral laws; it constructs resistances. "Effective" history differs from traditional history in being without constants. *Nothing in humans—not even their body—is sufficiently stable to serve as the basis for self-recognition or for understanding others.*[1]

Foucault and Nietzsche are often characterized as holding that the body is "socially constructed." But this is only part of their view. Both Nietzsche and Foucault also see the body as the basis of our being, a basis that has been covered up by the intellectualist philosophical tradition.

At the same time, however, the recourse to embodiment in Nietzsche and Foucault is not a reductionism to the biological. "Embodiment" is a concept that implies that there is a biological dimension to comportment, but embodiment is also a phenomenon that depends on other related concepts and thus on cultural context. "Body" may seem like an essence, or like what philosophers now call a natural-kind term (like 'water', 'heat', or 'gold'). But I see the concept of the body in Nietzsche as more like 'money', or 'love', or 'power', or 'justice'—phenomena that depend on their concepts and on culture.[2]

The particular difficulty that I want to address in the analysis of embodiment concerns the normative dimension that is raised when Foucault takes the body as the basis of critical resistance. His account does not simply describe how the body is *formed*, but it implies critically that the social construction of the body *deforms* it. There are some obvious objections, however, that need to be discussed. If there is nothing natural to the body, then how could one say that it has been deformed? How could any social construction be assessed as better or worse than any other? How could domination even be identified as such? Furthermore, if conscious agents are powerless to change or resist their acculturated understanding of how to comport themselves, what value is the sociological or genealogical effort to bring this process of bodily construction to light?

These questions show how problematic the hypothesis of the historicity of the body can be. In this chapter and the next I take Foucault and Bourdieu as two of the best recent theorists who start from the body's historical situatedness. My aim is to offer a reading that anticipates and obviates objections raised against their enterprises by those allied more with the assumption of universal invariants. I will be focusing on the issue of whether these theories of embodiment are internally consistent in their attempts to account for the possibility of critical resistance to domination given that their concrete analyses are often assumed to portray individual agents as powerless and ineffective in bringing about social transformation.

The Body as Resistance

To set up the problem more carefully, let me first look at Foucault as one way of working out how there could be a history of the body at the same time as the body is asserted to be the basis of our being. Foucault clearly derives his understanding of the critical potential of genealogy from Nietzsche. In "Nietzsche, Genealogy, History" Foucault sees the task of genealogical, critical histories as the double one of exposing both "a body totally imprinted by history and the process of history's destruction of the body."[3] Note that historical forces are said simultaneously not only to shape but also to destroy the body. But if the body is always already *in* history, if there is already a history of the body, was there ever anything the body was *before* history and that is now destroyed? Or is what gets destroyed never natural, but only the destruction of some previous destruction?

Hubert Dreyfus and Paul Rabinow have seen this problem in their book on Foucault. Insofar as the body is the basis to which genealogy ties its interpretations, the body should become the basis for the *critical* thrust of genealogy.[4] They are not convinced, however, that Foucault explains adequately *how* the body functions as the basis of critique and resistance. They conclude their book with a series of critical questions, including the following one about whether Foucault has not paid too high a price by abandoning Merleau-Ponty's phenomenological method in favor of Nietzsche's genealogical method:

Is the main philosophic task to give a content to Merleau-Ponty's analysis of *le corps propre?* Or is such an attempt which finds ahistorical and cross-cultural structures in the body misdirected? If there are such structures can one appeal to them without returning to naturalism? *Is one of the bases for resistance to bio-power to be found in the body?* Can the body be totally transformed by disciplinary techniques? Merleau-Ponty sees the body as having a *telos* towards rationality and explicitness; if he is correct how is it that power and organizational rationality are so infrequently linked in other cultures? If, on the other hand, power and rationality are not grounded in the body's need to get a maximum grip on the world, what is the relation between the body's capacities and power?[5]

Dreyfus and Rabinow see Foucault as somewhere between Nietzsche and Merleau-Ponty. From Nietzsche Foucault has learned about the malleability of the body, but they find Foucault "elusive" about whether the body is entirely malleable or not.[6] The reason for this elusiveness is, on their interpretation, that Foucault is also drawn to Merleau-Ponty's cross-cultural, ahistorical bodily constants. These constants include up-down asymmetry and size and brightness constancy in perception, plus social constancy in response to gestures, facial expression, and sexual significa-tion. But although Foucault has learned from Merleau-Ponty about knowers being embodied, Foucault wants to add the historical and cultural dimensions of the body's sit-uatedness that Merleau-Ponty supposedly ignored.[7] They then suggest that Foucault should have followed Merleau-Ponty so as to have the lived body as a position from which to criticize the practices of manipulation and formation that have also conditioned the investigator: "If the lived body is *more* than the result of the disciplinary technologies that have been brought to bear upon it, it would perhaps provide a position from which to criticize these practices, and maybe even a way to account for the tendency towards rationaliza-tion and the tendency of this tendency to hide itself."[8] The problem they see is that Foucault never actually specifies this "more" and has "remained silent" about what the bod-ily invariants that would be needed to ground this critique actually are.[9]

This critique of Foucault's silence about invariants would be devastating if invariants were the only way to fill out the "more" that the body must be for it to supply the point of resis-tance to the total reshaping of the body through bio-power. I would like to suggest two responses to that critique. The first is a counter-criticism and the second is a more constructive response.

The counter-criticism is simply the negative point that even if there are bodily invariants, they would not be all that is necessary to make an appeal to the body as the basis for critique and resistance. It is not necessary for Foucault to deny that there are invariants. Even if all human beings, whatever their culture or time, have felt pain, the more inter-esting question is how they have interpreted the experience of pain. I would speculate that the experience of pain is so conditioned by the cultural-historical interpretations of it that there is little more that can be said about it than that generally it is aversive.[10] The philosophical point is that invariance need not be denied altogether, but the very universality of such invariants may be so thin as to make them uninteresting, or too thin to answer the more interesting critical questions. Even if there are bodily universals, and Foucault need not deny that there are, these universals may be too thin to serve as the basis of the more concrete criticisms and resistances.

Thus, in describing his method of doing the "history of systems of thought," Foucault clarifies what he means by "experience" (which comes close to Merleau-Ponty's lived body but with the historical-cultural dimensions emphasized) and insists that he is not denying that there might be universal structures involved in experiences, even if experiences are always singular:

Singular forms of experience may perfectly well harbor universal structures; they may well not be independent from the concrete determinations of social existence. However, neither those determinations nor those structures can allow for experiences (that is, for understandings of a certain type, for rules of a certain form, for certain modes of consciousness of oneself and others) except through thought. . . . This thought has a historicity which is proper to it. That it should have this historicity does not mean it is deprived of all universal form, but instead that the putting into play of these universal forms is itself historical.[11]

Foucault is insisting that the universals by themselves do not determine how they are experienced (or interpreted) concretely. Correlatively, they cannot be the exclusive basis of criticism and resistance, because how they are embodied is also crucial, and criticism must also reveal how these embodied experiences are *transformable*. In describing his method for doing the "history of thought," Foucault writes,

> There is a third and final principle implied by this enterprise: an awareness that criticism—understood as analysis of the historical conditions which bear on the creation of links to truth, to rules, and to the self—does not mark out impassable boundaries or describe closed systems; it brings to light *transformable* singularities. These transformations could not take place except by means of a working of thought upon itself; that is the principle of the history of thought as critical activity.[12]

I infer from this reference to the critical activity of thought working on itself that Foucault construes his own genealogical enterprise as an effective form of critical resistance.

Beyond this defensive line of response to Dreyfus and Rabinow, however, lies a second, more constructive line of response. There is another sense in which the body is "more" than any particular way in which it has been "socially constructed." If the body can be shown to have been lived differently historically (through genealogy), or to be lived differently culturally (through ethnography), then the body can be seen to be "more" than what it now has become, even if this "more" is not claimed to be "universal," or "biological," or "natural." The contrast alone will not make us change, of course, but it will open the possibility of change. We will not be able to go back to the past or to step out of our culture entirely, but we may be able to find the resources in ourselves to save ourselves from the destructive tendencies that the contrast reveals.

To explain this constructive response in more detail, let me point to three examples from Foucault's work: his study of the normalization that occurs when "docile bodies" are shaped by disciplinary power (as depicted in *Discipline and Punish*), his genealogy of ethics, and his account of bio-power.

These examples bring out the point that only when genealogy can show the body to have been changed or even destroyed by historical forces does genealogy become effective, *critical history* in Nietzsche's sense, but without appeal to *a priori* principles or universal invariants. Criticism, Foucault explains in "What Is Enlightenment," will take a different form when it adopts the hypothesis of historicity instead of the assumption of invariance:

> ... criticism is no longer going to be practiced in the search for formal structures with universal value, but rather as a historical investigation into the events that have led us to constitute ourselves and to recognize ourselves as subjects of what we are doing, thinking, saying. ... And this critique will be genealogical in the sense that it will not deduce from the form of what we are what it is impossible for us to do and to know; but it will separate out, from the contingency that has made us what we are, the possibility of no longer being, doing, or thinking what we are, do, or think.[13]

Using Nietzsche's genealogical method, then, will enable Foucault in the following three examples to do a form of immanent critique of forms of power that produce material bodies.

Normalization

To take the first example, normalization is a crucial feature that is revealed in Foucault's history of punishment. Foucault is interested not only in how individuals get programmed by the social institutions in which they find themselves, but also in why they accept being programmed. He does not want to ask the question of political theory about where the right to punish comes from, but instead he asks the reverse question: "How were people made to accept the power to punish, or quite simply, when punished, tolerate

being so?"[14] Part of the answer concerns the use of "norms"
not only in prisons, but in other institutions (schools, for
instance, or hospitals, or factories, or armies) such that perhaps the entire society threatens to become "carceral": "The
judges of normality are everywhere. We are in the society of
the teacher-judge, the doctor-judge, the educator-judge, the
'social worker'-judge; it is on them that the universal reign
of the normative is based; and each individual, wherever he
may find himself, subjects to it his body, his gestures, his
behaviour, his aptitudes, his achievements."[15] Contrary to
the way critics often read Foucault, this passage shows that
he does not ignore the role of individual agency in the social
construction of subjectivity. Social beings are not zombies
who have no awareness and agency in their formation.
Foucault should therefore not be called an advocate of
"social construction" of subjectivity, if that phrase is understood in a mechanistic or deterministic way. The point of
Bentham's model prison, the Panopticon, is to train individuals to see themselves as being seen: "He who is subjected
to a field of visibility, and who knows it, assumes responsibility for the constraints of power; he makes them play
spontaneously upon himself; he inscribes in himself the
power relation in which he simultaneously plays both roles;
he becomes the principle of his own subjection."[16] In general, individuals are complicit in the process of their self-
formation and they learn to normalize themselves. Indeed,
normalization does not suppress individualization, but produces it. However, what it is to be an individual changes
once the disciplinary regime colonizes and supplants the
older, juridical regime.[17]

For present purposes it is important to see that Foucault
does not criticize normalization in the name of something universal. That would itself be simply a variant of normalization,

of thinking that there is a normal, natural, universal way to exist, and that criticism is possible only of the abnormal, or whatever falls short of the normal as an ideal. The mistake to which Foucault is pointing involves the way the normal is taken as a norm. He is not trying to substitute other norms, but instead he is trying to deflate the tendency to think that there can be only one set (presumably, one's own) of normal, socially normed ways to exist or that everything we do must be measured against such social norms. The point is not to make a better distinction between the normal and the abnormal, but to challenge the social use of that very distinction.

Disciplinary power is not all bad, however. As Nietzsche says about asceticism, learning to restrain oneself can be productive. Similarly, discipline, and especially self-discipline, has advantages and disadvantages. The critical resistance to normalization stems from the sense that normalization has spread too far in our lives, and is blocking many other viable forms of life. This constriction of possibilities is achieved when normalization asserts the norms as necessary, or natural, or universal. Foucault's history is intended to show that the modern understanding of how to punish was an arbitrary invention that at first seemed to be merely one convenient and efficient means among others, but later became the only possible means, and perhaps even an end in itself. As he says of Bentham's sketch of the model, panoptical prison, "A *real* subjection is born mechanically from a *fictitious* relation."[18] Power can be productive if it opens up new possibilities, but it turns into domination if its function becomes entirely the negative one of shrinking and restricting possibilities.

This general point can be illustrated more concretely by returning to the notion of embodiment and taking up a much debated issue in interpreting Foucault's theory of the body. Despite his claim that the body is thoroughly social and historical, Foucault is sometimes read as appealing to an unhistorical or "natural" or pre-social conception of the body. An often cited instance of such a slip is the line in volume 1 of *The History of Sexuality* where Foucault asserts: "The rallying point for the counterattack against the deployment of sexuality ought not to be sex-desire, but bodies and pleasures."[19] Another such passage comes from *Herculine Barbin,* where Foucault appeals to a "happy limbo of a non-identity."[20] Both of these passages are often taken as referring to a "natural" body that pre-exists and is deformed by a social-historical construction of the disciplined or normalized body. Citing Nancy Fraser's criticisms of Foucault, Steven Best and Douglas Kellner remark, for instance, that "Foucault contradicts himself in claiming that everything is historically constituted within power relations and then privileging some realm of the body as a transcendental source of transgression. He thereby seems to reproduce the kind of essentialist anthropology for which he attacks humanism."[21]

[margin note: Criticism of Foucault's body]

However, as more sympathetic readers note, Foucault is not contradicting himself.[22] David Halperin emphasizes that in context Foucault is insisting on the possibility of a *different economy* of bodies and pleasures. Thus, bodies and pleasures are not natural, unhistorical elements or eternal building blocks of human sexuality. Moreover, Ladelle McWhorter has pointed out that Foucault is making precisely the point that the very idea of the "natural" body comes into being at the same time as the idea of disciplinary power. In *Discipline and Punish* Foucault explicitly says that the "natural" or organic body is a new object that superseded the earlier conception of the "mechanical" body. In 1772 Guibert may think that he has "discovered" the natural body that resists the army's attempts to maximize bodily efficiency, but readers should not confuse Guibert's self-understanding with Foucault's. Foucault's genealogical explanation is that normalization is the grid of intelligibility that first gives the idea of the natural body a sense. Foucault is consistent in that he thinks that the conception of the body changed in the course of the seventeenth and eighteenth centuries, and that bodies will be lived differently as they are understood differently.

The "natural" body in Foucault's book thus is not some pre-social, unhistorical given on which normalizing social practices are then imposed at a particular point in time. The natural body is only a postulate to explain the resistance to discipline and normalization, and would not make sense independent of these historically contingent social practices. Perhaps one should not speak of this postulate as "fictitious" if that implies that it is avoidable. But Foucault does so to make his rhetorical point that within the regime the resulting subjection will certainly be experienced as unavoidable and therefore completely real. Thus, we must distinguish between the regime's self-understanding, which takes the body to be ahistorical, and the genealogical analysis, which calls this ahistoricality into question. Distinguishing these different perspectives enables Foucault to maintain cogently that the value of the genealogical demonstration of the historical construction of our bodily concepts and categories is proportional to the extent that it reduces the power that the illusion of ahistorical inevitability would otherwise have over us.

I myself would express this point in terms of the distinction between the *de re* and the *de dicto*.[23] It is important to understand that it is not Foucault who is claiming *de re* that there is a natural body that resists normalization, but rather the eighteenth century disciplinarians. Foucault will be misread if his *de dicto* statements (which address ways of speaking) are confused with *de re* statements (which are taken as referring to the things spoken about). Foucault sees the *de re* claims in the historical documents as *de dicto* assertions that depend on a certain way of speaking that is perhaps only now being superseded. Thus, he sees that talk about the natural body is historically conditioned by the discursive need to talk about something natural to which the norms are applied. But Foucault himself is not confusing the *de re* and the *de dicto*, for he understands that this appeal to the natural body is only a way of speaking that depends on the practices and intentions of normalization. The genealogist identifies the historical contingency of the *de re* claims, and thereby comes to understand them as *de dicto* ways of speaking. The genealogical analysis moves from inside the discourse to a position beyond the discourse such that we can understand how the discourse functioned without any longer feeling compelled to talk in just that way. Thus, for the genealogist the very idea of the "natural" turns out to be already discursive and normative, and not the pre-normative or pre-discursive reality that the eighteenth century disciplinarians thought they were referring to from inside their own discourse. Though from the genealogical perspective the relations are understood to be *de dicto* (or, to use Foucault's own word, fictitious), from inside the normalizing practices of the eighteenth-century Prussian army the "subjection," Foucault remarks, was nevertheless entirely "real."

The Historicity of Ethics

Even after Foucault shifted his attention from social normalization of the body to his later interest in the "genealogy of ethics," including the ideas of "ethical substance" and *ethos*,

he continued to think that domination could be distinguished from critical resistance even in a thoroughly histori-
cized account of ethical self-fashioning. Instead of offering a
Kantian or Habermasian theory of *a priori* moral principles
and procedures, Foucault follows Nietzsche's call for the
more concrete practice of critical *history*, that is, genealogical
critiques of false universals embedded in the specific ways
in which we have been socialized subliminally. In particular, we need more specific analyses of the concrete ethical practices, of what the Greeks call the *ethos* and Hegel
calls *Sittlichkeit* (in contrast to the abstract moral code, or
Moralität). Foucault thinks of the *ethos* as personal, but not as
private. An individual's *ethos* is publicly observable, and it is
visibly permeated by social norms and political codes.

The general method for investigating change in the *ethos*
is genealogy. Foucault is not doing a genealogy of *morals*,
since Foucault believes that the moral principles that people
espouse are fairly constant throughout history. He is doing a
genealogy of *ethics*, which involves describing what people
do more than what they *say*, with *embodied patterns of action*
more than with *conscious principles*. An example of this
genealogy of ethics comes from the interview "On the
Genealogy of Ethics: An Overview of Work in Progress," in
which Foucault suggests that changes in the *ethos* between
Greek, early Christian, and modern times imply that we can
learn that our present ethical and sexual self-understanding
is neither universal nor "natural." Foucault charts the shift
in what he calls "ethical substance"—a central term of
Hegel's. The history of ethics will thus be the history of
the changes in ethical substance (and other aspects of
Sittlichkeit, including the mode of subjectivation, or *mode
d'assujettissement*, which I discuss below). The moral code
containing the standard precepts or universal principles

does not change much, in Foucault's opinion. However, this lack of change is not what gives the code its "binding force." On the contrary, that the code does not change much, even though the meaning of what it is to be ethical (the "ethical substance") changes, suggests that the real ethical "glue" must be found at a more concrete level.

At this level Foucault is concerned to show that in the case of the ethics of sexual comportment, there have been major shifts in the understanding of what it is to be a sexual being. If his historical genealogy is correct, "sexuality" is a recent and strictly modern phenomenon that differs significantly from what the Greeks called *aphrodisia* or what the early Christians called the flesh. Each of these has its own formula based on the relative emphasis placed on each of the three poles of acts, pleasures, and desire. The Greek *aphrodisia*, for instance, is said to emphasize acts, with pleasure being subsidiary, and desire starting to bracketed with the Stoics. Early Christianity puts the emphasis on desire instead of on acts because the concern at least since Augustine has been to eradicate sexual desire. The modern formula emphasizes desire, "since you have to liberate your own desire," whereas acts are not very important, and pleasure—well, "nobody knows what it is!"[25] However, one takes this "history," the suggestion is that sexuality is neither an invariant essence nor a natural-kind term, but a culturally variable and transformable phenomenon.

3 poles

Further details aside, the reason for pointing out the historicity of ethics is not to suggest that these earlier self-understandings are viable *alternatives* for us today, because we cannot now go back to them. But they are also not *inferior* to ours, as a Kantian or Habermasian evolutionary model would imply. Foucault's point is rather that seeing that other peoples lived successfully with self-interpretations different

from our own should suggest that stultifying aspects of ourselves that we had assumed to be universal and natural
might in fact be arbitrary and contingent features that could
potentially be changed. On Foucault's account, then, we
are *not* locked into our present self-interpretation. Just as
Nietzsche thinks of the body not as a single unity but as a
plurality of (sometimes conflicting) drives, Foucault thinks
that we are always "more" than the one, dominant interpretation of ourselves that we tend to take for granted as both
universal and natural. Critical resistance thus flows from the
realization that the present's self-interpretation is only one
among several others that have been viable, and that it
should keep itself open to alternative interpretations.

The Life-and-Death Struggle in Bio-Power

My discussion of power so far has focused on what Foucault
calls disciplinary power. The question is whether the strategies of resistance against disciplinary power will be equally
effective against bio-power. As described in writings after
Discipline and Punish, bio-power is at once more insidious
and more obvious than disciplinary power. It is more insidious insofar as it functions in a more global or holistic manner and constitutes people's bodies not simply as individual
bodies but as generic ones. Medicalization is one way that
the generic body is constituted. Insofar as medicine is itself
regulated by the state, however, the operations of bio-power
are more visible. Although Foucault is often criticized for
ignoring the power of the state, he does in fact focus on state
power (and on racism) in his discussions of bio-power.

The differences between disciplinary power and bio-power
are perhaps best seen not in the *locus classicus* of volume 1 of *The
History of Sexuality,* but in the lecture that he gave at the Collège

de France on March 17, 1976. This lecture is published in the volume titled *"Society Must Be Defended."*[26] Here the presentation of bio-power is astonishingly reminiscent of Hegel's dialectical deconstruction of shapes of consciousness in *The Phenomenology of Spirit.* Despite Deleuze's attempt to separate dialectics and genealogy, Foucault's account of bio-power echoes Hegel's account of "life." Hegel's method is to show how the basic contradiction in a concept becomes apparent so that the phenomenon in question comes to be seen as manifestly incoherent. In the account of life, which precedes the famous life and death struggle of the lord and the bondsman, the contradiction turns on the fact that "life" seems to satisfy the criterion of "spirit" in being completely *sui generis,* self-constituting and autonomous. But precisely because life is so general, and indeed a completely generic notion, its emptiness quickly becomes apparent. For Hegel life turns into death insofar as particulars must die so that generic life can go on. Life even turns into a form of suicide insofar as death turns out to be essential to life. Similarly, Foucault's critical resistance to bio-power depends on the genealogical revelation that the life that bio-power promotes, and that we welcome, also turns out to make death even more of an enormity than it is for disciplinary power or the power of the sovereign. When taken to its limits, bio-power leads to a kind of suicide for life itself, and thus its basic contradiction becomes apparent. Whether Foucault was aware of building this dialectical turn into the portrayal of bio-power is not clear. But certainly his description of bio-power deserves a prominent place in the history of the philosophical reception of Hegel's famous story of the master and slave.

After having shown the difference between the power of the sovereign and what he calls disciplinary power in *Discipline and Punish,* Foucault then in his 1976 lectures distinguishes "disciplinary" power from what he calls "regulatory" bio-power. Are these two different *kinds* of power, as different from each other as disciplinary power is from the power of the sovereign? Sometimes he speaks of the movement from one to the other as if they were different kinds. At other times he seems to think of them as two different forms that bio-power can take, as when he speaks in one breath of the "disciplinary or regulatory bio-power" that gradually supersedes the power of sovereignty. However, if we are to take him at his word that he is not giving a *theory* of power as such, then this metaphysical question is the wrong one to ask. Instead, it is more appropriate to consider these not as two different kinds of power, but as different "techniques" or "technologies" of power. Because they can function at different levels, often at the same time, I prefer to think of them as levels of intelligibility rather than as metaphysically different things or as causally connected substances. As levels of intelligibility, they need not compete with each other and there need not be any question of reducing one to the other.

There is a further question to clear up in order to avoid confusion, and that is, what exactly is the relation of "bio-power" and "bio-politics"? If I am right that the distinction between disciplinary power and bio-power is not a matter of different kinds of power, but of different levels of explanation, then "bio-politics" simply means the strategies that are to be pursued in implementing bio-power. Foucault often uses the terms interchangeably, as when he speaks of the use of statistics as a way in which this bio-power becomes more deeply entrenched in our bio-political conceptions of appropriate means by which to order (or "govern") ourselves. Bio-political questions will thus be tied to questions of governmentality. Foucault defines governmentality in a broad sense as "the ensemble formed by the institutions, procedures, analyses and reflections, the calculations and tactics that allow the exercise of this very specific albeit complex form of power, which has as its target population, as its principle form of knowledge political economy, and as its essential technical means apparatuses of security."[27] Thus, in the concept of bio-politics, 'political' implies contestability, which in turn implies alternative strategies for realizing the social security that governmentality intends to achieve through social regulation.

With these terminological clarifications on the table, it is now possible to bring out the differences between disciplinary power and bio-power. Even if these are not different from each other in kind, they have emerged at different historical times. On Foucault's chronology, disciplinary power emerged in the seventeenth and early eighteenth centuries, whereas bio-power started to develop only at the end of the eighteenth century and was predominant by the nineteenth century.[28] Disciplinary power began to displace the power of the sovereign, even if the latter still persists as the official language of political power, including talk about rights. Disciplinary power is not unrelated to the traditional topics of political theory, but it purports to be a deeper level of explanation. It articulates the conditions for the possibility of social and political developments, including capitalism (with its need for a reliable labor force).

Bio-power is not, however, a deeper level of social ontology than disciplinary power. Bio-power does not suppress disciplinary power. If Foucault speaks of it as "non-disciplinary," this is simply because the mechanisms have a different scope and point in another direction. Whereas disciplinary power addresses itself to our bodily being, bio-power addresses "l'homme-espèce," which could be translated as "species-being."[29] This apparent allusion to Marx is not a denial of the importance of the way the social "dressage" configures the individual body without the subject's awareness. But it does bring out how the individual body is also a generic body, one that can be statistically explained by reference to populations. Bio-power offers an explanation of the body through statistics about birth rates, death rates, census, and the like. Statistics are as indispensable to bio-power as architectural space is to the disciplinary construction of the body.[30]

Bio-power is thus a more global perspective on our life processes than disciplinary power. Both are focusing on knowledge about the body that the agent does not have: disciplinary power because it works on us in ways that are too subtle or "micro" to be perceived, and bio-power because it is so "macro" insofar as it represents a perspective that is too large for us to incorporate into our personal intentions. Bio-power does not reduce us to a statistic so much as it sees broad trends of population that escape our individual plans.

Bio-power also has its own political agenda, one that stands in marked contrast to the model of sovereignty that is being displaced. Whereas the sovereign had the right to allow someone to live or to cause them to die ("le droit de faire mourir ou de laisser vivre"), bio-power is the right that one has to be caused to live or to be allowed to die ("le droit de faire vivre et de laisser mourir").[31] The course of March 17, 1976 then reflects helpfully on the differences between disciplinary power, which is focused on the dressage or training of the individual body, and regulatory bio-power. Regulatory bio-power is equally concerned with the body rather than with a different kind of object, namely society. However, the new object is the multiplicity of bodies, i.e., "population." Is population merely a statistical artifact and less real than individual bodies? Foucault's social ontology recognizes that the opposite can be the case as well: individual bodies are subject not only to causal laws but to statistical laws, and processes such as the medicalization of more and more aspects of our lives are as real as any of our direct bodily experiences.

Medicine is not the only manifestation of bio-power, but it is a paradigm case of bio-politics insofar as its mission to prolong life represents a benefit we all want to have at the same time that it takes control of our lives (and our deaths) in ways that we might regret. Similarly, looking not merely at the end of life but back to the beginning, it seems obvious that the medical ability to push back the limits that separate normal and premature births, and even to change the conditions of conception, is not without its costs as well. Bio-power works more globally and generically than disciplinary power. Its intent is to bring about general effects, such as prolonging life, decreasing disease, or increasing the birth rate. Instead of the concern for the details of an individual body, medicine works more globally and generically, for instance, by finding the particular pill that will cure all cases of a disease, or of a certain kind of pain, or of moods like depression. Medicine may not be perceived as "power over," but in fact it runs through our entire lives. There is a tendency, for instance, to think that there is little that cannot be cured by taking a pill. Certainly medicine benefits our lives, but its undeniable "power to" improve and prolong life also allows us to abandon our responsibility for our moods, our minds, and our bodies.

Bio-power is thus in the service of "causing to live" and it apparently intends to ignore the materiality of death, which it simply allows to happen. Few would want to resist the ways in which modern scientific medicine accomplishes its goals of increasing life expectancy and decreasing mortality rates. Yet once again, the promise is so generic that the goal

hides the reality. Most people think that they would want
to live longer, but they may not be taking into account
that sometimes the quality of life is such that longer life
may be undesirable. What people want is not eternal life,
but eternal youth, and even that could lead to undesirable consequences, such as overpopulation. The generic
promise of ideal goals can allow people to buy into bio-
power without understanding its actual costs and inevitable
disappointments.

Traditional theorists of power have criticized Foucault for
confusing two distinct conceptions of power: "power over"
and "power to." But bio-power is a convincing case of
a form of power that is both "power to" and "power over."
As such, it is a positive form that power takes. Although
Foucault had often insisted that power was positive and
productive and not simply negative and repressive, this
point was hard to see when the topic was disciplinary
power. When the topic is bio-power, it is easier to see that
we might very well welcome a form of "power over." We
might think of it as power over disease, or pain, or infirmity,
and not as power over ourselves. But in fact it is power over
ourselves, and this is because disease, pain, and infirmity
are an inevitable part of our material lives and therefore
inescapable features of our embodied selves.

The contradiction at the heart of bio-power is brought out
best by Foucault when he shows the connections between
bio-power, racism, and genocidal discourse that can ultimately turn suicidal. If bio-power is more concerned with
the global or generic body, and discipline is more focused on
the individualized body, bio-power is more obviously a
matter of state regulation and it involves a certain biologizing discourse. Racism is thus the paradigm that Foucault
had been lecturing on that year. Of course, something like

racism existed before the start of bio-power in the late eighteenth century. For Foucault, that form of racism was simply
the ordinary "ethnic" hatred that people have for others
who are different. Foucault is interested in the emergence of
a new type of racist discourse, one that employs biological
notions such as degeneracy, inferiority, and purity. He calls
this racist discourse "statist" rather than "ethnic" because of
the obvious ways in which the state uses it to justify practices such as segregation, apartheid, and even genocide.
Although he emphasizes fascistic statism, he also speculates
that the origins of socialism are equally racist. He notes, for
instance, that socialism of the "Soviet type" has used medicalizing discourse to incarcerate political dissidents and to
suppress ethnic differences.

Whether the political arrangement in question is fascist or
socialist, racist hatred and genocidal tendencies can even
turn back on the state itself. Life thus encounters its contradiction and becomes suicidal. Foucault suggests three
examples of this dialectical self-deconstruction. One
example is Hitler's declaration at the end of the war that the
German economy and the means of sustenance for the German people should be destroyed. Hitler was thus in effect
calling on others to follow him into suicide. Another
example is the atomic bomb, and Foucault recognizes the
irony that the project of aiding all life produced the means to
destroy all life. In *The History of Sexuality* he remarks: "The
atomic situation is now at the end point of this process: the
power to expose a whole population to death is the underside of the power to guarantee an individual's continued
existence."[32] The best example of the paradox of bio-power,
however, would be the easily imaginable case of a virulent
virus, produced by biotechnology but somehow getting out
of control and destroying all other forms of life on the

planet. The threat that this case could become real shows the
paradox of bio-power in its most basic form: the attempt to
promote life in a generic sense could end up leaving only
one generic form of life. The virus would display its biological superiority by being the last form of life.

The point of these examples is thus to emphasize the often
insidious ways in which the discourse of bio-power envi-
sions making life better and purer. The discourse may not be
explicitly adversarial and may not posit others as outright
enemies. Rather, as in the case of colonialist racism the
intention is not so much to eliminate adversaries who are
equal, but to purify the population of inferior biological
strains. If exposing this duplicity could be a step toward the
suicide of bio-power in a manner that is reminiscent of
Hegel's dialectical deconstructions in *The Phenomenology of
Spirit,* the difference is that Hegel is criticizing concepts, or
shapes of consciousness, or figures of *mentalité* that could be
called ideologies. But Foucault is not pointing to an ideological stance like social Darwinism. He does not think that bio-
power is a case of ideology. This abstention from the notion
of ideology is a major methodological difference between
Hegelian dialectic and Nietzschean genealogy and it is my
topic in chapter 5. In Foucault's genealogical account bio-
power is not an ideology that shatters as soon as its contradictory nature becomes conscious. Instead, bio-power is
more materially a technology of power with advantages
that people will be reluctant to forgo. The contradiction that
bio-power tries to cover up is that death is the underside of
life, and there is nothing more material or inescapable than
death. Foucault's emphasis on bio-*power* is thus intended to
emphasize the materiality of population in the same way
that disciplinary power brings out the materiality of embodiment. The materiality of both technologies of power is

marked by the fact that their disadvantages are ignored or misrecognized as perceived advantages. For the most part, people welcome the benefits of these technologies and do not perceive them as forms of power. Only the critical capacity of the genealogical account will make resistance possible by making the insidious features of these technologies of power evident.

Resistance, however, does not involve appeal to values that transcend bio-power. On the contrary, it invokes the same "right" to life and health that is inscribed in bio-power. The language of rights comes, of course, from the sovereignty model. However, Foucault does not think that the traditional juridical model could comprehend the idea of a right to life until bio-power became dominant. Foucault sums up the history of resistance to bio-power by remarking that "life as a political object was in a sense taken at face value and turned back against the system that was bent on controlling it."[33] Resistance to the underside of bio-power in the name of life itself is thus once again a strategy of turning the system back against itself. This is not surprising, for in a normalizing society there is no better source of norms for resistance than the norms of that society. The resistance is more likely to be effective, of course, when the norms are made manifest through a genealogical critique.

Foucault's Social Ontology of Resistance

Foucault recognizes that he has to explain the conditions for the possibility of resistance, and he does so by building resistance into power relations from the start. Power, as he conceives it for both disciplinary power and bio-power, is not what would be in effect if determinism were true, and if an individual had only one course of action open. Power for

Foucault implies having more than one option open. Domination, in contrast, occurs when people buy into constraints that entrap them in asymmetrical relations that blind them to their real range of possibilities. Conceptually, all domination is power, but not all power is domination. Domination is exclusively power over, whereas power in a broader sense can be positive and productive. Foucault cites the pedagogical relation of student and teacher as a case of power that is not necessarily domination (although it often is).[34]

Foucault insists against his critics that his theory does not dismiss freedom and individual agency. Instead, he maintains in an interview from January 20, 1984, that one could not speak of power unless one could also speak of freedom. Correlatively, where power is found, there resistance will be found as well: ". . . in order for power relations to come into play, there must be at least a certain degree of freedom on both sides. . . . This means that in power relations there is necessarily the possibility of resistance because if there were no possibility of resistance (of violent resistance, flight, deception, strategies capable of reversing the situation), there would be no power relations at all."[35] Resistance thus does not come on the scene secondarily, only in response to power. Instead, resistance is found in the social ontology from the start. Without a power network it would not even make sense to speak of either resistance or domination, and patterns of resistance and domination are the signs that a power network exists. Moreover, power needs resistance, and would not be operative without it. Power depends on points of resistance to spread itself more extensively through the social network.[36] There is an apparent paradox in that resistance does not always only disrupt power. Sometimes resistance serves the ends of domination more than it inhibits them. Foucault cannot guarantee in advance that the genealogical unveiling of domination will be effective and liberating. But genealogical analysis can at least aim at challenging domination at every level. Even if genealogy presupposes that there is no society without power relations and without some domination, it can still have the emancipatory aspiration of reducing the asymmetrical relations of domination to a minimum.

Given that resistance does not always subvert domination, but on the contrary, is often taken over and exploited in such a way as to increase domination, how is emancipatory resistance to be distinguished from co-optation and compliance? Co-optation is the phenomenon where domination defuses resistance not by trying to suppress resistance, but on the contrary, by appearing to allow such resistance to express itself. Critical activity that looks as if it is aimed at minimizing domination may instead be only an illusion. Insofar as power functions more effectively the less visible it is, the critical activity may be serving rather than subverting power if what looks like resistance is really just an appearance that hides the insidious spread of normalizing processes.

Can the genealogist distinguish, then, a case of effective resistance from one of co-optation by the forces of normalization? Foucault does not think that universal principles will help in making this distinction, and he also rejects the explanatory role of a notion such as false consciousness.[37] However, he does seem to think that cases of co-opted resistance can be distinguished from a special group of cases of effective resistance. These special cases are, curiously enough, instances where domination's strategies of co-optation are themselves co-opted. Critical resistance in these cases involves using the very mechanisms of power to destabilize and subvert domination. Foucault does not go into much detail about such cases, but the following examples may help to clarify his analysis of effective resistance.

(1) One such example is provided by ecological movements that successfully resisted technological destruction of the environment. The destructive technology claimed to be based on scientific truths, but ecology won by "playing the same game differently."[38] The ecological movement succeeded not by opposing science, but by generating new scientific approaches that countermanded the narrowness of the technological conception of science. To illustrate this critical destabilization further, I will look at some other examples of this process of reversing power relations from Foucault's studies of discipline and sexuality.

(2) Another example is provided in *Discipline and Punish* in the chapter on "Illegalities and Delinquency." His main point brings out the usual direction in which co-optation works. Prisons are apparently designed to reduce delinquency. But if delinquency were in fact eliminated, the prison system would also be eliminated. What happens in fact is that the prison system establishes a permanent need for itself by stabilizing and perhaps even increasing the category of delinquency, almost as if the prison system had a functionalist drive toward self-preservation and self-enhancement. "This delinquency," Foucault remarks, "is a result of the system; but it also becomes a part and an instrument of it."[39] Citing examples such as prostitution and police informants, Foucault asserts that delinquency, or controlled illegality, is useful to the illegal interests of the dominant groups,[40] and is produced and exploited for the "profit and power of the dominant class."[41] In other words, illegality is controlled and co-opted to serve the interests of the dominant class, which itself often depends on and is complicit with this illegality. But Foucault also suggests, somewhat briefly, that this direction of co-optation can be reversed. What he calls "popular illegalities" represent acts of resis-

tance to the new codes that were introduced in the period 1780–1848.[42] Illegal practices such as the refusal to pay taxes or to comply with conscription, or workers' revolts through such practices as absenteeism, pilfering raw materials, or machine-breaking, became linked to political attempts to overthrow power. Foucault understands these strategies of resistance as attempts to turn the system against itself: "A whole series of illegalities was inscribed in struggles in which those struggling knew that they were confronting both the law and the class that had imposed it."[43]

(3) A further example where resistance reversed the usual direction of co-optation is the case of the invention of the category of "perversity." In volume 1 of *The History of Sexuality*, Foucault argues that perversion is not an ahistorical phenomenon, but a relatively recent way of speaking that dates from the nineteenth century. In other words, the nineteenth century doctors might have thought that they *discovered* perversion, but the genealogist sees perversion as a product of a specific medical approach to the body and thus as a category that was *invented* by nineteenth century medicine. As Foucault says more explicitly in an interview in *Power/Knowledge*, the "emergence of perversion as a medical object is linked with that of instinct" only since the 1840s.[44] On his account of ways of speaking about sexuality, up to the end of the eighteenth century the focus was on matrimonial relations via three major explicit codes: canonical law, civil law, and Christian pastoral.[45] But then in the nineteenth century less was said about matrimonial relations, and instead "sex" was discussed much more in terms of "unnatural" relations.[46] Foucault summarizes this change by suggesting that the libertine (Don Juan) was replaced by the pervert. The old category of the sodomite (who was thought of as engaged in a temporary aberration of behavior, not as having a distinctive personality) was replaced

by the new category of the homosexual, that is, someone who is a distinctive kind of person, with a determinate "soul."[47] Rather than seeing the Victorian period as setting up barriers to perversion, Foucault sees modern bio-power as producing and multiplying singular sexualities.[48] "The growth of perversions . . . is the real product of a type of power on bodies and their pleasures."[49] Although the intentions were to repress sexuality, modern societies have produced an explosion of unorthodox sexualities,[50] and Foucault cites an arcane list from the time with such categories as zoophiles, zooerasts, auto-monosexualists, mixoscopophiles, gynecomasts, presbyophiles, sexoesthetic inverts, and dyspareunist women.[51] Contrary to its inventors' intentions, then, power does not mean less sex, but more sex, that is, more ways of speaking about and instantiating sexuality. Also contrary to its inventors' intentions, perversion became a locus and means of resistance. So-called homosexuality, once invented, learned to speak on its own behalf and demand recognition of its legitimacy.[52] It learned to seize and reverse discourse, and it provides an example of how discourse can be used both for and against power.

(4) In an interview titled "Body/Power," Foucault gestures toward other examples of this reversal of co-optation as well. Thus, the social system may try to make the bodies of children or soldiers more useful by valuing the mastery of the body gained through gymnastics, sports, exercise, and drills. But Foucault points out that the body may then turn around and challenge other social norms: health may become more important than economics, or pleasure more important than marriage or "decency": "Suddenly, what had made power strong becomes used to attack it. Power, after investing itself in the body, finds itself exposed to a counterattack in the same body. . . ."[53] However, Foucault is aware that power is

insidious and that it may be able to reverse this reversal in turn. He quickly adds that "the impression that power weakens and vacillates here is in fact mistaken; power can retreat here, re-organise its forces, invest itself elsewhere . . . and so the battle continues."[54] An example of this response is the way the revolt of the body gets co-opted. If control by repression ("don't do this, don't do that") meets resistance, Foucault suggests that other sorts of control can be introduced. Overt repression might be replaced by the more alluring and more effective control by stimulation, for instance, where sun-tan products and films seem to say "Get undressed—but be slim, good-looking, tanned!"[55]

Foucault sums up his account of resistance in volume 1 of *The History of Sexuality* by insisting that power and resistance will be found together: "Where there is power, there is resistance."[56] Resistance does not come from "outside" the power configuration, for it would not make sense to talk of power unless there were also points of resistance that played the role of adversary or target. Moreover, Foucault insists on the plurality of these points of resistance. There is "no single locus of great Refusal, soul of revolt, source of all rebellions, or pure law of the revolutionary."[57] These multiple points of resistance produce social cleavages and fracture unities, and thus have the effect of generating new regroupings that will in turn encounter new points of resistance.

Critique as Desubjectivation

Given this multiplicity of points of resistance plus the ever-present danger of the co-optation of resistance, what allows Foucault to distinguish between good or bad, valid or invalid resistances? To deal with this perennial question, one must begin with Foucault's analysis of subject-formation [*assujettissement*] and then look closely at how critique functions. One ordinary translation of the word *assujettissement* would be simply "constraint," and it is Foucault's subtle ear for the *sujet* in the middle of the word that gives it the additional technical meaning that can be translated as subjection, subjugation, or subjectification. For Foucault there is always some mode of subjectification involved in our self-understanding. In the interview "On the Genealogy of Ethics," for instance, he defines the *mode d'assujettissement* as "the way in which people are invited or incited to recognize their moral obligations."[58] Examples are a beautiful existence (for the Greeks), divine commands (for Christians), or rational, universal rules (for Stoics and for Kantians).

Governmentalization is what "subjugates" or "subjectifies" people by defining for them the legitimate answers to questions about what counts as a person, what counts as a proper relation to one's gender, or what rights a citizen has. Foucault thus does not start his genealogical analysis of the process of subject-formation from the question of how neutral subjects let themselves be dominated. There are two reasons for this. First, neutrality is a myth. "There is no such thing as a neutral subject," Foucault remarks. "Everyone is forcibly the adversary of someone else."[59] Second, he believes that subjects do not exist prior to relations of domination, but are in fact manufactured in and through these relations. His theme, he says, is not "the genesis of sovereignty, but the fabrication of subjects."[60] In short, the working hypothesis of Foucault's genealogical approach is not that subjects produce domination, but that domination produces subjects.

Given this account of subject-formation or *assujettissement*, critique is then the desubjugation or desubjectivation [*désassujettissement*] of the subject. This means that critique functions not by providing an alternative account of who you are and what you ought to do, but by dissolving your sense of who you are and disrupting your sense of what the right thing to do is.

In the light of this account of critique as the desubjectification of a subjectivity initially fabricated under relations of domination, how then does Foucault deal with the problem of normativity? To understand Foucault correctly, one must remember that the Nietzschean analysis of the body is at stake, not a Cartesian account of consciousness or even a Kantian view about the self. Foucault makes clear in an interview with D. Trombadori (in 1978) that Nietzsche, not phenomenology, is the model for this moment of desubjectivation. The phenomenologists try to recapture the meaning of everyday experience in order to rediscover "the sense in which the subject that I am is indeed responsible, in its transcendental functions, for founding that experience together with its meanings"; for Nietzsche (and Bataille and Blanchot), in contrast, "experience has the function of wrenching the subject from itself, of seeing to it that the subject is no longer itself, or that it is brought to its annihilation or its dissolution."[61]

[margin note: Trying to find how the ego affect experience]

In a May 1978 interview titled "Questions of Method," Foucault attributes desubjectivation to critique, but not to a form of criticism that tells people what to do. He insists that no one should expect to find advice or instruction in his books that will tell them "what is to be done." On the contrary, his critical project is "precisely to bring it about that they 'no longer know what to do,' so that the acts, gestures, discourses that up until then had seemed to go without saying become problematic, difficult, dangerous."[62] He insists that this effect is intentional, and he defines critique as follows: "Critique doesn't have to be the premise of a deduction that concludes, 'this, then, is what needs to be done.' It should be an instrument for those who fight, those who resist and refuse what is. Its use should be in processes of conflict and confrontation, *essays in refusal*."[63] This interview also shows that for Foucault resistance will be more efficacious precisely because critique does not give reformers explicit directives, but instead brings them up against a limit-experience that disrupts their deepest convictions and their sense of who they are.

The mode of being that Foucault is envisioning here is expressed by his use of the idiomatic French phrase *se déprendre de soi-même*, which Paul Rabinow discusses informatively.[64] This expression can mean "freeing oneself from oneself," but because that rendition seems to beg the question about voluntarism, it is better translated as "distancing oneself from oneself," or "detaching oneself from oneself," or the translation that I propose: "dissolving oneself." This expression is related to, but stronger than Foucault's notion of *égarement*, or "straying from oneself," as in this passage in *The Use of Pleasure*: "After all, what would the value of the passion for knowledge be if it resulted only in a certain amount of knowledgeableness and not, in one way or another, and to the extent possible, in the knower straying afield from himself."[65]

These terms are connected to the idea of the limit-experience. Kant's enterprise was to define the limits of what can be known, limits that Kant thought that we could not exceed. Hegel challenged this project by asking: If there were limits to knowledge, in what sense could one know that? The philosophical knowledge that there are limits to knowledge enables us to distinguish legitimate empirical knowledge from unjustified uses of reason alone without any sense experience. But then that *philosophical* knowledge is not itself the kind of *empirical* knowledge that is justified by positing those limits. Hegel thought that the Kantian claim to know both that there were limits and what the limits were was already to have exceeded these limits. But whereas Hegel inferred that there was therefore nothing that could not be known, and thus that absolute knowledge was possible, Nietzsche insisted on the perspectival character of knowledge. "Absolute knowledge" would be an oxymoron for Nietzsche, since it would imply a "God's eye perspective" or a "view from nowhere." The limit-experience for the Nietzschean would not be like the Kantian limits that enabled us to know who we were and to exist comfortably in our world. Instead, the Nietzschean limit-experience would be one where our limits were shattered, such that our understanding of ourselves and our world broke down and required us to question our most deeply entrenched beliefs and practices.

This Nietzschean account of limits can be seen in the following passage from Foucault's lecture "What Is Enlightenment?": "The critical ontology of ourselves must be considered not, certainly, as a theory, a doctrine, nor even as a permanent body of knowledge that is accumulating; it must be considered as an attitude, an ethos, a philosophical life in which the critique of what we are is at one and the same time the historical analysis of the limits impressed on us and an experiment with the possibility of going beyond [or exceeding] them [*de leur franchissement possible*]."[66] "Going beyond" is not quite the right translation for 'franchissement', nor is "crossing" (as in "crossing a border"), because those spatial notions involve the positing of another side, whereas the Kantian point about limits is that there is no other side. But the idea is clear. For Foucault, the force of critique is that the encounter with one's limits dissolves one's background belief that there are no other ways to experience the phenomena in question. Insofar as the dissolution of this background belief amounts to dissolving fundamental beliefs about oneself, it opens up other possibilities and reshapes one's sense of what can be done. Critique is thus a crucial condition of freedom.

I conclude from these various passages that Foucault can in fact speak not only coherently but also cogently of critique as a *désassujettissement,* a desubjectivation and dissolution of the subject. On the normative question about when and how domination ought to be resisted, Foucault's answer is that one should not expect philosophy to provide an *a priori* principle that will permanently settle such a question. The genealogical histories that investigate power relations will be more effective in showing what is called for in a particular context. The most that Foucault can say as a critical theorist (as opposed to his concrete work as a critical historian) is that because power always meets some resistance, domination is bad because it misrecognizes that power itself implies openness and possibilities. The asymmetry introduced by domination works against this openness and against possibilities, and thus provokes and validates resistance.

In sum, to use the Nietzschean language of the later Foucault, the point of critique is to enhance the lives and the possibilities of individuals, to allow them the space to try to create themselves as works of art. They may not succeed in this self-fashioning, but that failure should be due only to themselves, and not to social domination. Therefore, domination must be resisted if only because it restricts the range of possibilities open to agents. That is why Foucault saw his own philosophical ethos as constantly exposing and challenging oppression. The point of his own critical resistance was to do whatever was possible to make sure that the games of power were played with the minimum of domination.

Post-Critique: Judith Butler

There is a question that remains about whether Foucault has explained in enough detail the problem of where critical resistance comes from. This issue becomes especially acute if one considers that on Foucault's account of normalization, there are no other norms than those supplied by the society itself. As a postscript to this chapter I would like to add a discussion of this problem as reflected in Foucault's May 1978 lecture titled "What Is Critique?" plus a brilliant commentary by Judith Butler titled "What Is Critique? An Essay on Foucault's Virtue."[67] The happy conjunction of these two documents marks an original form of critical theory that I call post-critique.

Judith Butler invites this label when she poses the problem Foucault faces as how to deal with the question "What good is thinking otherwise, if we don't know in advance that thinking otherwise will produce a better world?"[68] *Penser autrement* is, of course, Foucault's own slogan for what he hopes to accomplish. Butler is reminding us of the charge originated by Nancy Fraser and taken over by Jürgen Habermas that critique is worthless and resistance is directionless "if we do not have a moral framework in which to decide with knowingness that certain new possibilities or ways of thinking otherwise will bring forth that world whose betterness we can judge by sure and already established standards."[69] Butler believes that this question reduces contemporary debate to an impasse "within the critical and post-critical theory of our time."[70] This impasse gives rise to the need for post-critique because the debate has reached limits that show an incoherence within the categories by which social life is ordered. Whereas Kantian theorists want to stay within these categories, Foucault is instead allying himself, on Butler's reading, with "a Left cultural tradition post-Kant" that challenges these ordering categories.

Much as Foucault's interpretations of Nietzsche express his understanding of his own situation and methodology, Butler's description of Foucault's position is so poignant that it seems to apply to her own methodological self-understanding as well. Both can be seen as practicing a style of thinking that attempts to destabilize the limits of the present order. Their practices represent a form of critical resistance to a power that, in Butler's words, "sets the limits to what a subject can 'be,' beyond which it no longer 'is' "; this power "seeks to constrain the subject through the force of coercion, and the resistance to coercion consists in the stylization of the self at the limits of established being."[71]

Butler's terms here might seem to go beyond Foucault's insofar as she speaks of the stylization of the self. Such locutions suggest a degree of voluntaristic self-fashioning that might seem inconsistent with Foucault's insistence on the ways in which both disciplinary power and bio-power condition bodies at levels that are too micro or macro to play a role in conscious intentions. However, Foucault does speak of autonomy in this lecture, and he defines critique as "the art of voluntary insubordination, that of reflected intractability."[72] Foucault thus does not rule out the efficacy of voluntary reflection in critique.

Voluntarism is not really the issue, though, since Foucault and Butler are both trying to describe processes that are not readily accessible to consciousness. I have just provided

Foucault's account of what critique will or will not be able to do, but Butler thinks that there is still a more difficult question that should be thought through. That is the question about how critique *can* have that effect. Butler's contribution is to provide a "psychic" explanation of power in addition to Foucault's "social" explanation. In *The Psychic Life of Power* she argues that the psychic explanation is not prior to the social explanation. On her account, the process of subject-formation is thoroughly social. Furthermore, the *psyche* is not the same as the *subject*. The psyche is that which exceeds and resists the identity of the subject-position. Butler's critique of Foucault draws on the Lacanian view that the unconscious reveals the "failure" of identity, and that, as Jacqueline Rose says concisely, "there is resistance to identity at the very heart of psychic life."[73]

For Butler a crucial question posed by this lecture is: What does Foucault mean when he begins his lecture by remarking that "there is something in critique which is akin to virtue" and that he is going to speak about "this critical attitude as virtue in general"? For Butler this point about virtue is the centerpiece of this lecture, and her subtitle for her commentary is "An Essay on Foucault's Virtue." However, I take her account of virtue to be an original contribution of her own. Foucault does not seem to have developed his thoughts about virtue much in this lecture, and it is not a central topic in other variants of Foucault's related discussions of Kant's essay "What Is Enlightenment?" including the two interviews from 1978 that I have just cited. In the course of her interpretation Butler suggests that 'virtue' replaces 'resistance' in Foucault's account of critique.[74] However, I do not find the terms to be mutually exclusive. Foucault could well be describing both the *acts* and the *attitude* with which the acts are performed. Acts of resistance will be virtuous then if they are carried out in the right way (that is, with the critical attitude). Foucault's reference to virtue could thus be taken as a supplement to and not as a replacement for the account of critical resistance. If virtue is, in Butler's words, both "an act of courage, acting without guarantees" and also "the perspective by which the subject gains a critical distance on established authority,"[75] then virtue is just another name for critical resistance.

What strikes me as especially insightful in Butler's account is the connection of critique to practice. The critical attitude must be directed toward a particular form of power, and it cannot hold itself aloof from concrete historical and social practices. If Foucault's idea of connecting the critical attitude to virtue is to reinforce the idea of practice, virtue in general would then be the result of constant attention to the habits that would build the critical attitude more deeply into our conduct. I take this to be the central argument of Butler's essay. On Butler's reading, virtue involves "the practice by which the self forms itself in desubjugation, which is to say that it risks its deformation as a subject" by asking "Who will be a subject here, and what will count as a life?"[76]

To unpack this definition, I would point out that, insofar as the particular virtues that Butler cites—insubordination and reflected intractability—have as their point the desubjugation of the subject imposed by governmentalization, they must in some sense be practiced voluntarily. But the voluntary has limits. As Butler makes especially clear in a later essay, "Bodies and Power, Revisited," the social norms that are already in place are the only possible context for resistance. These norms define who one is, and because one is attached to oneself, resisting these norms through insubordination puts one's own sense of who one is at risk.

I think that it is Butler's virtue, even more than Foucault's, that she sees how much the critical attitude represents such a thorough-going risk to "the capacity to sustain a sense of one's enduring status as a subject." In rejecting the particular virtues reinforced by the dominant social paradigms, one does not become free of constraints. To make this point clear, one must understand the role that "interpellation" and "foreclosure" play in the desubjectivation that comes about through the disruption of the subject's sense of itself. Interpellation results when one hears oneself called by a word that categorizes, objectifies, or reifies one in an injurious manner. Interpellation teaches one psychologically what one's social identity is and what the consequences of that identity are. Foreclosure is a psychoanalytic term that refers to a basic feature of the production of a subject whereby the subject is produced by being *subordinated,* and is in some sense precisely this subordination. The subject subjects itself, shackles itself, and in effect, it desires its own subjection. For Butler, power precedes the subject: "Power not only *acts on a subject* but, in a transitive sense, *enacts* the subject into being."[78]

The major puzzle then becomes to explain two points: first, why the subject desires its subjection, and if that is true, then second, how the subject can want to resist this subordination when the subordination makes the subject what it is. The answer to both of these questions depends on the effect of foreclosure, which has the consequence that desire is made possible by the attempt to prohibit it. "Through the neurotic repetition," Butler argues in *The Psychic Life of Power,* "the subject pursues its own dissolution, its own unraveling, a pursuit that marks an agency, but not the *subject's* agency—rather, the agency of a desire that aims at the dissolution of the subject, where the subject stands as a bar to that desire."[79] For one to persist as oneself, one must either "desire the conditions of one's own subordination" or the subject "must thwart its own desire."[80] In terms of the structure of interpellation, this means that the subject either accepts the social identity that interpellation imposes on it, or it turns against its attachment to itself. Agency for Butler results from this ability of the psychic to emerge from the social, but then to turn back on the social. Only by accepting, occupying, and taking over the injurious term, says Butler, "can I resist and oppose it, recasting the power that constitutes me as the power I oppose."[81]

The importance of critique, then, is the way that it promotes the desubjectivation of the subject insofar as critique problematizes and makes apparent both (1) how governmentalization forecloses or blocks ways in which people can generate their own styles of living out their differing understandings of what it is to be a person within a particular ordering of social categories and (2) at what points this foreclosure becomes visible, whether in discontinuities or epistemic breaks or internal contradictions. Examples of the disclosure of social foreclosure might be those that I have provided earlier, e.g., life's suicide in bio-power, or the use of the history of ethics to show the non-absolute character of sexuality. If a particular social order is possible, it is also possible for that order not to be the case, and both Foucault and Butler think that critique can open a door to a possible reversal of the power system.

The danger of allowing self-reflection the capacity of resistance and transformation is that it disrupts Foucault's Nietzschean sense of the body. If in answer to the question "Where does resistance come from?" Foucault were to say "From an 'originary freedom,'" he would be violating his own social ontology. He does in fact come close to saying this at the end of his talk. There he speaks of an unqualified will not to be governed, whereas earlier on he had insisted that there was never an anarchistic will not to be governed *at all*, but only ever a resistant will not to be governed in a particular way or to such an extent. When a questioner then challenges this apparent contradiction, he corrects his unqualified usage and says "I do not think that the will not to be governed at all is something that one could consider an originary aspiration. I think that, in fact, the will not to be governed is always the will not to be governed thusly, like that, by these people, at this price. . . . I was not referring to something that would be a fundamental anarchism, that would be like an originary freedom, absolutely and wholeheartedly resistant to any governmentalization."[82]

Butler is fascinated that Foucault even "mentioned"—although he did not "use" the term—"originary freedom." She notes that he himself toys with the thought of originary freedom when, in the give and take of the question period, he adds (playfully, I think): "I did not say it, but this does not mean that I absolutely exclude it."[83] Butler dwells on the possibility that although he was not saying that there is originary freedom, he nevertheless seems, significantly, to "post it, mention it, say it without quite saying it."[84] Although I like the idea of "post-it" notes, which can be stuck on the text and then removed without a trace, I myself am not persuaded by Butler's praise for Foucault's "oddly brave" act of taking the risk of having uttered a phrase that would completely undermine his analysis of power. I think that he is clear that his starting point is the Nietzschean body, and not the Kantian autonomous self. The virtue of Foucault's approach to critique, in my view, is that it shows the incoherence of the social order, not of its own social ontology.

I do agree, however, that Butler supplies a convincing psychological explanation of why one resists. One resists not merely because one is constrained, but because one recognizes that one identifies with these constraints insofar as they become one's identity by making one who one is. At this point I think that the question "What does one resist?" should be answered carefully. Resistance is never simply to constraint in general, because one is always constrained by something or other. There is no originary freedom with absolutely no constraints. Resistance comes when one senses not only one's dependence on these constraints, but also one's tendency to give in to them.

My guess is that what Butler likes in Foucault, and what she thus theorizes not only as his virtue but as virtue in general, is the way his thought is formed in "disobedience to the principles by which one is formed."[85] Virtue in general, then, would be the practice of risking one's deformation as a subject by resistance not to the constraining principles per se, but to one's *attachment* to them insofar as they constitute one's identity. Living with constraints is not what is bad, because power is inevitable. The question is whether one is doing so out of a tranquilized, conformist attitude, or out of a reflective, critical attitude. Butler's importance in contemporary critical theory comes from her effectiveness in giving independent arguments that the latter attitude is more virtuous than the former. If her argument "goes beyond," "exceeds," or "crosses" Foucault's, that *franchissement* attests to the value of her own sustained work on the question "Why resist?"

3   Bourdieu: "Agents, Not Subjects"

interesting

In the range from Merleau-Ponty to Nietzsche, Foucault stands very close to Nietzsche. Pierre Bourdieu, in contrast, resists the relativism that threatens the Nietzschean side of this spectrum and stands in a lineage that is closer to Marx and Merleau-Ponty.[1] However, Foucault and Bourdieu can profitably be put on the same spectrum insofar as Bourdieu can be read as deepening Foucault's account of how subjectivity is constructed through power relations by providing a more detailed sociological theory of this process. The central idea of this theory is Bourdieu's account of the habitus, which always is situated in what Bourdieu calls a field. The analysis of the habitus and the field can be taken as Bourdieu's way of adding the social dimension to Merleau-Ponty's theory of embodiment. But Bourdieu does not follow the earlier phenomenological program entirely, for he does not see the social dimension as secondary to perception. I read Bourdieu as maintaining that the perceptual is itself conditioned by the social. Showing this will require some interpretation, however, and will depend on the general issue of how Bourdieu sees the relation between the biological and the social features of embodiment. Once these issues are clarified, I can then go on to the central issue of this book and ask whether Bourdieu's approach allows for conscious, critical resistance to oppressive socialization.

Merleau-Ponty's Phenomenology

"All consciousness is, in some measure, perceptual consciousness," says Maurice Merleau-Ponty in *The Phenomenology of Perception*.[2] With this slogan Merleau-Ponty intends to show that previous philosophy went wrong in emphasizing consciousness and ignoring embodiment. Merleau-Ponty does not deny consciousness, or even what he calls the cogito, but he affirms that the cogito is always *incarnated* or embodied, in contrast to the disembodied Cartesian cogito or Kantian ego. Neither the Cartesian cogito nor the Kantian ego is located in space, which is outer; hence, each is essentially "inner." For Merleau-Ponty the distinction between the inner and the outer still obtains, but from the standpoint of embodiment the relations are reversed: "Inside and outside are inseparable. The world is wholly inside and I am wholly outside myself."[3] "The world is wholly inside" because my body has incorporated the skills and practical know-how of how to go about doing things in the world. Like Nietzsche, Merleau-Ponty sees the body as providing the basis for one's orientation to the world. Objectively, there is no up or down, or left or right, to the universe. Only one's body is located in such a way as to make such orientation possible.[4] The uniqueness of orientation is what makes it "essential to me not only to have a body, but to have *this* body."[5] "I am wholly outside myself" because the body is not an object, or a fixed point of reference in the world, but a "motor subject" that is an "original intentionality" that makes space possible.[6] The mobile body is the condition of the possibility not only of our experience of space, prior to geometry's abstract concept of space, but also "of all expressive operations and all acquired views which constitute the cultural world."[7]

What happens to the constituting subjectivity that Kant referred to as the transcendental unity of apperception? Who is having my experiences if not me? In Merleau-Ponty's terms, the question is "How I can be the constituting agent of my thought in general"—that is, "How subjectivity can be both *dependent* yet *indeclinable,*"[8] Merleau-Ponty's answer depends on rejecting both Hume's conception of subjectivity as a succession of psychic acts and Kant's transcendental synthesis of these acts. Subjectivity does not imply "private sensations"[9] that are isolated from one another from one moment to the next. For Merleau-Ponty I am "one single experience inseparable from itself, one single 'living cohesion,'"[10] such that "it is through one present thought that I achieve the unity of all my thoughts."[11] To say that subjectivity is dependent and indeclinable is to say that "it does not constitute the world," but it finds itself with the world all around it, like a *field.*[12] Thus, on Merleau-Ponty's theory I am always in a situation. Being always situated does not mean that I cannot change my point of view, because I am not tied to any one perspective. However, "I must always have one [perspective], and can have only one at once."[13] The world in which I find myself is the *field* of experience. Merleau-Ponty says "I am a field, an experience."[14] I will show shortly how this conception of the field is adopted and adapted by Bourdieu.

As for the role of language in experience, Merleau-Ponty's view has the consequences that I am not a disembodied knower and that there is no absolute knowledge. Consciousness, i.e., the *intention* to mean something, does not in fact make words mean what they do.[15] Merleau-Ponty uses the word 'outrun' to describe the sense in which the meanings can exceed our intentions. He says that intention outruns speech,[16] and that "language outruns us" because of "a surplus of the signified over the signifying."[17] Knowledge for Merleau-Ponty is always had against the background of my past experience. Insofar as we cannot thematize every aspect of this background, much of my knowledge remains tacit. Indeed, much of my sense of myself remains implicit, and thus, Merleau-Ponty speaks of the tacit cogito, "myself experienced by myself."[18] The tacit cogito ("the presence of oneself to oneself") takes the place of Kant's transcendental unity of apperception and is anterior to philosophy. It knows itself only in specific situations, e.g., dread of death or of another's looking at me.[19]

This insistence on the tacit cogito becomes a problem when Merleau-Ponty wants to account for freedom, for usually freedom depends on the transparency of the cogito to itself. Why does Merleau-Ponty still insist on freedom? His response is that "there is no case in which I am utterly committed; but in this case I do not withdraw into my freedom; I commit myself elsewhere."[20] What then is freedom? In contrast to Sartre, who maintains that there is a strict either/or whereby human conduct is either completely determined or absolutely free, Merleau-Ponty argues that freedom is situated in the world, and "the world is already constituted, but also never completely constituted."[21] For Merleau-Ponty freedom is always situated in a field, and thus, neither determinism nor absolute choice is strictly true.[22] The field restricts the possibilities, but it does not determine only one possible outcome. To say that freedom implies a field is to say that freedom does bring the obstacles to freedom into being, but only in terms of a "sedimented" situation.[23] Sedimentation includes various attitudes toward life into which

I have inculcated myself.[24] I have developed a style of existing and this style conditions what I do.[25]

To conclude this summary of Merleau-Ponty with an example, Sartrean idealism reduces "being a worker" to the consciousness of being a worker.[26] Merleau-Ponty insists, in contrast, that I *exist* as working class, and this supplies my motives for being revolutionary and my judgments, e.g., "I *am* a worker." Contrary to Sartre, then, I am situated in a social environment that is always already there. "My freedom . . . has not the power to transform me instantaneously into what I decide to be."[27] Furthermore, I am not alone in the world. "My life must have a significance which I do not constitute; there must strictly speaking be an intersubjectivity."[28] With this background, I can now go on to show how Bourdieu's theory draws on but significantly modifies Merleau-Ponty's view.

Bourdieu: Habitus and Field

Bourdieu makes Merleau-Ponty's notion of embodiment more concrete with his notion of the habitus. To understand the habitus one must recognize the difference between that idea and more traditional philosophical notions of habit. Standardly, habit is contrasted to deliberation or decisions of the will. However, Bourdieu views this bifurcation as an oversimplified account of agency. To generate a more complex account, he criticizes Pascal's advice to act as if one believed, with the expectation that habits of action will lead to the actuality of belief. Bourdieu is persuaded by Bernard Williams that "one cannot both believe *p* and believe that the belief that *p* stems from a decision to believe *p*."[29] Bourdieu argues that the attempt to explain social action will fail if one tries to work from a framework in which actions are

caused exclusively either by voluntaristic decisions of reason or by reaction to mechanisms that are external to agents.
Instead, he wants an account of agency whereby action is
reasonable even if it is not the product of reasoned design.
Action can be seen to be "intelligible and coherent without
springing from an intention of coherence and a deliberate
decision."[30]

Bourdieu can thus be read as providing a more detailed
version of what Foucault calls "intentionality without a subject." Indeed, Bourdieu uses as metaphors for the habitus a
conductorless orchestra or a train laying its own rails.[31] He
also gives as an example "the intentionless invention of regulated improvisation" of the virtuoso who finds in his or her
own discourse the triggers for further discourse: "In other
words, being produced by a *modus operandi* which is not consciously mastered, the discourse contains an 'objective intention' . . . which outruns the conscious intentions of its
apparent author and constantly offers new pertinent stimuli
to the *modus operandi* of which it is the product. . . ."[32] The
habitus thus does not work via rigid mechanical causation, or
like an algorithm that allows for only one output. Instead, it
has a certain plasticity due to the fuzziness, irregularity, and
even incoherencies of a few principles that must be "easy to
master and use."[33] This plasticity allows for the generation of
improvisations. Bourdieu's insistence on this plasticity obviates not only the mechanistic explanations of objectivistic
theories of social construction, but also the subjectivistic
explanations of phenomenological theories (especially Sartre's).
Bourdieu intends the habitus to be beyond the usual antinomies of free will and determinism, or conscious and unconscious agency, or even the individual and society.[34]

Consciousness can try to achieve the same effects as the
habitus does, but it cannot do so in the same way. Anthro-

pologists, he believes, cannot simply bewitch themselves and really live the beliefs in witchcraft or magic.[35] As a sense for what is practically required, the habitus has a deeper urgency that "excludes all deliberation."[36] Bourdieu characterizes the habitus as the system of "structured, structuring" or "durable, transposable" *dispositions.*[37] ('Transposable' means that the habitus is adaptable enough to reproduce itself as circumstances change; 'transposable' thus does not imply that the habitus itself can be transformed.) Is he claiming that the habitus is even deeper than perception is for Merleau-Ponty? It seems so, for the habitus is acquired from early experience and then forgotten; it becomes a "second nature"[38] that is "the basis of the perception and appreciation of all subsequent experiences."[39]

But if the habitus becomes *second* nature, what came first? Biology? Bourdieu does not deny biology, but he sees the biological as always entwined with the social. Sometimes he seems to imply that the biological can be analytically separated from the social. In his famous early essay on "The Kabyle House or the World Reversed" he seems to be finding pairs of universals combined into an ordered set that explains how both the Berber house and the Berber universe are structured: "Thus, the house is organized in accordance with a set of homologous oppositions—high:low :: light:dark :: day:night :: male:female :: *nif:h'urma* :: fertilizing:able to be fertilized."[40] Even in the later *Logic of Practice* he speaks of the "biologically preconstructed aspect of this [sexual] gymnastics (penetrating or being penetrated, being on top or below, etc.)."[41] In a footnote he mentions the possibility "that specifically biological determinations of sexual identity may help to determine social position (e.g. by favouring dispositions more or less close to the established definition of excellence which, in a class society, are more or

less favourable to social mobility)."[42] But this footnote follows a sentence claiming that social determinations constitute not only social identity, but "probably also the sexual
dispositions themselves."[43] He also cites evidence that
awareness of sexual differentiations comes into being simultaneously with perception of social differences, such as
those between the differing social roles of the father and the
mother.[44] His considered view must be, then, that the habitus is precisely the ability to unify what is socially necessary
and what is biologically necessary. This produces "a biological (and especially sexual) reading of social properties and
a social reading of sexual properties, thus leading to a social
re-use of biological properties and a biological re-use of
social properties. . . . In a society divided into classes, all the
products of a given agent, by an essential overdetermina-
tion, speak inseparably and simultaneously of his/her
class—or, more precisely, his/her position and rising or
falling trajectory within the social structure—and of his/her
body—or, more precisely, of all the properties, always
socially qualified, of which he/she is the bearer: sexual
ones, of course, but also physical properties that are praised,
like strength or beauty, or stigmatized."[45]

Bourdieu interprets his own method as being different
from the phenomenological search for a perceptual level
prior to the social level. Instead, the body is where the practical belief is instantiated, and one is born into the habitus,
which is both bodily and social. This embodiment increases
rather than decreases the intelligibility of action, Bourdieu
says, insofar as "it is because agents never know completely what they are doing that what they do has more
sense than they know."[46] Conscious representation will
never capture this practical knowledge, which is built into
such things as bodily postures (bowing, etc.) that immedi-

ately recall associated thoughts and feelings. Adapting Marcel Proust, Bourdieu says that "arms and legs are full of numb imperatives."[47] These imperatives may seem insignificant (e.g., "sit up straight," "don't hold your knife in your left hand"). In the end, however, they amount to a whole system or bodily hexis that may seem perfectly "natural," but that Bourdieu shows to be an embodied "political mythology."[48] The bodily hexis and the habitus are thus two sides of the same coin. Are there any actions that are not structured by this bodily hexis and its social habitus? The answer, apparently, is "no." Bourdieu writes: ". . . in fact all the actions performed in a structured space and time are immediately qualified symbolically and function as structural exercises through which practical mastery of the fundamental schemes is constituted. . . . [T]he whole social order imposes itself at the deepest level of the bodily dispositions. . . ."[49] The body is thus the bottom line, but the body is thoroughly colonized by the social. The body does not function as a phenomenological invariant, but is permeated everywhere by the historical. In *Pascalian Meditations* Bourdieu thus confirms his critique of the lack of a sufficient understanding of the social and the historical in the phenomenology not only of Husserl and Schutz but also of "even the otherwise very enlightening analysis by Merleau-Ponty."[50] "The body is in the social world," remarks Bourdieu, "but the social world is in the body (in the form of *hexis* and *eidos*)."[51]

Strictly speaking, the body is not in the entire world all at once, but instead the habitus is in what Bourdieu, following Merleau-Ponty, calls a "field." Fields are not the world per se, but are like regions of the world, such as the political, the religious, the scientific, or the academic fields. One might think that the habitus was the subjective aspect while the field was the objective aspect. However, this reading would reintroduce the opposition between subjectivist and objectivist explanations that Bourdieu wants to avoid. The distinction is characterized by Bourdieu as the difference between the feel for the game and the game itself. To pursue this connection between a field and a game, I note that the "game itself" is not a physical object on the order of a tree or a table, which could exist even if there were no people. In contrast, a game is a social object, in the sense that unless there were players there would be no game. At the same time, if the game did not exist, there could be no "players." The plural is important here, because games are social in the further sense that there must always be able to be more than one player. Of course, there are many games that one can play alone (solitaire, for instance). But if the game has rules, then it can by played by anyone who can understand those rules. Games are thus objective in the sense of being public, and not subjective in the sense of being essentially private. Just as there can be no private language in Wittgenstein's sense, I do not think that there can be a private game or field in Bourdieu's sense.

When one is playing a game, the game absorbs the attention of the players and defines their world for them, as long as they are "playing." Bourdieu observes that "the game presents itself to someone caught up in it, absorbed in it, as a transcendent universe, imposing its own ends and norms uncondition-ally."[52] The disanalogy between a game and a field shows up here, for people can easily stop playing a game, but it is almost impossible not to be caught up in a field. Unlike ordinary games, which one can decide to play or to stop playing, social fields, which are "the products of a long, slow process of autonomization," are such that either one is "born into the game" or one can enter it only after long apprenticeship.[53] There is no way to do science, for instance, outside the scien-

tific field. If one does step out of a field, even if simply to go to
lunch, one immediately steps into another field. That is why
Bourdieu thinks that Sartre mischaracterizes the waiter in the
café who is serving the lunch. Sartre analyzes the waiter as
comporting himself like an actor playing a part. On Sartre's
account, the waiter is in bad faith because he is trying to make
himself into an object. Bourdieu, in contrast, sees the waiter as
being less like an actor and more like a child who imitates his
father. Acquiring a habitus and an understanding of the field
is not a matter of "pretending," but of learning how to walk or
talk with the skills of an accomplished adult.

Of course, when the graduate student gets a job as a
waiter, he may well feel above such a job, and he can signal
his distance from the job in countless ways "precisely by
affecting to play it as a *role*."[54] Bourdieu amusingly extends
Sartre's description of the waiter to that of the intellectual.
To be an intellectual thus is to be like the waiter in *every*
aspect of life. The intellectual tries to generate "the scholastic illusion of distance from *all* positions."[55] The intellectual
wants to give the impression of being distanced from every
meaningful social field, and that is what makes the intellectual seem ridiculous in Bourdieu's eyes.

a shade of grey

This example is especially intriguing because Bourdieu is
himself an intellectual, and he has a bad conscience about
that aspect of himself. In the introduction to *Pascalian Meditations* he writes:

I have never really felt justified in existing as an intellectual; and I
have always tried—as I have tried again here—to exorcise everything in my thinking that might be linked to that status, such as
philosophical intellectualism. I do not like the intellectual in
myself, and what may sound, in my writing, like anti-
intellectualism is chiefly directed against the intellectualism or
intellectuality that remains in me, despite all my efforts, such as the

difficulty, so typical of intellectuals, I have in accepting that my freedom has its limits.[56]

But is not this move of disavowing his own desire to be an intellectual precisely the move that makes him an intellectual? If one accepts the analysis of what it is to be an intellectual much later in the book, then Bourdieu is exemplifying the intellectual's strategy of trying to stand at a distance from all possible social positions, including that of the intellectual. Bourdieu cannot avoid being an intellectual even when he would like to disavow those tendencies in his own thought, because that disavowal only makes him a hyper-intellectual, that is, someone who knows that an intellectual tries to stand at a distance from any subject-position and then tries to stand at a distance from that position as well. An intellectual who knows what an intellectual is can therefore not stop being one. On the contrary, that person becomes, like Bourdieu, an exaggerated intellectual: one who thinks that he or she is not one, but who therefore is one.

In another critique of intellectuals in *The Rules of Art*, Bourdieu says that they are "two-dimensional figures" who ignore what really invests them with the specific authority that they have.[57] When intellectuals speak, they do so with the ambition of being universal. However, in reality they are merely the mouthpieces of the "historical unconscious" of a "singular intellectual field" that is ventriloquizing through them. Real communication, he believes, cannot be achieved, as Habermas thinks, by looking at the single universality that the individual intellectual projects. Instead, in intellectual debate (between Foucault and Habermas, for instance), genuine communication will not be possible unless the parties understand what I would call the "multiple universalities" that are attempting to speak. That is, for Bourdieu we have to listen not merely to the universal propositions, but to the different kinds of historical unconscious that are trying to be heard. More important than the universals are the "specific histories of intellectual universes that have produced our categories of perception and thought."[58]

The point of these examples is that any field can be seen as involving illusions. Those who are not caught up in a game, perhaps because they are not allowed to play it, see how the players are perpetuating these illusions. Socioanalysis is itself a preeminent technique of showing fields to be illusions. On the one hand, then, Bourdieu's parody of the intellectual rebounds on himself. On the other hand, though, insofar as the habitus is always in some field or other and does not usually have the option of stepping out of a given field to see it as an illusion, Bourdieu is right to insist on the necessity that the field imposes on what agents can or cannot do. Perhaps one need not play a given game, but then "no one can benefit from the game, not even those who dominate it, without taking part in the game and being taken in by the game."[59] To take oneself off the board, as one does in chess by laying down one's king, is thus a "social death" and an "unthinkable option."[60]

Not a causal notion, the field does not determine every move that agents make, but it makes any particular move intelligible. Furthermore, agents have different levels of skill. A field is established "through the practical strategies of agents endowed with different habitus and quantities of specific capital, and therefore with unequal mastery of the specific forces of production bequeathed by all the previous generations and capable of perceiving the space of positions as more or less wide spaces of possibles in which the things that offer themselves as 'to be done' present themselves more or less compellingly."[61] There is no "level" playing field in the real social world, although one may be taken in by the illusion of equity. The illusion that the field is level may be part of what perpetuates the illusion that the field is real. This belief in the reality of the field helps to hide its arbitrariness. Simply thinking about the arbitrariness of all social relations, however, clearly does not make particular ones go away. That is because this practical belief is not a state of mind for Bourdieu, but a "state of the body."[62] The body is a "memory pad" for the "most serious social injunctions" that make one who one is.[63]

Agents vs. Subjects

Now that I have sketched Bourdieu's account of the habitus and the social field, I will examine two standard criticisms of his theory. The first is that individuals have very little free play within the habitus. The second is that Bourdieu insists so strongly on the habitus's ability to *reproduce* itself that there is no room to account for social *transformation*.[64] That is, there appears to be little attention in Bourdieu to the possibility of critical resistance, including its component concepts of individual agency, social critique, and historical change.

Bourdieu has several lines of response to these criticisms, but it should be evident that his general strategy is to account for critical resistance by starting from the account of situated freedom that Merleau-Ponty developed in opposition to Sartre's radical freedom. There is enough free play either in the habitus or in the field, he believes, to allow for the possibility of critical resistance, even if resistance rarely succeeds in bringing about genuine social transformation. On Bourdieu's account, although the habitus is all-pervasive, it also has a degree of plasticity, and thus does not entirely preclude agency, whether individual or collective. Bourdieu is not a determinist. On the contrary, the notion of the habitus is intended to *explain* agency. Bourdieu thinks that structuralists such as Lévi-Strauss and Althusser are misguided in reducing agents to structural epiphenomena. Social agents are not rule-following automata, and Bourdieu thinks that Husserl, Merleau-Ponty, and Heidegger are on the right track in giving non-mechanistic and non-intellectualist (i.e., anti-Cartesian) accounts of the relation of agents and the world. He insists, however, that he means "agents, not subjects."[65]

What does this distinction mean? Agents have a feel for the game and for what the social situation requires, but this practical sense is usually not the result of reflective reason or explicit deliberation as it supposedly is for a subject. The intuitive feel for the game is not self-conscious, but the result of embodied dispositions. For Bourdieu in *The Logic of Practice*, the important theoretical task is to give an appropriate account of the practical sense that agents have. Practical sense fixes *pertinence*, and thus social perception is selective.[66] Practical mastery is a form of what Nicholas of Cusa called "learned ignorance" insofar as it "does not contain knowledge of its own principles."[67] Practical mastery does not need explicit rules and norms, and indeed, the attempt to make the rule explicit can be a major obstacle both to the appropriate action and to the construction of an adequate theory of practice.[68] Bourdieu maintains that an agent cannot reflect without some loss of a sense for the practice or of the feel for the game.[69] For instance, the agent cannot raise the question, what is the point of this practice? For Bourdieu, "the very nature of practice is that it excludes this question."[70] As Heidegger also points out, the question arises only when there has been a breakdown—that is, when what Bourdieu calls the "automatisms" no longer function for the agent.[71]

When Bourdieu says that *agents* are not *subjects*, he means that they are doers of deeds that are intelligible only against a background of social practices and within a social field. The source for this distinction between agents and subjects could well be Nietzsche, who sees the doer as a fiction that follows from rather than precedes the deed. On the Cartesian model of the sovereign subject, the decision to act follows from reasons that would ideally be transparent to the actor who exists prior to the action and who decides to act. On the Nietzschean model of the engaged agent, the agent comes into being only through action, and action flows more from background practices and social conventions than from explicit decisions. A rather blunt way to express this point would be to say that "subjects" think that for the most part they know what they are doing. "Agents," in contrast, for the most part do not know what they are doing. Or better, "agents" do much of what they do without needing to think explicitly about it.

Defenders of Nietzschean agency therefore see defenders of Cartesian subjects as self-deceived cognizers who misrecognize their own complicity in maintaining substantive social dissymmetries that those who are better off take to be procedurally legitimate. In contrast, defenders of Cartesian subjects maintain that the Nietzschean account of agency treats people as social zombies by disregarding the role of self-conscious reflection in meaningful, purposive action. Of course, drawing the contrast this bluntly caricatures each position, and it makes the agential mode seem counterintuitive. However, this contrast shows what the agential account will have to explain, namely the relation of the agent to the background practices. On the agential model, the background constrains the agent and leaves only limited room for the agent's own ability to decide and choose. But constraint does not only narrow down possibilities. On the contrary, constraint makes action possible, and is thus enabling and not necessarily disabling. A model such as Sartre's whereby persons are radically free makes action more difficult to explain because even our preferences seem to be chosen. But then, how could we choose our preferences? If we had no preferences from the start, then there would be no preference that would lead to choice X rather than choice Y.

Although the background constrains choice and action, and thus seems to be at odds with the ideal of freely chosen action, in fact there are good arguments that the background explains action better insofar as some constraint is necessary to make a particular action intelligible. Our capacities are not such that we can reckon with an infinity of possibilities. Action is intelligible only within a field that delimits alternative courses of action. The agent is an agent because there must be some room for maneuver, but the agent is not a "subject" because it maneuvers within a field of intelligibility that it can never entirely articulate and master.

A further implication of this agential model is that the background practices are the source of the norms that are applied in evaluating actions and their outcomes. But then, if the norms are internal to the practices, how do we rise above the practices and evaluate them? Bourdieu insists that although our concepts are always perspectival, this perspectivism does not entail relativism. Understanding requires objectivity, for without objectivity the perspectivist could not claim that understanding is perspectival. I note that even Foucault speaks of the course of inquiry leading to a point where "one finds that one is looking down on oneself from above."[72]

For Bourdieu norms are built into the background practices, which cohere in the habitus. The habitus is both a skill and a norm, for a norm is nothing more than a social skill. That is to say, a simple skill does not have a standard of correctness outside its situated goal. Nevertheless, as socialization inculcates agents with various skills, coordination becomes necessary and the norms required by coordination come to be shared by other social agents. These norms can even transcend the particular culture and come to be shared by larger collectivities. For Bourdieu, then, there are no normative universals apart from concrete, contextual interpretations. However, Bourdieu believes that sociology and science in general must posit objectivity. Without objectivity there would not only be no reason to assert the truth of one's perceptions and beliefs, there would also be no standpoint for assessing and possibly criticizing the actions of others or oneself. Truth is crucial, Bourdieu argues in *Pascalian Meditations* (supposedly against Richard Rorty and other alleged postmoderns), and "if there is a truth, it is that truth is a stake in struggles."[73] Only the objective portrayal of social dissymmetries that try to remain hidden will have an emancipatory effect, one that leads to constructive social criticism and effective political action.

In replacing the disengaged Cartesian subject with the situated worldly agent, Bourdieu wants to avoid subjectivistic explanations that rely too much on conscious reasons people give for their comportment. He also wants to avoid strictly objectivistic explanations that totally discount the subjective feel that agents have for their actions. In particular, he does not want his theory to be taken as a variant of either ideal rational choice or Sartrean radical choice.

Taking the first of these false alternatives, Bourdieu recognizes that the feel for the game may seem like the result of rational calculation, but Bourdieu insists that agency in a practical situation is not explicable on a rational-choice model:

> The conditions of rational calculation are practically never given in practice: time is limited, information is restricted, etc. And yet agents *do* do, much more often than if they were behaving randomly, "the only thing to do." This is because, following the intuitions of a "logic of practice" which is the product of a lasting exposure to conditions similar to those in which they are placed, they anticipate the necessity immanent in the way of the world.[74]

The rational-choice model thus may give the right account of the outcome, but it misses much about how that outcome was produced.

As for the second model, Sartre's theory of radical freedom in *Being and Nothingness* tends to discount the field, and thus, the social and environmental influences on choice. For Sartre the agent meets with objective resistance but is always free to reinterpret the nature of the goals and projects to be pursued. Although decisions are generally not the result of conscious deliberation, for the early Sartre they are still explained largely by reference to subjectivity. In contrast, Bourdieu thinks that the habitus explains agency better than Sartre's model of radical choice precisely because it recognizes that what must be explained is always choice within a structured situation that individuals do not themselves consciously structure. The habitus is built up from early experiences that are themselves prior to or simultaneous with the emergence of our subjective sense of our individual identities. But the weight of this early experience, according to Bourdieu, leads to self-reinforcement and resistance to change, as protection against crisis.[75] We tend to prefer the familiar problems with which we have already coped, and we build up *non-conscious, unwilled* strategies for avoiding the perception of other possibilities. This leads Bourdieu to see the force of the habitus as deeply conservative. What agents take as free choice in a present that is not determined by the past, but which anticipates and shapes the future, is really a projection of the past that represents the need to make the present as much like the past as possible. Bourdieu substitutes this *presence of the past* for Heidegger's *anticipation of the future*.[76] What looks to a philosopher such as Heidegger as possibilities coming to us from the future are really, for Bourdieu, the result of the *reproduction* of past objective structures.

In sum, the habitus does help to explain how individual agency is possible because it explains how our perceptions of possibilities are narrowed down to a range within which we can comport ourselves with enough play to feel as if we are choosing freely and meaningfully. Bourdieu does not rule out our sense of "personal" style, since this is a social fact that must be recognized. But he does see personal style as "never more than a deviation in relation to the style of a period or class."[77] Individuals are treated as essentially identical if they share the same social habitus.[78] This habitus constructs the present world but it also turns the "present of the presumed world" into "the only one [the habitus] can ever know."[79] The habitus explains how we perceive the possibilities for action that we do. At the same time that it explains agency, however, its explanation is that social agency leads more to replication and confirmation than to transformation: "The habitus is the principle of a selective perception of the indices tending to confirm and reinforce it rather than transform it."[80]

The thrust of the habitus is therefore conservative. But one must distinguish between the phenomenon of the habitus and the sociological *theory* of the habitus. The question then becomes "Is Bourdieu's *theory* itself incapable of social critique and resistance?" Commentators have noticed that he does not address himself to cases of social transformation or historical change. But Bourdieu is himself critical of social classes (for instance, the petite bourgeoisie) and social phenomena (such as officialization and symbolic violence). He sees sociology as reflexive, as a socioanalysis that, like psychoanalysis, can dispel the social myths that perpetuate domination.[81] He is not a fatalistic functionalist even if he does see an extremely high degree of necessity in how social behavior is produced. Yet this perception of necessity is precisely the motivation to resist that necessity through the deployment of a scientific sociology that will unmask the social self-deception or misrecognition that perpetuates the illusion of necessity:

I am often stunned by the degree to which things are determined: sometimes I think to myself, "This is impossible, people are going to think that you exaggerate." And, believe me, I do not rejoice over this. Indeed, I think that if I perceive necessity so acutely, it is because I find it particularly unbearable.[82]

What he must think is that the necessity is never total, and that the socioanalysis that portrays this necessity itself leads to resistance insofar as necessity is abhorrent.

Unfortunately, there is also a "winner loses" dilemma here: the more strongly that necessity is portrayed, the less successful resistance will appear to be able to be. Bourdieu does not seem to feel the full force of this dilemma, for he insists instead, without much argument, that we should opt not for sociologistic resignation, but for a "rational utopianism" that uses "the knowledge of the probable to make the possible come true."[83] I infer therefore that he is not really talking about necessity as fatalistic determinism or functionalism, but only ever about probability. In his own terms, we should see the habitus not as a deterministic, causal explanation, but only ever as an interpretation or a model that makes the social comportment intelligible. In Bourdieu's own language, we should not confuse the model of reality with the reality of the model.

The example of gender illuminates how Bourdieu's approach could have a critical thrust. In his portrayal of traditional Berber culture he shows the male/female opposition to be so basic that most other binary oppositions reflect it as well. But he is clear that there is a political mythology here: "male order is so deeply grounded as to need no justification: it imposes itself as self-evident, universal. . . ."[84] The deep necessity thus does not imply that the ordering is justified, but it works precisely to veil possibilities that would flow from recognition of the lack of justification: "male *sociodicy* owes its specific efficacy to the fact that it legitimates a relation of domination by inscribing it in a biological which is itself a biologized *social construction*."[85] Biology itself, when put to social use, becomes a socially constructed category that can serve to constrict social possibilities.

He also offers a reading of Virginia Woolf's *To the Lighthouse* as portraying "the domination of the dominant by his domination."[86] That is, women are portrayed as being able to ignore the *illusio* that leads men to engage in the central games of society. He argues in *Masculine Domination* that women can escape this normal will to dominate. By living through a Bourdieuian socioanalysis, they can attain a lucid view of the games that males play in their "desperate, and in its triumphant unawareness somewhat tragic, effort that every man has to make to rise to his own childhood conception of manhood."[87] Generalizing from the relation of Mr. and Mrs. Ramsey, Bourdieu asserts that women can see through to the vanity involved in the games, and he believes the story shows that women have "the *entirely negative* privilege of not being taken in by the games in which privileges are fought for."[88]

In sum, Bourdieu's reflexive sociology is clearly intended to be critical, however fatalistic his theory and practice seem. I prefer to emphasize the plasticity and flexibility of the habitus over its more reactionary and fatalist-sounding elements. After all, Bourdieu does think that conscious control of the habitus is possible, but only after the socioanalysis brings the influence of the habitus out of the tacit background into the explicit foreground. He therefore asserts that "not only can habitus be practically transformed (always within definite boundaries) by the effect of a social trajectory leading to conditions of living different from initial ones, it can also be *controlled* through awakening of consciousness and socioanalysis."[89] At the same time he is critical of the efficacy of "consciousness-raising" and of the "conscious, free, deliberate act of an isolated 'subject.' "[90] But I will point out that the *appearance* of determinism and resignation is generated precisely by the extent to which action is theorized as stemming much more from the body and its opaque dispositions than from conscious intentions. The strategy of moving the body from the periphery of our theories to their centers is not without its dangers. The more pervasive and inaccessible the practices of bodily socialization are made out to be, the less criticism and resistance may seem to be possible or worthwhile.

Bourdieu vs. Derrida

The emphasis on the body motivates Bourdieu to distance himself from Derrida's emphasis on language and from what Bourdieu calls the "divinization of the text."[91] At the same time he also objects to J. L. Austin's speech act theory for not recognizing that the power of performatives is a social power first and foremost, and that Austin could not even talk about the illocutionary force of speech acts such as promises without social power being already at play. The minister's ability to say "I thee wed" or the chancellor's ability to award a degree are possible not because of the structure of language alone, but because of the institutions in which these utterances are authorized. After all, the University Chancellor usually begins her speech that grants the degrees by saying "By the powers invested in me. . . ."

Bourdieu may think that this emphasis on the social is necessary to avoid falling back into the language of consciousness. However, linguistic structures are not conscious, and they may even condition how consciousness functions. Bourdieu is himself aware of this power of language, for he criticizes philosophers such as Heidegger for exploiting it. Bourdieu charges Heidegger with manipulating ordinary language and transforming it into an elevated style where ordinary words are given technical meanings that are then said to show essential truths that were hidden in ordinary usage. In sum, Bourdieu criticizes Austin for making ordinary language basic, and he criticizes Heidegger for saying that ordinary language is not basic. Is he trying to have it both ways at once?

It is hard to imagine that Bourdieu really believes that he could escape the scholastic field of philosophy that he castigates. He talks about the "magic" that takes place as a result of the interplay of the habitus and the field. At the same time, he criticizes Heidegger for his verbal conjuring tricks, such as inventing false etymologies or turning ordinary words into magical technical terms that purport to show

what is really going on. Heidegger's conjuring tricks are
designed to make us wonder how we could have missed
such insights when they were there in plain sight in the
ordinary words all along. Yet Bourdieu is an accomplished
rhetorician in his own right, and his rhetorical skills certainly must be part of the explanation for his own success in
the academic system that he loves to hate. One of Bourdieu's
favorite techniques is to use oxymorons so that something
intelligible emerges despite the apparent verbal contradictions. Examples would be his characterizations that I have
just cited of the habitus as "the intentionless invention of regulated improvisation"[92] or as "conductorless orchestra-
tion."[93] Furthermore, although Bourdieu chastises Heidegger
for attempted proof-by-etymology, Bourdieu is not above
suggesting that connections between roots of words show
connections between apparently unrelated phenomena, as
between virtue and virility, given the Latin root, *vir*.[94]

As a final example, one of his most characteristic and effective uses of tropes involves chiasmus, or turning a phrase
back on itself in parallel. The magic trick of socioanalysis is to
show, for instance, the confusion of "sliding from the model
of reality to the reality of the model."[95] Socioanalysis is said
furthermore to reveal how "the appropriation of the function
by the nominee is also appropriation of the nominee by the
function."[96] Socioanalysis may also lead one to doubt "the
reality of resistance which ignores the resistance of 'reality.'"[97] In effect, Bourdieu's skillful use of this rhetorical
device shows how, by reversing the words, a basic confusion
could have been avoided. Even when there is not a complete
reversal of meaning, he still likes to criticize those (probably
including Foucault) who "experience revolutions in the order
of words as radical revolutions in the order of things."[98]
However, as these examples show, Bourdieu himself likes

revolutions in the order of words. Both his skill and the authority of the field reinforce the reader's tendency to assume that these rhetorical flourishes encapsulate hard-won scientific truths about the social order.

These linguistic and stylistic issues are tied to a basic critique that Bourdieu levels against Derrida (and probably Foucault as well). Bourdieu disagrees strongly with Derrida about the role of language and the distinction between language and its authority. Bourdieu challenges Derrida (and Austin) for failing to ask where the authority comes from that enables the same utterances to lead in some cases to successful performance and in other cases not. His answer is that it is not enough just to look at the level of the utterances. One must also ask about the social sources of authorization. Bourdieu's thesis is that Derrida's approach forgets that "authority comes to language from outside."[99] He gives the example from Homer of the custom in ancient Greece whereby a person who was authorized to speak was given a staff-like *skeptron* to hold. Bourdieu maintains that the apparent authority of the holder of the skeptron is itself an illusion, one that has to be *mis*recognized to succeed. For Bourdieu there is often nothing but what he calls "social magic" involved in who gets authorized to speak and who does not. There are always masqueraders, "who disguise a performative utterance as a descriptive or constative statement." The spokesperson is really no better than the masqueraders, and Bourdieu defines the spokesperson as "an impostor endowed with the *skeptron.*"[100]

Why does Bourdieu imply that everyone who presumes to be authorized to speak is an imposter? Is everyone who speaks necessarily co-opted by the authorizing authorities? Is there no critical speech act that could be the basis for resistance? Certainly some people do know more than others on certain topics. In *Excitable Speech* Judith Butler takes issue with Bourdieu insofar as she thinks that he theorizes the status quo and does not take into account how the same language can be turned back against the social authority. Extending the idea of the performative, she gives the example of Rosa Parks sitting in the front of the bus and thereby starting the emancipatory resistance to racial discrimination.[101] However, Bourdieu does seem to be aware of how resistance at the marginal edges can succeed in challenging the social authorization. That is probably his reason for asserting the counterintuitive claim that there are always masqueraders. Masqueraders are more likely to be aware of the social arbitrariness of who gets to hold the *skeptron,* and more likely to turn the language against the authorities.

This point involves a question of political strategy, however, whereas I think that the real philosophical issue here is that Bourdieu should be distinguishing several separate theses about the background conditions of intelligibility. The general charge is that the intelligibility of much of what agents do is conditioned by implicit background practices that cannot be made explicit all at once. However, there are at least three controversial views about whether these background practices can be made explicit through critique and then become the basis for resistance. The first is that there are *bodily* skills that exhibit a practical know-how that cannot be articulated entirely in the explicit knowing-that of theoretical assertions. The second is that there are also *social* skills that would break down if they were articulated and thematized explicitly. The third thesis is that there are phenomena that necessarily exceed any and all attempts to articulate them.

Whereas Bourdieu could accept the first and second theses, I think that Derrida accepts the third and Bourdieu does not. Bourdieu is interested in theorizing the practices as they are practiced, which means coming up with a notion of "agents" who are neither "subjects" nor "zombies." In contrast, concepts that are candidates for the third thesis will be disclosive conditions that make the uncovering of particular entities possible but that cannot be uncovered themselves. Derrida calls these notions *quasi-transcendentals*. If I understand him correctly, a quasi-transcendental is not transcendent, which (for Kant) implies having the metaphysical status of *ultimate reality*. *Quasi-transcendentals* are transcendental because they exceed attempts to make them explicit. This insistence on the excess of a quasi-transcendental means that it escapes complete articulation in any particular context, and that it can be iterated only in an other context (although it would exceed that context as well). A quasi-transcendental is something that transcends a context, but only from within yet another context. It is not part of the God's eye view of everything or the "view from nowhere." That is why it is a *quasi*-transcendental, for it only ever appears contextualized. That is, it transcends any particular context, but it is only ever found in some context or other. It appears not as a *repetition*, which is always the *same*, but as an *iteration*, which is like a repetition except that it alters because the context is different. As Derrida uses the term, iteration is repetition but with alteration.

Quasi-transcendentals need not be thought to be ineffable. The point is rather that they are the constitutive conditions of practices (and not themselves identifiable as practices). They might involve 'context' or 'iterability' in claims such as "there is no contextless point of view" or "there could be no meanings that are not iterable (i.e., repeatable, but with some alteration of meaning)." They are therefore not discrete, "ontic" phenomena so much as what makes practices significant. They could thus be said to be *organizing significances.* Other examples of quasi-transcendentals may include Heidegger's clearing, Nietzsche's will to power, Levinas's Other, and Laclau's "infinite play of differences" (i.e., society). However, for now I am concerned with Derrida's quasi-transcendentals, especially justice and *différance*, which have the feature of *undecidability.* Undecidability is a well-known term and for a long time has been the crux of deconstruction. Unfortunately, the concept gives the impression that deconstruction could never take a normative stand. If basic alternatives such as right or wrong, good or bad, and true or false could not be decided, deconstruction would seem to be useless for ethical, political, or even aesthetic resistance.

Derrida corrects this view in his important essay "Force of Law: The 'Mystical Foundations of Authority.'" As Derrida recognizes in his essay, if decisions could not be made, this would threaten "the whole *subjectal* axiomatic of responsibility, of conscience, of intentionality, of property."[102] I stress the word 'subjectal' here as a contrast to 'agential'. Derrida now says that undecidability does not mean that decisions cannot be made. It only means that for a decision to have been a free decision there must have been some prior sense in which the choice of going one way or the other on a decision seemed *underdetermined.* 'Underdetermined' is my term, and is introduced as a gloss on Derrida's statement in "Force of Law" that "if it were guaranteed, the decision would be reduced to calculation and we couldn't call it just."[103] The "aporia" is supposedly that either there is some rule that determines the decision, but then the decision is not free; or it has not been made in accordance with a rule, and then it is not just.

To Bourdieu, Derrida's analysis would certainly sound sophistic. Bourdieu could argue that this account threatens to turn undecid*ability* into undecid*edness*. If the claim is merely the psychological one that any decision must have initially gone through some uncertainty before deciding on one rather than the other, that is too trivial a point to be an aporia. If the claim is that decisions are arbitrary because there is never sufficient justification for the outcome, that is a more philosophically interesting claim, but it depends on a dubious conception of *justification.*

Because Derrida thinks of justification as an impossible achievement, he believes that decisions can never be just. Each decision (by a judge, for instance) seems to have to be *ex nihilo* in that it has to take on itself the question of whether the principle or rule that it invokes was valid in the first place. The judge's decision sets itself above the law and effectively suspends the law. Yet as a decision it declares that the particular rule of law was always in effect and that it determined the outcome of this decision. The decision is said to be a *performative* that exceeds itself. It is violence at the beginning, because it represents a *break* with past law, and it is violence in the outcome, because it imposes its interpretation on the present *in the name of* the justice of the law. The law is deconstructable, then, because although it pretends to a legitimate constative that is sanctioned by justice, a *genealogical* analysis shows it to be a performative that enacts a form of violence. The law depends on violence being misrecognized as legitimate.

This theory might only reinforce Bourdieu's belief that deconstruction involves a radical skepticism about the political, the ethical, and the aesthetic. However, Derrida tries to rebut that charge in this essay by saying that *justice* is different from the law. His "deconstructive genealogy" tries to show that the law claims to be just but is in fact violence. But he does not claim to deconstruct justice itself. Justice is undeconstructable, he asserts, and he even says that deconstruction is justice. Furthermore, he claims that deconstruction is not opposed to but in fact is guided by the "classical emancipatory ideal."[104]

For both Foucault and Derrida, then, genealogy is practiced in the name of emancipation. While I doubt that Bourdieu would consider Derrida's claim that justice is undeconstructable a sufficient account of the social reality behind language, Bourdieu also claims that his own method of reflexive sociology is emancipatory. Insofar as that claim is crucial in understanding Bourdieu's account of critical resistance, I will now turn to an evaluation of it, saving an assessment of the prospects of Derrida's enterprise of deconstructive genealogy for later in this book.

Bourdieu's Social Ontology of Resistance

Refusing the assumption of transhistorical bodily invariants and hypothesizing instead the historical situatedness of the body carries theoretical risks. A major task becomes that of explaining how the social fabric makes resistance possible. Furthermore, if the theorist sees the empirical application of the theory as itself a form of social critique or destabilization, then that methodological possibility also must be consistent with the ontological explanation of both domination and resistance.

There are thus at least two ways to hear the question "How is critical resistance possible?" This question could be taken as a request for practical, political guidelines about how to distinguish what is socially evil from what is socially good, and how to overcome the evil. But although both Foucault and Bourdieu have been politically active as private individuals, their theories do not aspire to legislating *a priori* precepts about the form that criticism and resistance must take in different circumstances. The contingencies of each situation will require *phronesis,* or the practical wisdom to see what the singular situation demands.

But they do not ignore the question altogether, for it can also be understood along the lines of Kant's famous question "How is experience possible?" Here the question is less one of practical politics than of social ontology (where "social ontology" means only a heuristic theoretical model of the features of the social, not a foundationalist claim to metaphysical necessity). Of course, Foucault and Bourdieu reject the approach of transcendental philosophy, but they do try to explain the conditions for the possibility of resistance. That is, they offer some account of how social reality can produce a phenomenon like resistance, even if they desist from *prescribing* the forms that it must take in each and every case.

Perhaps because of the influence of Merleau-Ponty and Heidegger, Bourdieu's social ontology does acknowledge that there are some universals. But these are not universal principles such as Kant or Habermas think are necessary to ground criticism and resistance. Instead, Bourdieu speaks of the universal characteristics of *bodily* existence "such as the fact of existing as a separate biological individual, or of being confined to a place and a moment, or even the fact of being and knowing oneself destined for death."[105] Unlike Habermasian universals, these particular universals that Bourdieu cites do not point to a context-independent standpoint from which to judge a particular social configuration. Instead, Bourdieu's universals entail that there is no such ideal context-independent standpoint, and that the given society alone provides the grounds for evaluation and criticism:

Doomed to death, that end which cannot be taken as an end, man is a being without reason for being. It is society, and society alone, which dispenses, to different degrees, the justifications and reasons for existing; it is society which, by producing the affairs or positions that are said to be "important," produces the acts and agents that are judged to be "important," for themselves and for the others—characters objectively and subjectively assured of their value and thus liberated from indifference and insignificance.[106]

The Kantian universalist is therefore misguided in trying to assess social situations from a God's-eye point of view. For Bourdieu such a point of view is still a particular social point of view that is failing to recognize itself as such. The social cannot be transcended:

Indeed, without going so far as to say, with Durkheim, "Society is God," I would say: God is never anything other than society. What is expected of God is only ever obtained from society, which alone has the power to justify you, to liberate you from facticity, contingency, and absurdity. . . . The judgement of others is the last judgement; and social exclusion is the concrete form of hell and damnation.[107]

Consequently, when asked specifically about Habermas's desire for universal norms, Bourdieu responds in a historicist way and asks about the social conditions that would prompt someone to have an interest in the universal. He admits to such an interest himself. However, what is more important to him than knowing universals is knowing reflexively the limits of his own vision. I see Bourdieu as rejecting both absolutism and relativism, and striving instead for reflexivity. Self-analysis reveals not simply first-order knowledge of the object domain, but a second-order knowledge of "the instruments of knowledge in their historically determinate aspects."[108]

In brief, universals are less interesting to Bourdieu than the desire for universals, which is socially conditioned. A

theory that aspires to universals without reflexive awareness of its limitations will produce distortions by ignoring
the social conditions for the production of truths. Bourdieu
recognizes that the universalist's desire for a self-founding
theoria is tempting, but he believes that it must be tempered
by a more historicist reflexive critique:

> I discover that one becomes a sociologist, a theoretician, so as to
> have an absolute point of view, a *theoria*; and that, for as long as it
> is unrecognized, this kingly, divine ambition is a tremendous cause
> of error. So much so that, to escape even a little from the relative,
> one absolutely has to abdicate from the claim to absolute knowl-
> edge, uncrown the philosopher-king.[109]

This reflexive critique not only admits its own fallibility, but it
is also essential in revealing the historical conditions for its
own aspirations to *theoria*. Bourdieu believes that failing to
recognize these historical conditions will trap us in misrecog-
nitions of ourselves and our situation. Unlike the universalist,
he thinks that self-understanding is attained better by starting with a more historicist attitude. Unlike those whom he
labels postmodernists, however, he does not think that this
historicism leads to skepticism about truth and reason.
Instead, he thinks that this methodological historicism serves
the defense of truth and reason better than Habermas's universalism. Bourdieu's reflexive historicism makes us more
conscious of the fact that truth is not simply epistemic, but
also something that is *valued* and thus contested in what
Bourdieu calls the "politics of truth" within a given scientific
field.[110] Similarly, rationality is not atemporal, but it is a function of the particular canons and principles at a given
moment. Denying the historicity of rationality and the politics of truth will trap us in the illusion of being free and not
needing to resist. The methodological hypothesis of histori-

cism is thus closer to the truth than methodological universalism, and Bourdieu believes that it leads more effectively to practical resistance and emancipation.

How can socioanalytic resistance be certain, however, that it is emancipatory and not simply submissive? Bourdieu's account, as reconstructed aptly by Loïc Wacquant, starts from the recognition of how problematic resistance is, and how difficult it is to distinguish resistance from submission.[111] What he calls the unresolvable contradiction of resistance is that whereas resistance might seem liberating and submission alienating, in fact resistance is often alienating while submission can be liberating.[11] Thus, the dominated can resist by trying to efface the signs of difference that have led to their domination. But this strategy has the same effect as assimilation, and could well look like submission. Or the dominated can instead try to dominate their own domination by accepting and accentuating the characteristics that mark them as dominated. But this too does not look much different from giving in to domination.

Since I have been discussing Bourdieu's views about gender, let me offer as an example the debate among feminists about whether the category of the "feminine" must be rejected altogether, or whether it is still possible to be feminine even if the category itself has been a means of furthering male domination of women. The dilemma is that insofar as someone continues, for instance, to wear feminine fashions or to check her appearance constantly, she will risk being seen as submitting even if, as a feminist, she understands herself to be resisting the patriarchal gaze. But if she refuses to wear what she likes just because of how it will be perceived, that too may amount to being co-opted and assimilated. Addressing Sandra Lee Bartky's well-known essay "Foucault, Femininity and the Modernization of Patriarchal Power," Elizabeth Grosz writes: "The practices of femininity can readily function, in certain contexts that are difficult to ascertain in advance, as modes of guerrilla subversion of patriarchal codes, although the line between compliance and subversion is always a fine one, difficult to draw with any certainty." Grosz then adds the important point that outside a given power network (or social "field," a Bourdieuian could say) there is no way to describe an action as either resistance or compliance: "Its enmeshment in disciplinary regimes is the condition of the subject's social effectivity, as either conformist or subversive."[113]

This example problematizes Bourdieu's account of the complicity of the dominated in their own domination.[114] On Bourdieu's social ontology, whether this submission is voluntary or involuntary is beside the point, for *the dispositions which incline them to this complicity are also the effect, embodied, of domination.*"[115] That is, the dominated will not experience their existence as the result of intolerable domination because their own dispositions fit the social field in which they find themselves.

If this is Bourdieu's outlook, it seems to be too pessimistic an assessment of the possibilities for resistance to patriarchy. He does not seem to appreciate the creative potential of using the practices of femininity for the purposes of what Grosz calls the "guerrilla subversion of patriarchal codes." So although Grosz agrees with Bourdieu that it is difficult to say where the line is between subversion and compliance, she does not think that it is impossible to tell the difference. Some days one's efforts at subversion will be misinterpreted as compliance, but other days one may be more successful in challenging the dominant codes and revealing the code of domination that they mask.

Like Bourdieu, Foucault is also aware that domination functions more effectively when the arbitrariness of the asymmetrical relations remains invisible. However, he is not as skeptical as Bourdieu about subverting domination. The question is: What might help to make relations of domination visible and thus to call for critical questioning and resistance to them? As I indicated, Bourdieu's answer is the socioanalysis itself. He thinks that the reflexivity of the sociological insight into how asymmetrically the social situation is structured can neutralize the force of the bodily dispositions. Bourdieu thus believes that objective, scientific knowledge can be emancipatory. The better we understand the external constraints on our thought and action, the more we will see through them and the less effective they will become.[116]

Social self-knowledge thus can lead to effective resistance. The contribution of socioanalysis is that it reveals that comportment generally understood as freedom may in reality be illusory. As Bourdieu remarks, "paradoxically, sociology frees us by freeing us from the illusion of freedom, or, more exactly, from the misplaced belief in illusory freedom."[117] The idea is that social determinants have more effect the less they are perceived. When they come to be perceived and acknowledged as determinants, that in itself will provoke resistance. The greatest illusion is the false belief that one is free from social determinants. This illusion of being free from determination allows the determinants to be even more effective. Believing that one is free thus makes determinism more likely to be true. Conversely, coming to recognize social determinants as such can potentially be liberating.

Reflexive sociology is itself therefore understood to be a form of critical resistance. It aspires to objectivity and reason in the sense that it grasps the truth of a social configuration. But it recognizes that its own stance is produced by its own social configuration, so it does not claim insight into trans-historical structures or *a priori* principles.

Despite this nod to the historical, Bourdieu's epistemo-logical claims are stronger than Foucault's. Bourdieu's stress on scientific explanation implies that a particular socio-analysis must be taken as the one right explanation of the social structure. In discussing Bourdieu's own rhetorical strategies and why these made him more of an intellectual rather than less of one, I have shown some reason to doubt the emancipatory efficacy of socioanalysis in the final moment of self-knowledge.

In contrast, I think that Foucault stands on firmer ground in that he does not claim the status of science for genealogy. In the tradition of critical theory, he would probably settle for the suggestion that a particular genealogical account was one of several possible interpretations. But Foucault could nevertheless say that the account was a valid interpre-tation. Like Bourdieu, Foucault does not believe that knowl-edge is a matter only of domination. On the contrary, he could maintain that the knowledge represented by a suc-cessful genealogical unveiling of asymmetries and false uni-versals can itself be an efficacious means of resisting domination. For domination to be resisted effectively it must first be revealed.

The problem with this response as an interpretation of Bourdieu is that it is not clearly compatible with the strong statements (especially in earlier writings) about how inac-cessible the habitus is to conscious recognition and transfor-mation. Whether Bourdieu has really explained how neutralization and destabilization of the habitus would be possible is a matter of continuing debate. If the reading of Bourdieu that I have provided is correct, the most sympa-thetic line of defense depends on emphasizing the plasticity of the habitus. The interplay of the habitus and the field structures how the world is intelligible, but this grid of intelligibility does not strictly determine what we do. Bourdieu is really offering us an account of the intelligibility of action and not one that explains how action is causally generated.[118] There is room for the perception of different possibilities within the social field, and thus for improvised courses of action. Insofar as this grid of intelligibility functions by narrowing the range of perceived possibilities, becoming more reflexive about the grid itself would in fact seem to widen the range of perceived possibilities and thus to weaken the grip of the compulsions to compliance.

Post-Critique: Philosophy and Race

As a postscript to this chapter, I would like to offer some reflections on a provocative question that was recently posed to academics who write about Continental philosophy: Why have twentieth-century Continental philosophers not paid more attention to race? This question puts any philosopher on the spot, insofar as race could always be thematized more than it has been in the past. The critical resistance to racism has been a paradigm, and I include my own post-critical reflections at this point because they draw on Bourdieu's reflexive sociology in a way that is intended to show how well suited that method is for a discussion of such a question.

But first, a useful exercise would be to note other topics that Continental philosophers tend to ignore, and to figure out why. Until relatively recently, for instance, gender was not discussed, even if sex was. Class was a concept left to sociology to study. In addition to race, class, and gender (but among these, gender and race especially), there are other aspects of human facticity that have been ignored. Emmanuel Levinas criticized Martin Heidegger by remarking that the Dasein is never hungry. Continental philosophers have indeed paid little attention to hunger, to war, to disease, to infirmities, or to physical disabilities. At the same time, Levinas also pointed out, they have ignored enjoyment by overemphasizing anxiety, fecundity by overemphasizing death, and accomplishment by overemphasizing failure.

The negative preoccupation with fear, death, and failure is the legacy of existentialism. However, despite existentialism's attempt to account for the individual and the personal, it was also universalistic. Jean-Paul Sartre was thought to be radical because of his analyses of sadism, masochism, sex, and seduction. Yet his enterprise was to give a universal account of what it is to be human. Similarly, although Heidegger was not an existentialist, *Being and Time* is a book that gives a general theory of the Dasein. There is not much attention in either theorist to differential features of the body, such as whether the body in question is male or female or black or white. In fact, it is difficult to tell whether Heidegger's Dasein even has a body. Heidegger tends to think of the body as an object, and as such, the body tends to be portrayed as a derivative phenomenon that presupposes the more primordial world-disclosure of the Dasein. Sartre does talk about the body, but he clearly does not like it very much. The body is usually something vile, especially the feminine, sexualized body, which he typifies in *Being and Nothingness* as the slimy.

Maurice Merleau-Ponty and Simone de Beauvoir begin to portray the body more positively, and also as more central to philosophy than the Cartesian cogito. De Beauvoir gives an account of gendered difference that shows the masculinist blindness in Sartre. Merleau-Ponty makes embodiment in general and perception in particular fundamental to the human experience of being located in a world. However, he produced no major study of race during his abruptly curtailed lifetime.

Given the question of why there is not more attention to race, one disingenuous response is that the study of race is the job of cultural studies or anthropology or sociology, but not of philosophy. This "division-of-labor" argument supposedly spares philosophers the burden of delving into social practices that are beyond their experience. Equally self-deceptive is the "not-my-area" argument. Here the academic philosopher grants that race is a philosophical topic, but then suggests that along with other specializations such as philosophy of physics or modal logic, it is not among that person's areas of competence. Both of these arguments can mask what may be simply a refusal to think.

At this point, though, a closer look at Continental philosophy itself as a profession, rather than at the psychology of its professors, may be illuminating. The model here is Bourdieu's reflexive sociology. Applying his model of the relation of habitus and field, Bourdieu shows the ways in which the academic field has built-in patterns of misrecognition that academics rely on so that they will not have to see the illusions that their profession perpetrates. We have seen the irony of Bourdieu's analysis of the intellectual, for instance, for always trying not to be the sort of person with a particular past, and for generating "the scholastic illusion of distance from all positions."[119] For Bourdieu this attempt to escape every meaningful social field is a form of hypocrisy since one necessarily has to be involved in some social fields.

In context, Bourdieu is analyzing not just the intellectual in general, but his own background in philosophy. However, since the task is not to offer a psychological or biographical explanation, the focus should be on the theory and not the person. His analysis can thus be expanded and applied to philosophy itself, even if he does not do so in exactly the following words. His point is that the scholastic illusion is a feature of philosophy itself in its aspiration to stand outside and to comprehend every particular standpoint. The illusion that philosophy transcends its facticity or particularity is precisely what prevents its practitioners from seeing their own situatedness.

Bourdieu's notion of the field could lead to the construction of an explanation of how the field of philosophy may be blocking the study of the particularity of race. The argument would depend on the claim that philosophy tends to neglect race because philosophy's emphasis on shared features that people have in common leads to a general neglect of particular bodily differences. In *Racist Culture: Philosophy and the Politics of Meaning*, David Theo Goldberg argues that the modern liberal philosophical tradition has denied the moral relevance of otherness, and that by ignoring difference, philosophy historically has failed to take race seriously.[120] Goldberg provides textual evidence that modern liberal philosophers such as Kant and Hume insisted on the natural stupidity of nonwhites, and even Mill thought that they were incapable of self-government.[121]

If Goldberg is right, and if the neglect of race is itself racist, is it possible to conclude that philosophy itself as an academic field (in Bourdieu's technical sense of the term) is racist? A strong version of this conclusion could imply that philosophy as a subject matter *causes* racism, or at least a certain indifference to racial difference. However, as I maintained earlier, Bourdieu should not be construed as offering a causal account of the generation of action. Instead, the field and habitus should only be taken as a model or a grid of intelligibility for social comportment. Therefore, the strong, causal claim goes beyond what Bourdieu's account would warrant. The conclusion that could be drawn is that philosophy as a field has been and continues to be unduly blind to differential phenomena such as race. However, without the causal claim, one could reasonably hope that this blindness could then be criticized, resisted, and corrected.

Although Bourdieu does not make this argument about philosophy and racism himself, if he accepted it he would probably add that it applies to universalists and pluralists alike. Bourdieu thinks that the concern of philosophy for the universal often ignores "the conditions of access to the universal" and it "generally serves to justify the established order, the prevailing distribution of powers and privileges—the domination of the bourgeois, white, Euro-American heterosexual male."[122] Pluralism is no better off because the cynical rejection of the hegemony of the universal can be merely another way "of accepting things as they are."[123] This cynical relativism is for Bourdieu the more dangerous of the two attitudes because it can give itself "an air of radicalism."[124] The appearance of radicalism is an illusion that masks philosophy's co-optation and its inability to alter the status quo.

Any field involves arbitrary assumptions and exclusions that then cannot be perceived once one is authorized to play the game. Those who become skilled at the game do not experience the rules that the field imposes on what agents can or cannot do as constraining but as enabling. Because the skilled are so good at maneuvering in the field, they will experience as entitlements the same structures that outsiders may perceive as impositions. Skilled insiders may not think of themselves as biased, but in fact Bourdieu thinks that they are co-opted by the habitus. In hiring a new faculty member, for instance, he thinks that while there is conscious attention to the signs of competence, the acceptability of candidates depends to a large extent on their habitus, that is, "the barely perceptible indices, generally corporeal ones— dress, bearing, manner—of dispositions to be, and above all to become, 'one of us.' "[125]

This conclusion is not in itself very surprising. What is surprising is that Bourdieu did not list the most obvious corporeal indication: race. Most people are aware that preferences for some people and exclusion of others are misrecognized, and that apparently rational concerns about competence are often based on an unarticulated sense of compatibility. What Bourdieu's analysis of the self-deception of philosophy brings out is the way that the academic field of philosophy causes its practitioners to think that philosophy can be done in only a certain way, or that there are only certain kinds of questions that are philosophical. This is not to say that there are no philosophical questions about race. But the questions tend to be primarily ethical and political ones, where racism is just a case or an example of the more general evils of oppression and exclusion. For instance, philosophers can ask normative questions about why racism is wrong, or why ideally skin color should be of no more consequence than eye color is now. However, there are also metaphysical questions that could be asked. Insofar as racism is generally essentialist, for instance, it could be contested by appeal to social construction or at least to human malleability. Even phenomenological questions about the experience of racist exclusion are pertinent to philosophy. So there is no reason to think that the questions about race that are strictly speaking "philosophical" are limited to a small corner of the field.

Insofar as Continental philosophy usually breaks through the sub-divisions imposed by the mainstream Anglo-American philosophy, it does seem to be precisely the place where one would expect more discussion of race. In fact, the claim that race has been ignored is not entirely accurate, and it is now time to point to some examples. Bourdieu's concern has just been noted. Sartre's introduction to Fanon's *Wretched of the Earth* is another example, as are his play *The Respectful Prostitute* and his newspaper articles condemning the racism he observed during his travels in the United States. Sartre also offers a trenchant analysis of anti-Semitism in "Portrait of an Anti-Semite." There he argues that racial bigotry is not simply a minor failing of a person, but a sign that the person's entire being is flawed. Furthermore, in *Being and Nothingness* he provides a powerful interpretation of a scene from a William Faulkner novel of a Klan murder of a man named Christmas. On this reading, racism becomes the paradigm for all forms of hatred, which Sartre sees not as the hatred of one or some others, but of all others. Racism is thus not just the resentment of a particular group, but of all humanity as such, including oneself. Sartre's analysis thus reaches farther than cultural studies would perhaps be willing to go insofar as Sartre does not hesitate to universalize the hatred in racist speech and conduct.

The poststructuralists have also paid more attention to race than is often supposed. Jacques Derrida has several essays in which he criticizes apartheid. As I point out in the next chapter, he also includes "opposition to racism" as a "European" duty, along with opposition to nationalism and to xenophobia. Furthermore, his recent autobiographical reflections have brought out the extent to which he was himself in his childhood subjected to state-imposed prejudice. Thus, as a Jewish child in Algeria his French citizenship was suspended. As for Foucault, although he is sometimes charged with neglecting all three of the categories of race, class, and gender, in fact there was a period when racism was his central concern. As we have seen, in volume 1 of *The History of Sexuality* he offers a novel historical account of the emergence of biological racism. Even more pertinent is the account that links state racism to bio-power, as discussed in chapter 2. Whereas racism in the age of bio-power can be practiced with efficiency on a massive scale, its rhetoric is a throwback to an earlier vocabulary of blood and family that is drawn from the sovereignty model of power. Foucault's genealogy of bio-power brings out both the horror and the contradiction of this conjunction of the reality of genocide and the rhetoric of racial cleansing. Foucault describes vividly how rhetoric and reality can go hand in hand in the complicit construction of social evil.

Poststructuralism has been a significant influence on more recent approaches to the study of race. As one example of the influence of poststructural social theory on subsequent post-critical social theory, I go back to the years shortly after Foucault's death to look at the complex relation of Cornel West to Michel Foucault. I say the relation is complex for although in 1985 West is enthusiastic about Foucault as a new paradigm for the study of race, by 1989 the attitude is more critical. In 1985 West wrote "The Dilemma of the Black Intellectual," which he describes in *The Cornel West Reader* as his "most widely quoted and controversial piece."[126] Here he accepts many of Foucault's tactical points, including the rejection of the favorite code words of both Marxism and bourgeois humanism: 'science', 'taste', 'tact', 'ideology', 'progress', and 'liberation'.[127] Insofar as such terms suborn intellectuals (particularly those who are African American) and induce them to go along with the established institutional means of domination and control, the code words must be resisted. However, West is not against institutions per se. Although he rejects the Kantian problematic, he is willing to adapt Kant's rhetoric to his own purposes, as when he quips that "an intelligentsia without institutionalized critical consciousness is blind, and critical consciousness severed from collective insurgency is empty."[128] The struggle is not over "the truth," but over control of the vast institutional mechanisms that give a regime of truth its status. However, like Bourdieu, West is wary of thinking of "intellectual work" (an oxymoron) as a form of "oppositional political praxis" that allows African Americans to fit comfortably into the "bourgeois academy of postmodern America."[129] In this essay, then, West sees in Foucault's tactics "the possibility of effective resistance and meaningful social transformation;" however, he cannot buy into the Foucaultian "rejection of any form of utopianism and any positing of a telos."[130]

"On Prophetic Pragmatism," published in 1989, is a more specific program statement. After embracing Foucault's genealogical mode of inquiry, West rejects Foucault's antiromantic suspicion of any talk about "wholeness, totality, telos, purpose, or even future."[131] He disagrees with three features of Foucault's work: its insistence on asking the Kantian transcendental question about the conditions for the possibility of subject formation, the degree to which it downplays human agency (both individually and collectively) insofar as it reifies discourses, disciplines, and techniques, and its failure to do more than provide "solely negative conceptions of critique and resistance."[132] West's own program of prophetic pragmatism is more than willing to articulate ideals of democracy, equality, and freedom. As a pragmatist, he rejects the Kantian type of transcendental *worth looking into.* ?

question as "a wheel that turns yet plays no part in the mechanism."[133] He then remarks: "Like Foucault, prophetic pragmatists criticize and resist forms of subjection, as well as types of economic exploitation, state repression and bureaucratic domination. But these critiques and resistances, unlike his, are unashamedly guided by moral ideals of creative democracy and individuality."[134]

In wanting to go beyond Foucault, West is leaving behind the historical limitations of poststructuralism and looking to a more positive and constructive program of post-critique. Certainly the field of Continental philosophy should pay more attention to race. In fact, the recent publication of several books and anthologies by Continental philosophers on race begins to fill the gap. Moreover, as I have indicated, Continental philosophy can in fact point to some examples in its history where it did analyze race in provocative ways. As the field moves more into alignment with other areas of the humanities and social sciences, its own parameters will broaden to include questions that were previously, perhaps, not considered to be sufficiently "philosophical." If this change represents progress in the academy, there is still some distance to go before it is reflected in real social change as well. However, intellectual cynicism about the past will only decrease the chances of change in the future. In the present, therefore, if the choice is between cynicism and hope, Cornel West's pragmatic program of proactive hope is likely to be the more productive attitude.

4   Levinas and Derrida: "Ethical Resistance"

Levinas: Intersubjectivity and the Face

Emmanuel Levinas approaches philosophy in a markedly different way than Foucault and Bourdieu. Writing at an earlier moment when Sartre and Merleau-Ponty are still at the forefront of French philosophy, Levinas must stake out his own standpoint by contrasting it to that of these phenomenologists, and to Heidegger as well. But despite Levinas's critique of these philosophers, there is still a sense in which his approach to philosophy is closer to theirs than it is to the poststructuralists. Most pointedly, he still aspires to "first philosophy," that is, to a foundational account of human existence. In contrast to Foucault, then, Levinas's theory may appear unhistorical and *a priori*. What makes Levinas so distinctive, however, is the importance he gives to the ethical. His reason for doing first philosophy is to make ethics primary, where ethics is used in the broad sense of unenforceable obligation. This primacy of the ethical contrasts with French phenomenologists for whom ethics was either something of an afterthought or else a promissory note tacked on after the main phenomenological theory was worked out in the magnum opus.

For poststructuralists such as Foucault and Derrida the lack of attention to the ethical also became problematic. One reason attention has returned to Levinas's early work and in particular to *Totality and Infinity* (first published in 1961) is that he makes the ethical so central, whereas the phenomenologists and the poststructuralists alike seem unable to provide an ethics. Of course, Foucault starts to make up for this lack in his last years by his historical studies of the ethics of the care for the self. But the later Foucault continues to be a thoroughgoing historicist. A significant point of difference between Foucault and Levinas is thus that whereas they are both pluralists, Foucault is much more historicist.

Given these contrasts, how does Levinas account for critical resistance, and how persuasive are his foundationalist claims about human existence? His explanation of resistance is closely tied to his views about the alterity of self and other. The uniqueness of these views comes from his insistence on preserving the difference and alterity of this relation rather than trying to bridge or assimilate the difference in the manner, for instance, that the Hegelian master-slave dialectic does. Because of this emphasis on difference, Levinas becomes interesting in relation to Derrida's notion of *différance*. I will discuss the relation of Derrida and Levinas later in this chapter. Now, however, I want to focus on Levinas's account of ethical resistance, and to do that, I should first make clear his account of intersubjectivity in general and the face of the other in particular.

To broach the issues about intersubjectivity I will start with a disagreement between Levinas and Merleau-Ponty. The larger issue is how one first becomes aware of others. This question is tied in turn to the question of how one becomes aware of oneself. Moreover, does this self-awareness come before the perception of others, or is self-awareness possible only on the condition of the perception of others?

The case in point concerns Merleau-Ponty's interpretation of Husserl on the phenomenon of the handshake.[1] The analyses of the handshake lead to three different cases or paradigms. The first considers the case of shaking hands with oneself. That is, the right hand touches the left hand, but the left hand, instead of remaining "touched" like a sheer object, starts to perceive the right hand. Merleau-Ponty sees this event as a paradigm of the *body* (not simply consciousness) becoming self-aware: "Thus I touch myself touching; my body accomplishes 'a sort of reflection'" and the body itself becomes a "perceiving thing," a "subject-object."[2]

This first paradigm prepares one for understanding that there are other such "perceiving things." I become aware of others not as Descartes and other philosophers thought—that is, through comparison, analogy, projection or what Husserl calls "introjection." Instead, says Merleau-Ponty, "the reason why I have evidence of the other's being-there when I shake his/her hand is that his/her hand is substituted for my left hand, and my body annexes the body of another person in that 'sort of reflection' it is paradoxically the seat of. My two hands 'coexist' or are 'compresent' because they are one single body's hands. The other person appears through an extension of that compresence; he/she and I are like organs of one single intercorporeality."[3] In other words, on Merleau-Ponty's reading of Husserl, the second paradigm of shaking the other's hand is like the first paradigm of shaking one's own hand. He believes that one feels the other's hand to be feeling one's own hand. Just as one's own left hand can switch from being touched by one's own right hand and become the hand that is doing the touching, Merleau-Ponty ventriloquizes Husserl into asserting that one touches the other's hand and then feels one's own hand being touched. For both of these phenomenologists this example is intended to show that the awareness of others is not based on indirect inference from one mind to another mind. Instead, the awareness is of an embodied person for another embodied person: "it is the [other person] as a whole who is given to me with all the possibilities . . . that I have in my presence to myself in my incarnate being, the unimpeachable attestation."[4]

Levinas wants to offer a third but entirely different account of the emergence of intersubjectivity, that is to say, of the awareness of the other as like the self but different from the self. First of all, he thinks (correctly, I would say) that Merleau-Ponty's Husserlian account of the phenomenon of the handshake is wrong. Can one really feel the other's hand feeling one's own? Levinas thinks not. But he also thinks that the phenomenologists are wrong not only about the phenomenon of the handshake, but also about the philosophical issues underlying their analysis of the handshake. The phenomenologists' paradigms overemphasize *cognition* and ignore what Levinas sees as the more primordial *ethical* relation to the other. For Levinas ethics is most primordially involved in the encounter with the *face* of the other. Even though Merleau-Ponty is emphasizing the primacy of the pre-theoretical over the theoretical, the *pre-theoretical* is still the pre-*theoretical*. The relation of sociality is still thought of most essentially as a matter of *knowledge*. Levinas then objects as follows:

In the phenomenological theory of intersubjectivity it is always the *knowledge* of the alter ego that breaks egological isolation. Even the values the alter ego takes on, and those attributed to it, are based on a prior knowledge. The idea that a sensibility could reach the other *otherwise* than by the "gnosis" of touching, or seeing . . .

seems foreign to the analyses of the phenomenologists. The psychism is consciousness, and in the word "consciousness" [conscience] the radical "science" [science] remains essential, primordial. Thus, sociality does not break the order of consciousness any more than does knowledge [savoir], which, cleaving to the known [su], immediately coincides with whatever might have been foreign to it.[5]

In contrast to the phenomenologists, then, Levinas asserts the primordiality of the ethical relation to others over the cognitive relation. Furthermore, whereas the cognitive relation tries to overcome difference and establish the unity of intercorporeality, the ethical relation for Levinas must be based, not on overcoming the radical separation from the other, but precisely on establishing and preserving this radical separation and difference. This difference is not experienced thematically: "Thought alert to the face of the other is the thought of an irreducible difference, a difference which is not a thematization and which disturbs the equilibrium of the impassible soul of knowing."[6] This irreducible difference is said to "resist" attempts to articulate and to thematize it. Experienced not as an epistemological gap that is to be bridged, but instead as a summons, this ethical difference is one that is to be respected by a sense of responsibility to the other, even if one is not in any way culpable.

Here again there is a disagreement with Heidegger. Heidegger's *Being and Time* starts with the insistence on *Jemeinigkeit* (which means "mineness," or my sense that my experiences are my own). Whereas Heidegger thinks this sense of mineness is primordial, Levinas thinks that in fact the sense of self implied by mineness is derived from relations to others:

It is as if, in virtue of this fraternity, my relation to the other no longer went back to a prior intimacy of what had once been *mine* [contra

Heidegger]. . . . Rather, it is as if my very self were constituted only through a relation to others, a relation that was gratuitous with respect to accounting for what may be mine and what another's.[7]

The summons of the other is thus a pre-cognitive matter that makes the sense of self possible. The summons by the other is prior to any explicit self-knowledge or reflexive self-awareness. Levinas is far from the Cartesian theory that the sense of self is primary and the sense for the other is derived. There may be a vestige of Cartesianism even in Heidegger if Levinas's reading of *Jemeinigkeit* is correct. Moreover, in insisting on the *ethical* dimension of the relation of self and other, Levinas is breaking with the Cartesian emphasis on the epistemological dimensions of this relation.

Returning to the example of the handshake between two persons, Levinas sees that the two hands even when clasped in a handshake in fact do not belong to the same body. He therefore shifts the paradigm to the encounter with the face of the other:

It is that radical separation, and the entire ethical order of sociality, that appears to me to be *signified* in the nakedness of the face illuminating the human visage, but also in the expressivity of the other person's whole sensible being, even in the hand one shakes.

Beginning with the face—in which the other is approached according to his or her ineradicable difference in ethical responsibility—sociality, as the human possibility of approaching the other, the absolutely other, is signified [*signifiée*]—that is, commanded.[8]

Levinas thus thinks that it is a *weakness* of the phenomenologists' account that it dissolves the "difference of strangeness." Levinas does not want an account of sociality as the *integration* of parts in a whole.[9] The relationship to the other, even in love and the caress, is not a fusion.[10]

More generally, as he says in *Totality and Infinity*, the aim is a pluralist philosophy in which "the plurality of being

would not disappear into the unity of number nor be integrated into a totality."[11] He invokes pluralism because the
face-to-face relation has to respect the unique subjectivity of
the other.[12] Indeed, the ego and the other cannot be a single
cognition because the conjuncture of the same and the other
breaks the totality. This conjuncture is best represented by
"the *direct* and *full face welcome* of the other by me."[13] This
passage is worded carefully to make several points. First,
Levinas's insistence that this relation is a *welcome* represents
a critique of Sartre. Sartre follows Hegel's master-slave
dialectic and takes the look of the other at oneself as a *threat*
to oneself and to one's autonomy. In contrast, Levinas sees
the person not as isolated and autonomous from others, but
as ethically involved with them from the start.[14] Second, the
welcome of the face is not just a modification of Heidegger's
being-with-others, since "the Other continues to face me"[15]
and to be unassimilable. Heidegger is, of course, accounting
for everydayness when he spells out this notion of being
involved in an undifferentiated way with others. But Levinas
thinks that this blurring of the difference between self and
other is not only phenomenologically inexact, but also ethically dangerous. The third point that Levinas is making
is directed against Hobbes and Hegel and also against
Sartre. All three of these theorists see the primordial relation between self and other as one of struggle, or war. For
Levinas, in contrast, the primordial relation to the other is
not war or struggle for recognition, but welcome and peace.
He thus gives a significantly different account of resistance.
Resistance is not primarily a matter of violence, as it would
have to be on the Hegelian master-slave dialectic or even on
Foucault's model of power. Instead, resistance is experienced
as a summons from the other precisely not to do violence to
the other. Resistance is thus fundamentally ethical, and *ethi-*

cal resistance is primordially non-violent: "The 'resistance' of the other does not do violence to me, does not act negatively; it has a positive structure: ethical."[16]

However, even if Levinas insists that peace, or the "non-allergic presence of the Other,"[17] must come first, before war and conflict, the relation to the other is not an easy one. Speaking of the alterity of both death and the other person, Levinas writes in *Time and the Other:*

> Existence is pluralist. . . . The other [*L'Autre*] is not unknown but unknowable, refractory to all light. But this precisely indicates that the other is in no way another myself, participating with me in a common existence. The relationship with the other is not an idyllic and harmonious relationship of communion, or a sympathy . . . through which we put ourselves in the other's place; we recognize the other as resembling us, but exterior to us; the relationship to the other is a relationship with a Mystery.[18]

Again, this passage cuts against Heidegger's view that for the most part one is not separated from others, but that one starts off with the identity that is given to one by the inauthentic "they-self" [*das Man*]. Levinas's larger point is that philosophy is misguided if it tries to break down alterity, or to illuminate the opaqueness of otherness. Instead, philosophy must learn to recognize and preserve the mystery of otherness.

Given Levinas's critique of Merleau-Ponty's notion of the lived body as still too representational and cognitive,[19] one could perhaps wonder if Levinas's theory really takes the body seriously enough. Even his account of the caress, which contrasts to Sartre's, suggests that the caress aims beyond the body. Similarly, the face is not really the physical features, but the look of an other who is not actually "seen" in a literal sense: "The face does not give itself to be seen. It is not a vision. The face is not that which is seen, . . . not an

object of knowledge [une connaissance]."[20] But Levinas says
this because he wants to break with the traditional metaphysical privilege given to vision since Plato.[21] Indeed, he
wants to break with the privilege given to all the senses.
Levinas seems to accept the Heideggerian critique that the
privileging of vision fails because it forgets the clearing that
makes the perception of entities possible even though it is
not itself perceived.[22] But Levinas also believes that in the
theorizing of sensation, whether visual or tactile, the alterity
of the object is lost insofar as the object becomes simply a
content that is enveloped in the identity of the I.[23] In contrast, the face is not the physical countenance: it refuses to be
contained and is "neither seen nor touched."[24]

Given Levinas's critique of the senses, the face is theorized better through language than through sensation.
Speaking solicits the other, but it recognizes the divergence
between my interlocutor and me. The other contests my
meaning and thus puts the I in question, rather than simply
confirming it. "The formal structure of language thereby
announces the ethical inviolability of the Other."[25]

But once again Levinas constructs his own view by going
beyond Merleau-Ponty.[26] Levinas accepts Merleau-Ponty's
criticism of the "myth" of a disincarnate thought preceding
language and speech. Levinas agrees that "thoughts" of an I
that thinks are not prior to, but require, the "I can" of the
body. But Levinas believes that Merleau-Ponty's model of
corporeal intentionality is still that of an internal monologue. Levinas objects to the idea of the monologue that "the
presentation of the face, expression, does not disclose an
inward world previously closed, adding thus a new region
to comprehend or to take over."[27] In contrast to the mono-
logical model, Levinas believes that the face-to-face relation
must be at the basis of language. As I understand him, he is

saying that language cannot be understood if the model includes only a speaker and a thing spoken about. As the philosopher of language Donald Davidson also argues, there must be at least two conspecifics (speakers) who can triangulate on an object. At least, I believe that this Davidsonian point is suggested in Levinas's claim that "In designating a thing I designate it to the Other."[28]

But Levinas is interested in ethics rather than philosophy of language per se. He therefore immediately brings out the ethical implications of this account of language. The fundamental point of expression is not to disclose being or to represent things, but to solicit concern: "The being that expresses itself imposes itself, but does so precisely by appealing to me with its destitution and nudity—its hunger—without my being able to be deaf to that appeal. Thus in expression the being that imposes itself does not limit but promotes my freedom, by arousing my goodness."[29] This "bond between expression and responsibility" is, for Levinas, the "ethical condition or essence of language."[30]

In making this point, Levinas undercuts his two competitors, Sartre and Heidegger. Sartre maintains that the other is a threat to one's freedom. With the Hegelian master-slave dialectic as the model, Sartre sees the relation between self and other as a struggle in which both try to assert their freedom but only one can triumph. For Levinas, in contrast, the encounter with the other first makes freedom possible. Freedom is for Levinas an ethical rather than a metaphysical issue. Freedom is tied to the summons that, as he says, arouses one's goodness. Similarly, in relation to Heidegger, Levinas thinks that the account of the Dasein is still too disembodied, too metaphysical, and it lacks sufficient attention to the ethical dimensions of the body. This point is brought out aptly when Levinas complains that "*Dasein* in Heidegger is never hungry."[31] This quip about hunger is not simply intended to be a self-regarding point, but it is instead an other-regarding claim. That is to say, at the level of the body there is an immediate ethical obligation to assuage the *other's* hunger.

More generally, Heidegger is faulted for stressing the negative and for not accounting for such central human phenomena as enjoyment. For Levinas the phenomenon of enjoyment is "'anterior' to the crystallization of consciousness, I and non-I, into subject and object."[32] Enjoyment shows that previous philosophers such as Kant theorized sensation by emphasizing vision and the look too much, instead of language and the welcome of the face, as Levinas does. By making the ethical a central dimension of his philosophy, Levinas is able to reconfigure the account of human existence. He also makes ethical resistance a primordial feature of this account, and it is now time to focus on that issue.

Levinas: "Guiltless Responsibility"

Looking at the ethical implications of Levinas's philosophy, the first thing to emphasize is how the face resists attempts at domination. The face supplies its own resistance, not in the name of universal concepts such as justice, guilt, or responsibility. Levinas believes that these ethical notions are made possible and explained by the fundamental phenomenon of the face, which is prior to conscious reflection. He thinks that goodness really can flow only from a face-to-face relation where one encounters and cares for the other's subjectivity.[33] As I will explain, this relation leads to his notion of "guiltless responsibility" which is at the center of his account of ethical resistance.[34]

In an analysis reminiscent of Sartre on how the project of hate necessarily defeats itself, Levinas gives as an example of ethical resistance the inability to eliminate the face even by the murder of the other. Killing aims at dominating the other, at reducing the other to something that can be controlled by power. But Levinas suggests two ways in which the project fails. First, he mentions what I take to be the familiar point that murder does not exert power over the sheer transcendence of the other and the unforeseeableness of the other's reactions. Secondly, however, he makes the more subtle point that power fails because power must dominate another comparable power, for instance, physical resistance. But the defenseless eyes of the other suggest "the resistance of what has no resistance—the ethical resistance."[35] The primordial expression, the first word, of the face is, then, "you shall not commit murder." This message is not an explicit perception and is not offered as a Hegelian analysis of the emergence of self-consciousness, but as a more primordial phenomenon.

For Levinas, then, the face supplies the basis of ethical resistance, which is the resistance of the powerless. Justice, legal right, and other principles follow from this primordial ethical phenomenon of the face:

One has to respond to one's right to be, not by referring to some abstract and anonymous law, or judicial entity, but because of one's fear for the Other. My being-in-the-world or my "place in the sun" [Pascal], my being at home [Heidegger], have these not also been the usurpation of spaces belonging to the other . . . whom I have already oppressed or starved, or driven out into a third world; are they not acts of repulsing, excluding, exiling, stripping, killing? . . . A fear for all the violence and murder my existing might generate, in spite of its conscious and intentional innocence. A fear which reaches back past my "self-consciousness". . . . It is the fear of occupying someone else's place with the *Da* of my *Dasein*; it is the inability to occupy a place, a profound utopia.[36]

Contrary to Hegel, I do not first feel myself threatened when I confront the other; instead, I realize that I threaten the other and that the other is my fundamental responsibility. In an eloquent passage, Levinas writes:

... in its expression, in its mortality, the face before me summons me, calls for me, begs for me, as if the invisible death that must be faced by the Other, pure otherness, separated, in some way, from any whole, were my business. It is as if that invisible death, ignored by the Other, whom already it concerns by the nakedness of its face, were already "regarding" me prior to confronting me, and becoming the death that stares me in the face. The other [person's] death calls me into question, as if, by my possible future indifference, I had become the accomplice of the death to which the other, who cannot see it, is exposed. . . . [37]

Contrary to Heidegger, moreover, I am really more concerned with the death of the other than I am with my own death. Levinas notices the dissymmetry between my relation to myself and my relation to others, as Heidegger did, but he comes to a different conclusion:

The idea of dissymmetry seems very important to me; it is, perhaps, the most important way of conceiving of the relationship between self and other which does not place them on the same level. You know my quotation from Dostoevsky: "Everyone is guilty in front of everyone else and me more than all the others." That is the idea of dissymmetry. . . . But the idea of dissymmetry is another way of saying that in the perseverance in being we are all equal, but . . . that the death of the other is more important than my own. . . . [38]

Actually, the quote from Dostoevsky is a bit misleading insofar as it suggests that guilt is the fundamental relation and the basis of our responsibility. But in other places Levinas emphasizes that we are responsible even if we are guiltless: "The more innocent we are, the more we are responsible."[39] Put even more succinctly, Levinas sees us as "responsible without being culpable."[40]

Responsibility is thus an original condition and it is not derived from specific acts:

Prior to any act, I am concerned with the Other, and I can never be absolved from this responsibility. To use an expression close to my heart, "Even when he does not regard me, he regards me." Consequently, I shall speak of the responsibility of those "who have done nothing," of an original responsibility of [humans] for the other person.[41]

Playing on two senses of regard (the sense of "seeing" and the sense of "mattering to"), Levinas construes the ethical relation whereby the well being of the other matters to me as a primordial rather than a derived condition. On this view, responsibility is even prior to freedom. "Responsibility for my neighbor dates from before my freedom in an immemorial past, an unrepresentable past that was never present and is more ancient than consciousness of."[42] Normally, this claim would seem strange, for the usual philosophical order of priority would imply that one could not be responsible unless one were free. Furthermore, being free would imply being conscious to some extent of one's actions and their consequences. But for Levinas, responsibility precedes freedom and consciousness, and it supplies the content on which the agent acts.

This last quote brings out how *unhistorical* Levinas's account is. He is trying to be even more fundamental than phenomenology. Although he is moving away from philosophy that privileges consciousness, he is still doing "first philosophy." In comparison to Foucault, for instance, there is no sense in which there could be a *history* of ethics. Foucault's account of the change in *ethos* contrasts sharply with Levinas's account of how structures of the body (especially the face) provide the foundation for our ethical relations to others. For Levinas resistance is explained not by appeal to universal concepts and principles, but by the fundamental and universal phenomenon of the face. From Foucault's genealogical perspective, Levinas's project would be a late variant of speculative metaphysics. Bourdieu and Foucault prefer more specific analyses, and suggest that the contrasts alone serve to break down the illusion of necessity and to open up possibilities of other ways of existing. Rather than try to adjudicate this contrast now, however, I want to bring Derrida into the picture. In particular, I want to show that despite Derrida's sympathy for and appreciation of Levinas's work, the unhistorical dimension of Levinas's theory becomes a central issue.

Derrida and the Deconstruction of 'Death'

In future histories of twentieth-century European thought poststructuralism will probably be noted mainly for its neo-Nietzschean critique of the Cartesian cogito and its emphasis on language and power instead of the earlier phenomenological concern for subjectivity and individual freedom. However, this picture of poststructuralism is more appropriate to its early years in the 1960s and the 1970s than it is in subsequent decades. Chapter 2 brought out the ethical turn in Foucault's last writings. The recent reawakening of interest in Levinas is also due largely to the prominence of the ethical in his thought. Ethics becomes so important because the Nietzschean influence on poststructuralism raises the specter of nihilism. If individual subjectivity is no longer conceived as the originator of action and the arbiter of values, then the agent seems unable to have much effect on social processes and thus to lack the capacity for critical resistance. The philosophical task therefore becomes one of accounting for the possibility of critical intervention and responsible agency.

Like Foucault, Derrida also challenges the Cartesian conception of subjectivity, and it is not surprising that his early linguistic turn was also followed by a later ethical turn. Levinas's work provided Derrida with a paradigm for thinking about the ethical, even though Derrida's first essay on Levinas raised substantive problems about Levinas's approach. Derrida and Levinas both theorize the irreducibility of difference. They resist Kantian attempts to make moral philosophy a matter mainly of justifying universal principles for ideal rational agents. They also object to Hegelian attempts to assimilate otherness and to see the other as the mirror of the self.

From Derrida's point of view, though, both Levinas and Heidegger seem to be aiming at foundationalist, unhistorical accounts of human agency, and Derrida is skeptical of such aspirations to "first philosophy." In turn, however, Derrida's own critics accuse deconstruction of being unable to account for positive ethical and political action, and generally as being disengaged from ethical and social issues. In response, Derrida has insisted that he has not ignored the practical and normative dimensions of philosophy. On the contrary, a central effect of deconstruction is to break down the philosophical distinction between the theoretical and the practical. In contrast to Heidegger, for instance, for whom death as such could not be a political issue, Derrida sees death as essentially political. As he says, death engages "the political in its essence."[43] The same holds for deconstruction. Indeed, although deconstruction is accused of being apolitical, the strong animus with which it was and still is received suggests how deeply political it is. In this section I explore the conception of the ethical and the political that emerges in recent writings by Derrida on death.

Death may seem a strange topic to include in a book on critical resistance. How can death be resisted, when it is inevitable? How can it be criticized, if it cannot be corrected? These questions about death might also lead to questions about whether there is any connection between death and ethics. If we think of ethics as the formulation of universal principles or the categorical imperative, then there will seem to be little connection. However, that conception of ethics requires a certain conception of what it is to be a moral human being. The conception of ethics shared by philosophers as diverse as Levinas and Heidegger addresses this broader question about what it is to be a person, and thus their ethical writings are intermixed with ontological claims. In *Being and Time,* for instance, only being-toward-death makes it possible for one to resist the conformism and normalization imposed by anonymous others (that is, by what Heidegger calls *das Man*). Only the individualization that results from facing up to one's own death makes it possible for one to establish one's own identity and integrity in one's life. If a philosopher disputes the Cartesian conception of the knowing subject (as a disembodied thinker) and the Kantian conception of the practical subject (as an individual, rationally autonomous, rule-governed cogitator), then the task becomes one of offering a different account of what it is to be an embodied, socialized person. Changing the conception of social agents will also lead to differing accounts of critical resistance.

The first step in thinking differently about what it is to be a person is to consider other dimensions of death than the biological. Is death only a *biological* limit imposed *by* the body? Or is it also a *cultural* limit imposed *on* the body?

When faced with such a binary opposition, Derrida's usual answer is to say "neither/nor," which is the form that aporia takes when the alternatives are the only possibilities.[44] Thus, it is not surprising that Derrida suggests that death is neither simply cultural nor simply biological.[45] The concept of death has no borders, he says (playing on several senses of borders), and it will exceed conceptual demarcation or closure.

Despite this neither/nor, however, Derrida does seem more interested in death as a cultural and historical phenomenon. Crossing borders, he says, "on change la mort."[46] That is to say, changing cultural contexts and national borders results in changes not only of currencies and of languages, but also of death. He thus sees death as central to the very idea of "culture," such that to speak of culture is *essentially* to invoke cultural practices for dealing with death. Influenced by Philippe Ariès on the history of death, Derrida insists not only that "all people do not die in the same way," but also that "culture itself, culture in general, is essentially, before anything, even a priori, the culture of death."[47]

In examining the ethical turn in Derrida, the specific issue that arises is whether the existential phenomenon of my own death is constitutive of the ethical, and what that claim implies. Philosophers such as Heidegger, Levinas, and Sartre disagree about this question, and if we are to understand Derrida's way of taking up the issue, we will have to explore his readings and criticisms of these philosophers. The concern in this chapter may be more with 'death' than with death per se, that is, with philosophical conceptions of death rather than the phenomenon of death. Of course, whether this distinction between the concept and the reality of death can even be drawn is a contested issue. How can one write a phenomenology of death when one's own death cannot be a phenomenon for oneself? Death seems to be beyond the limits for phenomenological description insofar as one's own death cannot be experienced precisely because one is dead. The deconstruction of 'death' has thus occurred in the realization that there is no referent for death (in the sense of one's own death), and that death is only a word. This is, in short, Derrida's deconstruction of 'death'.[48]

Someone might well ask, however, whether this result is adequate, or whether it trivializes death by making death seem to be merely a social construction. Is there not something more at stake than merely the word 'death' or merely a culturally variable phenomenon? The concern behind these questions is that there must be something more to death, something that we justifiably fear. This concern leads to further, more methodological questions: Does deconstruction deny language-independent reality? Or does it affirm such reality and claim only that human cognition cannot capture it as it is in itself? While debate has raged about these two questions, there is also a third possibility, for it could be asked whether deconstruction challenges the dichotomy between language and reality that is at play here. These are the conceptual issues that are at stake in Derrida's reading of philosophers such as Heidegger and Levinas on death. Death for Derrida is not so much a paradigm as an aporia, an unsolvable problem where the antitheses are either equally compelling or equally uncompelling, but in any case undecidable. Derrida speaks of the experience of the aporia as "interminable *resistance* or remainder."[49] To set the scene for an explanation of this resistance, I will first describe briefly the importance that Heidegger (following Rilke) gives to dying one's own death. Then I will discuss criticisms by Sartre and especially by Levinas of Heidegger's analysis of death, before returning to Derrida's

critique of both Heidegger and Levinas. For my purposes
the interest in this critique is that it continues to explore the
idea of ethical resistance at the level where a philosophical
account inquires into both the social ontology and the moral
psychology presupposed by that conception of philosophy
itself.

Heidegger on Being-toward-Death

In *Being and Time* Heidegger starts his analysis of human
existence or what he calls Dasein not with the isolated,
reflective individual standing at a distance from worldly
affairs, but with the familiar everyday activities in which
people are thoroughly immersed and in which they engage
skillfully and unreflectively. Everydayness is not in itself a
negative phenomenon. Even though Heidegger speaks of it
as "falling," the connotations are not pejorative. However,
he also speaks of it as "fleeing," which does suggest evasion
and self-deception. The pejorative language follows from
failing to face up to both the contingency and the uniqueness of one's situation and choosing to do what everyone
else would do, or to act how *das Man* would. Thus, although
a certain amount of doing what others do is a crucial part of
growing up in a culture, this acculturation turns into exces-
sive conformism when certain ways of thinking and acting
become the only recognized and sanctioned ways of comporting oneself. Even speaking of "*a* culture" is problematic,
for, as Derrida says in *The Other Heading*, "a culture never
has a single origin."[50]

Given this tendency for functional acculturation to turn
into dysfunctional conformism, *Being and Time* must explain
how the Dasein can break away from the conformist pressures of society and establish its unique identity or "authen-

ticity." The poet Rilke had already seen death as the key to this problem. Rilke distinguishes between the great death and the small death. Heidegger sees this distinction as the difference between my own death and the death of others. Evasion of my own death results by taking my own death as if it were like the death of another, which is not really a death since one lives on. Facing up to instead of fleeing one's own mortality thus becomes for Heidegger the key to authentic comportment and a life of integrity. Heidegger believes that my own death has a normative priority over the death of others (a claim that Levinas and Sartre dispute). Death is uniquely mine, he says, and is the one thing that nobody else can do for me.

For reasons that Hegel also had pointed out, death for Heidegger is critical because the possibility of death first makes it possible to see one's life as a whole. Given the immersion in the multitude of demands placed on one in everydayness, the possibility of rising above the multitude of demands and seeing life as a unified whole would seem highly unlikely. Only the possibility of death and the withdrawal of all these demands gives rise to a sense of the whole, even if only in the negative sense of all that would no longer be the case. Mortality is behind our finitude, and the recognition of finitude is what first makes it possible for certain things to matter to us more than others. An infinite life would lack the sense for what matters, and it might even lack the sense of selfhood that Heidegger is trying to explain.[51]

Sartre objects to the centrality of death in Heidegger's account. Finitude is not a function of mortality, Sartre argues, but of the temporal necessity of choosing one thing before another and being unable to reverse this sequence. Furthermore, Sartre rebuts Heidegger's claim that dying is the only thing that no one else can do for me. Sartre points out that no one else can love for me either, or do any number of other things for me. For Sartre, death does not individualize, contrary to Heidegger, and subjectivity is required if I am to recognize death as mine. Finally, Sartre maintains that death cannot be awaited, and is not really a limit on my freedom. In trying to take an attitude toward one's own death, Sartre thinks we are really only looking at ourselves from the point of view of the other. My own death is something I cannot experience, and thus is for Sartre merely a contingent brute fact that has no meaning for me.

Sartre can make these criticisms, however, only by failing to observe several distinctions that Heidegger made, and in particular, by confusing what Heidegger in §49 of *Being and Time* calls "being-toward-death," "perishing," and "demise." "Perishing" is the ending of something that lives. Dasein does not simply perish, however, because unlike lower forms of life, its ending matters to it and is a feature of the life itself, not simply a point at which life ends. In fact, Dasein cannot perish. The organism can end, but not Dasein, which never experiences its end.[52] Moreover, if perishing does not apply to one's own sense of existence, it also does not apply to the death of others. When other people die, we do not treat them as having simply ended, but we create elaborate rituals to show that they continue to matter to us. Cultural practices of burial confirm Heidegger's observation that a human corpse is not merely a lifeless thing, but that as something that has lost life, it deserves continued respect.

Heidegger uses the term 'demise', therefore, for the ending of Dasein, which involves more than merely perishing. But "demising" is not all there is to "being-toward-death." "Demise" is merely one aspect of Dasein's death (e.g., the biological and medical dimension). The event of demise is not what Heidegger sees as definitive of being-toward-death. Being-toward-death involves a way to be, and specifically, a way to be *toward* the end, which Heidegger distinguishes from being *at* an end. "Being-toward-death" is not the same as the event of "demise," and is a phenomenon of *life*, not of the moment of perishing.[53] Moreover, contrary to Sartre, being-toward-death is specifically said not to be a matter of taking up a certain *attitude*, but is more generally an ontological feature of our existence whereby we find ourselves "thrown" into a particular time and place which gives us our particular finitude.[54]

Levinas's Critique of Heidegger

Levinas would not agree with Sartre that death is irrelevant to living one's life. But, like Sartre, he takes issue with the ontological privilege that Heidegger and Rilke attribute to my own death over the death of others. Furthermore, whereas Heidegger and Sartre see ethics as following from ontology (or at least they see ontological claims as normatively neutral), Levinas believes that ethics is prior to ontology.

In the broad sense of ethics as unenforceable obligation, Levinas, unlike Sartre, does think that death is a critical ethical issue. In this broad sense of obligation, Levinas reverses the priority that Heidegger gives to my own death over the death of the other. For Levinas my own death is an impossibility that I will never reach. I therefore have no privileged phenomenological access to my own death, at least not enough to found ontology on it. Furthermore, from the ethical standpoint Levinas maintains that the death of the other is more fundamental than my own death. Responsibility is not first and foremost of-myself-for-myself, but for the Other.

Like Sartre, then, Levinas is critical of Heidegger's notion that only the anticipation of one's own death leads to an authentic life. But unlike both Sartre and Heidegger, Levinas draws different implications about freedom from this impossibility. Sartre has the most radical conception of freedom, and maintains that death is no more a limit on freedom than is birth. Freedom for Heidegger, in contrast, is circumscribed by death, and is thus more situated and finite. Dasein's anticipation of its own death first gives Dasein the possibility of completely clairvoyant insight into its life as a whole (in the *Augenblick* or moment of vision), and thus the possibility of freely taking charge of its existence. This freedom can be unwilling,[55] and is signaled by anxiety, which is the ontological condition of being-free-for the particular ontic acts of choice.[56] Freedom is not simply a matter of making particular choices, but it also involves accepting finitude and tolerating the fact that making one choice excludes all others.[57] Heidegger thus sees being-toward-death as an event of freedom. In the anticipation of death, the Dasein acquires the freedom that enables it to resist conformism and to pursue its own identity and integrity.

In contrast to both Sartre and Heidegger, however, Levinas sees death as the phenomenon wherein the subject reaches the limit of freedom and of the possible. Death is something the subject cannot master and in relation to which subjectivity remains passive. Death is the absolutely unknowable, and is thus the limit of the idealism whereby I think that *I* can constitute the world.[58] In contrast not only to Sartre's insistence on the radical freedom to which death is irrelevant, but also to Heidegger's situated freedom resulting from the anticipation of death, Levinas's account emphasizes the finitude of a freedom that cannot claim mastery over the ultimate alterity of death. In *Totality and Infinity*

Levinas suggests that the Heideggerian move of reconciling oneself to death is not sufficient to make one free. By implication, Sartre is also said to underestimate the capacity of torture, "stronger than death," to make a mockery of inward freedom. Closer to Hegel than to Heidegger and Sartre, Levinas insists that freedom is not merely inward, but that it must have the objective (social and political) means to realize itself. His critical encounter with Hegel's views about freedom leads us to understand that apolitical freedom is an illusion.[59]

Derrida's Rejoinders

Where does Derrida stand on the question whether one's own death is prior to the death of the other, or whether the death of the other has priority? At one point he sides with Levinas in that he infers that if I can never experience my own death, my sense of death is only ever extrapolated from the death of the other. As Derrida says, "the death of the other thus becomes again 'first,' always first" because "the death of the other, this death of the other in 'me,' is fundamentally the only death that is named in the syntagm 'my death.'"[60] The quotes around "first" suggest that Derrida does not want to play the traditional philosophical game of establishing which phenomena are most primordial. However, Derrida seems to be drawn to Levinas's claim that my sense of my own death is derived from the more originary recognition of the other as mortal. One could well infer that Derrida is more sympathetic to Levinas's general stance that one's sense of one's self is derived from and does not precede the encounter with the other. At least that seems to follow from his suggestion that the relation to oneself which constitutes the ego or what Heidegger calls "mineness"

(*Jemeinigkeit*) arises out of an originary experience of mourning. This originary mourning is said to institute "my relation
to myself" and to constitute "the egoity of the *ego* as well as
every *Jemeinigkeit* in the *différance*—neither internal nor external—that structures this experience."[61] Despite this proxim-
ity to Levinas's claim that the encounter with the mortality
of the face of the other precedes the reflexive sense of self,
Derrida claims that neither Levinas nor Heidegger nor Freud
have considered this originary mourning.[62] But Derrida does
not offer it as an alternative philosophical theory of the
constitution of subjectivity and intersubjectivity, since that
conception of theory is precisely what he wants to avoid.

Derrida's reasons for distancing himself from the triumvi-
rate of Heidegger, Freud, and Levinas are complex. Most
significant for my purposes, however, is his criticism that
their accounts of death purport to describe everyone everywhere in an unhistorical way. Given Derrida's historicist
views about the cultural specificity of death that I mentioned earlier, it is not surprising that he finds these theories
not to be universal, but on the contrary to be recognizably
embedded in and indebted to Western religious traditions.[63]
Thus, he suggests the necessity of a double reading of a
book like *Being and Time* (and, by extension, *Totality and
Infinity*). On the one hand, the book can be read in its own
terms as an existential analysis of death that gives a universal description that must be presupposed by any historical
or anthropological studies of death. On the other hand, the
book can be read as a vestige of Eurocentric onto-theology,
that is, "as a small, late document, among many others
within the huge archive where the memory of death in
Christian Europe is being accumulated."[64]

The charge that Heidegger's aspirations to a universal
account that goes beyond Judeo-Christian onto-theology are

undermined by his reliance on major onto-theological themes and concepts is not new. More interesting is the specific deconstruction that Derrida offers of the central notion of being-toward-death. If this deconstruction were successful, other Heideggerian notions such as authenticity, anxiety, and falling would also start to unravel. Even if the deconstruction is not entirely convincing, it succeeds in drawing attention to and casting doubt on the foundationalism of *Being and Time* (and presumably of *Totality and Infinity*). Let me first go into the details of the deconstruction before turning to the larger issue of foundationalism in philosophy. My purpose in considering these issues is to explore how a detailed textual deconstruction can represent critical resistance to the universalist aspirations of philosophy. This critique is not simply of metaphilosophical interest, but raises questions about the latent grip of onto-theology and Eurocentrism on conceptions of politics, ethics, and society.

The initial challenge to Heidegger's text concerns the distinction between perishing, demise, and being-toward-death. This distinction in turn depends on another distinction that at first seems rather marginal, but that Derrida sees as highly problematic. This second distinction that Heidegger relies on is that between humans and animals. In particular, language is the crucial feature that humans have and that animals lack. Animals are said not to have a relation to death. Animals merely perish rather than die in the human sense because they lack the linguistic abilities that are necessary to be aware of one's own death. To be aware of death for Heidegger is to realize the "possibility of impossibility." Levinas speaks similarly of approaching the moment when "nous ne 'pouvons plus pouvoir'" ("we are no longer 'able to be able'").[65]

Derrida's objection is that even if animals were said to lack a relation to death and to their dying (a premise that he denies), the same would have to be said of humans. Humans cannot experience their end either. Even if humans entertain the *possibility* of impossibility, the impossibility *as such* is beyond their ken. The phrase "as such" is important here, for although language may give us the ability to name death when animals lack this ability, that ability to name something might mislead us into thinking that we have access to the thing itself "as such." Derrida thus suggests that language may be deceiving us in the case of death, dissimulating our lack of access to our own death. "Who will guarantee," he asks, "that language is not precisely the origin of the nontruth of death, and of the other?"[66] Furthermore, if death is the possibility of impossibility, I have no more relation to my own impossibility than animals do. My grasp of death would then be due only to perishing and to the death of the other.[67] The distinction between perishing, demise, and dying is crucial to other distinctions, particularly authenticity and inauthenticity. Derrida's charge that this three-way distinction cannot be drawn sharply undermines Dasein's project of becoming authentic through a resolute relation to death. Insofar as authenticity is a central concern of Division Two of *Being and Time,* Heidegger's existential analysis begins to come undone.

Defenders of Heidegger have several lines of rejoinder to this critique. They could echo, for instance, Derrida's charges in *Aporias* (p. 38) that Levinas's critique of Heidegger ignores the distinction between demise and dying by pointing out that Derrida has not paid sufficient attention to the difference between demise and perishing. While I cannot experience my actual state of demise, I can experience its imminence and thus my being-toward an end. Furthermore, one could argue that Heidegger's notion of being-toward-death is more about life rather than death, in that its purpose is to explain how finitude is built into our experience of temporality. If this is a correct reading, of course, animals might not be qualitatively different from humans, so the examples used to illustrate perishing and demising would have to be changed. But plants would seem to perish and not to demise, so there would still be grounds for drawing such a distinction.

A more general problem with Derrida's critique arises from his conception of what a distinction is and what a philosophical attack on the distinction entails. At stake is the method of deconstruction in general. Derrida's target here and in other deconstructive readings is the ability to draw philosophical distinctions. The larger purpose in *Aporias* is to foil "every methodological strategy and every stratagem of delimitation."[68] Circumscription, or the drawing of sharp conceptual distinctions, is what he wants to show to be impossible. This obsession with blurring the lines of philosophical distinctions has been a central issue in the exchanges with John Searle. Searle argues that a distinction can be useful even if the lines are not entirely sharp. This seems right, for there is clearly a distinction between, for example, the face and the back of the head, even if we cannot say precisely where the face stops and the back of the head starts. Similarly, for most distinctions there are likely to be borderline cases where it is hard to decide on which side they should fall. But that does not mean the distinction is useless or that its application is undecidable.

In my view, then, the value of Derrida's analysis rests neither on this critique of what he calls circumscription, nor on his claims for the undecidability of distinctions such as perishing and dying. Instead, it lies in his calling into question the foundationalism of these philosophical accounts of death. Derrida is not offering another foundationalist account and he says expressly of the virtual debate where Heidegger, Levinas, and Freud compete for the most basic analysis, "my discourse was aimed at suggesting that this fundamentalist dimension is untenable and that it cannot even claim to have any coherence or rigorous specificity."[69] Heidegger's presuppositional (or "transcendental") arguments are intended to establish a foundation, and *Being and Time* clearly stands as a major work in the "great ontological-juridico-transcendental tradition."[70] However, Derrida thinks that raising doubts about the perishing/dying distinction will shift the interest in *Being and Time* away from its alleged demonstrations of ontological necessity.[71] This shift enables us to see through the way Heidegger overgeneralizes and universalizes a conception of death that in fact has an "irreducible historicity."[72] The same point would presumably apply by extension to Levinas and Freud.

Ethics without Foundations?

Does removing the foundationalist rhetoric in Levinas and Heidegger mean that their accounts of death and the other must be dismissed as well? Derrida's lengthy readings of these thinkers and his frequent return to them in his recent "ethical" writings on gifts, duty, death, and responsibility suggest on the contrary that they become even more useful. I find in these recent writings an interest in responsibility and duty that points to an effective program for critical resistance. In relation to critique, Derrida himself speaks in both *The Other Heading* and *Aporias* of a *duty* to criticize totalitarian dogmatism, and therefore of a further duty to cultivate "the virtue of such *critique, of the critical idea, the critical tradition,* but also submitting it, beyond critique and questioning, to a deconstructive genealogy that thinks and exceeds it without yet compromising it."[73] So critique is a duty, but it is important to go beyond critique and actually aim at positive social change. Critique cannot provide one with a good conscience, and in *Aporias* he insists that "one must avoid good conscience at all costs."[74] In *The Gift of Death* he laughs at those who label a certain skepticism about good conscience "nihilist," "relativist," "poststructuralist," or (worst of all) "deconstructionist."[75]

His point, I believe, has both a concrete and an abstract side. Concretely, he wants to know how anyone today could have a good conscience when, for instance, millions of children are dying of hunger.[76] More abstractly, I take him to be saying that a foundationless ethics would have to be willing to take back its judgments, and it could not claim theoretically that it was more than a possible interpretation of persons and their social duties. The form of its arguments will tend to be negative: without X there would not be Y.[77] An ethics that eschewed foundationalist claims could therefore not aspire to the certainty of good conscience, and it would see such self-certainty as misrecognizing the risk involved in responsible decision and normative engagement.

Although Derrida is thus an ethical pluralist who defends difference and alterity, he does not deny the social value of consensus and universal principles. Although he insists on the singularity of particular people, he recognizes the exemplarity of universality: "I have, the unique 'I' has, the responsibility of testifying for universality."[78] He then projects a list of European duties, including, for instance, the duty to welcome foreigners and to integrate them into the society, but at the same time to accept their alterity. More abstractly, he supports the duty of "respecting differences, idioms, minorities, singularities, but also the universality of

formal law, the desire for translation, agreement, and uni-
vocity, the law of the majority, opposition to racism, nationalism, and xenophobia."[79]

When Derrida rejects good conscience, he is not, of
course, suggesting that bad conscience is the proper moral
attitude. Rather, he is proposing a different moral psychology, one that is influenced by *both* Heidegger and Levinas
without emulating the vestiges of foundationalism in their
enterprises. Instead of starting with universal principles and
then explaining their application, moral psychology can
start from the singularity of death and of the other. Responsibility would be closely tied to death, whether the death of
the other or one's own death. Death is singular in that no
one else can die for me, and also in that I cannot take the
other's death away even by sacrificing myself on a particular occasion. "Everyone must assume his [or her] own
death, the one thing in the world that no one else can *either
give or take:* therein resides freedom and responsibility."[80]
Death must be taken upon oneself, and this recognition of
mortality as irreplaceability is what leads both to responsibility and to a sense of self: "The sameness of self, what
remains irreplaceable in dying, only becomes what it is, in
the sense of an identity as a relation of the self to itself, by
means of this idea of mortality as irreplaceability."[81]

Levinas would of course insist that responsibility is not
first and foremost to oneself, but to the other. In a reading of
Abraham and Isaac as depicted in Kierkegaard's *Fear and
Trembling,* Derrida complicates the issue and he appears to
be deconstructing ethics by emphasizing that in relating
responsibly to a particular other, I fail to relate responsibly
to all the other others. In sacrificing myself to the other, and
sacrificing what I could do for all the other others, Derrida
suggests that ethics itself has to be sacrificed. That is, insofar

as I relate ethically to one other, I cannot relate ethically to all the other others.[82] The Levinasian sentence that captures Abraham's paradox, "tout autre est tout autre" ("every other is entirely other"), suggests the tension resulting from the sense one has of being responsible for everyone else at every moment, at the same time that at any given moment one can act responsibly only toward a particular other. Paradoxically, then, to do my duty and behave ethically, I must behave unethically and fail to do my duty.[83]

This Kierkegaardian problem is compounded in that the particular other remains inaccessible to me because I cannot take away the other's mortality.[84] Levinas's critique of Kierkegaard insists that ethics is about singularity even more than it is about generality, and thus Kierkegaard's circumscriptive distinction between the ethical and the religious becomes blurred.[85] More generally, the sentence "tout autre est tout autre" deals with the relation of singularity and universality in ethical theory. Derrida glosses it as follows: " 'tout autre est tout autre' signifies that every other is singular, that every one is a singularity, which also means that every one is each one, a proposition that seals the contract between universality and the exception of singularity."[86] This play on the quantifiers 'each' and 'every' brings out theoretical tensions that in practice become existential dilemmas.

With this portrayal of the paradoxical character of ethics, Derrida should not be read as deconstructing ethics. Rather, he should be read, in my opinion, as trying to deconstruct any pretensions to the self-certainty of a foundationalist starting point for ethical theory. In other words, he is explaining the possibility of ethical resistance at the same time that he seeks to avoid the "good conscience" of a foundationalist, metaethical self-legitimation. Stripped of their transcendental arguments, Heidegger's notion of dying one's own death, and Levinas's sense of responsibility in the face of the other's mortality do not fade away, but in Derrida's hands they become innovative approaches to the moral psychology of ethical critique.

To sum up, this chapter has been concerned with a specific form of critical resistance, namely ethical resistance. Ethical resistance is construed by Levinas not as power resisting power, but as the resistance of the completely powerless. Ethical resistance may thus seem to be markedly different from the emancipatory social resistance that has been the topic of previous chapters. However, a faithful Levinasian who believed in first philosophy could argue that ethical resistance is so foundational that emancipatory social resistance would have to presuppose ethical resistance. Why would power be exerted in the name of social emancipation, the Levinasian might well ask, if this exercise of power were not at the same time a recognition of the obligation to the powerless?

However, to prove that emancipatory social resistance presupposed ethical resistance would require a stronger argument than I would want to make. The case that I have been advancing is that ethical resistance is a recognizable form of critical resistance, one that emerges from Derrida's adaptation of Levinas's ethical theory. Derrida's "ethical turn" is relatively recent, and thus is arguably better situated in the present post-critical period rather than the previous poststructural period.

In the Levinasian and Derridean accounts, both death and the other figure prominently. Insofar as death is less obviously relevant to the construction of a social theory that explains ethical resistance than the other is, let me clarify why death deserves so much attention. One might think that death is a matter for individual psychology and that it is irrelevant to the social. However, this inference would represent a failure to appreciate the centrality of death in the social ontologies of the philosophers against whom Derrida positions himself. Death is central to Hegel's analysis insofar as for Hegel the social requires the relation to death (and to work). Without death the relation to the whole would not be possible, and thus the being would lack the possibility for either selfhood or social community. For Heidegger, even though he is concerned with one's own death and how it leads to individual authenticity, being-toward-death is not purely private but involves a resolute relation to the world and to others. For Levinas the relation to the face of the other is a relation to the other's mortality. The point of Derrida's critique of Levinas is that death is an inherently social and historical matter, and not a purely personal, private concern. Derrida's argument about how death changes with the crossing of borders is intended to show how even death is configured by the social.

If Levinas connects ethics to the other, it must be noticed that for him death is often portrayed as the ultimate other. Death is what is most other to us. In the following passage, which I quoted earlier, it should be noted that he uses the word *autre* when the word *autrui* might have been expected:

The other [*L'Autre*] is not unknown but unknowable, refractory to all light. But this precisely indicates that the other is in no way another myself, participating with me in a common existence. The relationship with the other is not an idyllic and harmonious relationship of communion, or a sympathy . . . through which we put ourselves in the other's place; we recognize the other as resembling us, but exterior to us; the relationship to the other is a relationship with a Mystery.[87]

Autrui always means "other people," whereas *autre* is ambiguous and could mean anything that is other, not simply "others." If ethics is said to be a relation to the other, Levinas is being intentionally ambiguous about whether that other is death or another person. Of course, Levinas talks about the ethical resistance of the *face* of the other, and death does not have a face. However, the face is not the physical visage. What I see when I see the face of the other is precisely the mortality of the other. The other's mortality is thereby recognized as the ultimate source of the ethical obligation to ameliorate the need and the suffering of the other.

Death is thus central to ethical resistance insofar as death is at the core of ethics. That is, ethics is ultimately tied to a concern for death (both one's own death and the death of the other). If humans were not finite, mortal beings, there would not be much point in pursuing an ethical life. Kant's ethics, for instance, is based on the assumption that the answer to the question "Why be moral?" depends on being finite and not knowing the noumenal truth about whether the will is good or not.

Does one lose the ability to say that death is at the core of ethics if one gives up Levinas's pretensions to first philosophy, as Derrida does? The answer is no, because although death makes ethics possible, death does not determine the content of ethics. The fact that humans are finite creatures makes their choices significant, but finitude does not entail what ethical choices they are to make. That is what I mean when I say that the core of ethics is foundationless. On a reading of Levinas that avoids first philosophy, the content of ethics has to come from the relation not to one's own death, which would not have any consequences for judgments about how we ought to live. What will have such consequences is the other's neediness, and therefore the never-ending responsibility for the other.

The ethical resistance of the powerless others to our capacity to exert power over them is therefore what imposes

unenforceable obligations on us. The obligations are unenforceable precisely because of the other's lack of power. That
actions are at once obligatory and at the same time unenforceable is what puts them in the category of the ethical.
Obligations that were enforced would, by virtue of the force
behind them, not be freely undertaken and would not be in
the realm of the ethical. When read together, then, Levinas
and Derrida provide the outlines of a post-critical interpretation of ethics that is a serious alternative to more traditional (Kantian and Hegelian) accounts of the social
grounds for ethical comportment.

Post-Critique: Derrida and the Messianic

The ethical turns into the social and both Derrida and Levinas
offer accounts of that transition. However, neither has a social
ontology to offer. Levinas, of course, would not offer an
ontology because of the priority of the ethical over the ontological. Similarly, Derrida is opposed to the philosophical
task of doing ontology. He understands the word 'ontology'
in its traditional, metaphysical sense as the foundationalist
account of what there is. In contrast to the metaphysical way
of understanding what ontology is, "social ontology" would
seem to be an oxymoron if it relativized ontology to the
social. However, there is a way to use 'ontology' that circum-
vents metaphysics. If the term only points to what a given
social theory posits as the constituents of society, and if one
takes these references to constituents as ontological commitments of the theory rather than as necessarily real existents,
then there is no need to worry about slipping back into metaphysics. Different theories will have different ontological
commitments, that is, different understandings of the sorts of
social entities that there are. The reason to speak of a social

ontology is to bring out how each theory construes society as being composed of quasi-ontological constituents, for instance, power relations (Foucault) or the habitus and field (Bourdieu). Thus, in the phrase "social ontology" I mean 'ontology' to be understood only in an attenuated, non-metaphysical sense.

Derrida is so adamantly opposed to the use of the term 'ontology' by Marxist social theorists because an ontology in the metaphysical sense posits something that exists independent of theory. To use his phrase, ontology posits the existence of entities "outside the text." The early Derrida is famous for his denial of ontology in his claim that there is nothing outside the text. However, the later Derrida has granted that there are at least two universals that cannot be deconstructed and thus that transcend any given text. These two "quasi-transcendentals" are justice and messianicity. What keeps them from being "quasi-ontological" is that they are more like regulative ideals than like occurrently existing entities. For Kant, a regulative ideal is one that we have to think that we are approaching asymptotically, but one that we could never know we had achieved. I think that justice is a regulative ideal in this sense, and that is why Derrida does not equate it with the actual body of law in any given society.

Derrida's account of justice builds on Levinas. For Levinas there is not simply the relation to the other, there is also a relation to a third party who sees my relation to the other. In *Totality and Infinity* he says that this third party is ultimately "the whole of humanity which looks at us."[88] Thirdness thus leads to the judgment of justice. Because of its thirdness, the relation to the third party seems to come later than the relation to the face of the other. Yet although the third party is later conceptually, it is always already there in the look of the other. The regard of humanity is built into the face of the other and it turns that unobjectifiable presence of the face into the calculability of justice that comes from the judgment of the injustice involved in the relation to the other.

Just as Levinas's account of justice influences Derrida, despite some differences, so Levinas is an indispensable source of Derrida's account of messianicity as a regulative ideal for our communal and social activity. Levinas ties his notion of the third party to the prophetic voice. In *Totality and Infinity* he writes: "By essence the prophetic word responds to the epiphany of the face, doubles all discourse not as a discourse about moral themes, but as an irreducible movement of a discourse which by essence is aroused by the epiphany of the face inasmuch as it attests the presence of the third party, the whole of humanity, in the eyes that look at me."[89] Derrida extends this theme into his notion of messianicity without messianism. In "Marx & Sons" Derrida calls messianicity a "universal structure of experience."[90] Then he adds that messianicity is a "universal structure of relation to the event"[91] that cannot be deconstructed.[92] But even though it is a universal structure, it is not an ontological notion because it involves the coming of the event that would generate ontology in the first place.

However, insofar as Derrida's messianicity is a messianicity "without messianism,"[93] he goes beyond Levinas and strips the notion of its religious connotations, including a messiah. He thus turns messianicity into a basic structure not of theoretical knowledge (of which metaphysics is the ultimate paradigm), but of practical activity. A condition of praxis is that one not know how to calculate outcomes, and this unknowability and incalculability go toward making action an open-ended matter. I suggest that this open-endedness of practical action is the universal structure that

Derrida calls messianicity. In "Marx & Sons" he describes this messianicity as "une attente sans attente" ("a waiting without expectation").[94] This phrase is more reminiscent of Heidegger's being-toward-death than of Walter Benjamin's philosophy of history. The notion is not tied to a conception of universal history based on either progress, or decline, or cycles. Instead, messianicity is a basic condition of temporality and as such, it underlies the whole enterprise of the philosophy of history. Derrida corrects Fredric Jameson's impression that there is a utopian hope at stake here. For Derrida, Jameson is making a category mistake in putting Derrida's account of messianicity on the same plane as Walter Benjamin's utopian notion of the weak messianic force of history. Derrida's notion of messianicity is neither a form of optimism nor a form of pessimism (although he says that it is more optimistic than pessimistic). Messianicity makes both optimism and pessimism possible. It therefore also makes both utopian and dystopian politics possible.

For Derrida, then, messianicity is a fundamental condition of action in relation to time, and as such it involves the necessity of "waiting without waiting."[95] This means that on the one hand, we have to wait for our actions to have consequences, but on the other hand, we cannot simply wait, for we have to act. The messianic element involves a different experience of time from the typical bourgeois prioritizing of the present. Messianicity looks to the future, but it does so in a different way from what Derrida calls the apocalyptic. The apocalyptic rhetoric involves the assumption of teleological progress toward an eschatological endpoint. In the Hegelian story, the end of history is achieved when the development of freedom is complete as a result of predictable piecemeal advances. The Marxian story adds the idea of revolution as the final apocalyptic step of the developmental process.

In contrast to this apocalyptic story, messianicity separates the teleology from the eschatology. Messianicity drops the teleological story of progress, but retains the eschatological aspect whereby a breakthrough event can erupt at any moment. "*Anything but Utopian,*" Derrida writes in "Marx & Sons", "messianicity mandates that we interrupt the ordinary course of things, time and history *here-now;* it is inseparable from an affirmation of otherness and justice."[96] As an affirmation of otherness, messianicity must recognize that the future cannot be calculated, predicted, or programmed, but is always unexpected. As an affirmation of justice, messianicity also recognizes that the future is now, and that there is an injunction and a responsibility to act without delay. Although the messianic event cannot be simply willed to occur, its constant possibility precludes passivity or abstention and requires commitment.

Although Derrida shuns ontology, he has nevertheless built into messianicity an entire account of the temporality of action. Given this depiction of the relation of praxis and time, Derrida should not be accused of quietism. One version of quietism would be merely reactive resistance of the sort that is labeled "reformist." Reformists are held by Marxists to be afraid of the idea of revolution. Derrida insists, however, that deconstruction can avail itself of the trope of revolution. Just as deconstruction is not utopian, it is not anti-revolutionary. The source of the worry here is the common construal of poststructuralism and postmodernism as being opposed to the rhetoric of social progress. Because of this renunciation of the Hegelian idea of society's progressing by pulling itself up by its own bootstraps, it was assumed that anyone who was designated as "post" would have to reject the Marxian story of class struggle and revolution. Derrida explains in "Marx & Sons" that he does not reject either the idea of class, even if he finds it problematic, or the figure of revolution, even if he finds it complicated. He thinks that his understanding of messianicity shows that he is now incorrectly labeled as a poststructuralist or a postmodern.[97] Because of his critique of critique, which I noted previously, his more recent work could be appropriately identified as post-critical.

One Marxian notion that he does have reservations about is the idea of "ideology." Derrida suggests in "Marx & Sons" that "the word has perhaps seen its day."[98] He tends to agree with Rastko Močnik that there is a tension between the *idea* of ideology and the *theory* of ideology. As Močnik argues in *Ghostly Demarcations*,[99] the theory of ideology has a built-in blind spot to its own utterances. It can theorize the ideology that distorts other utterances, but it cannot access the source of its own utterances to examine the extent to which they also involve ideological distortions. Derrida suggests that the root of the problem here is the traditional notion of "theory," which implies a degree of objectivity that would be impossible to achieve. He recommends that one try to think differently about the theory of ideology, and he hints that thinking of it as an interpretation rather than as a theory would help.[100] He does not have time in that particular essay to pursue this critique of "ideology," but that critique is the concern of my next chapter.

5   Post-Marxism: "Who Is Speaking?"

Resisting "False Consciousness"

In *The German Ideology* Marx and Engels insist that when someone speaks, one should always ask oneself "Who is speaking and from where?" The contrast they intend is to the left Hegelians whom they criticize for trying to speak from above and outside the world. Resistance is thus thought to be more effective if it is not only critical but also self-critical. Lucien Goldmann repeats Marx's critique of the Hegelians in an attack on deconstruction in its earliest days. Goldmann follows not only Marx but also Lukács, and says: "To know what one is speaking about, Marx very justifiably requires that one know who is speaking and from where: it is necessary to know that one always speaks from within a world from which comes the structure of consciousness of the one who is speaking and who, in order to know what he [or she] is saying, must know this world and this structuration at the risk of otherwise remaining within an ideology."[1] This remark comes from lectures in Paris during the turbulent academic year that resulted in the events of May 1968. The target is apparently those, such as Derrida and Foucault, who follow Heidegger rather than Lukács in

[handwritten marginal note: fear of remaining within an ideology]

explaining the conditions for critical resistance by eliminating the vocabulary of subject and object. Such related terms as 'ideology', 'consciousness', and 'alienation' should also either disappear or be redefined. Goldmann's critique of Derrida is thus a continuation of Lukács's critique of Heidegger, which mirrors Marx's critique of the Hegelians in a famous line from *The German Ideology:* "Life is not determined by consciousness, but consciousness by life."[2]

Poststructuralism in general and Derridean deconstruction in particular do indeed seem to make Goldmann's desire to know who is speaking and from where impossible. Foucault applauds the indifference in Beckett's line " 'What does it matter who is speaking,' someone said, 'what does it matter who is speaking.' "[3] From Derrida's perspective the ethical importance of "who is speaking" is undermined if what is said is not the result of a transparent intention to utter a decidable meaning. The early Derrida might be read as going a step beyond Marx if, contrary to Goldmann, the meaning of language is not constituted by the "who," but the "who" is constituted by language (or *différance*). Similarly, the deconstructive strategy brackets Goldmann's appeal to a real "world" *from* which one speaks (the "where"), and *about* which one speaks (the referent). Deconstruction thus challenges the ideal that Goldmann in the initial quote takes as self-evident: "to know what one is speaking about." Goldmann thinks that not knowing what one is speaking about runs "the risk of otherwise remaining within an ideology." In contrast, deconstruction can be seen as suggesting that there is no "otherwise," that there is no case in which one knows *fully* who one is, from where one is speaking, and what one is speaking about.

The critique of deconstruction from a neo-Marxian standpoint is repeated frequently throughout the rest of the century. For instance, Terry Eagleton makes much the same criticism as Goldmann does. In *The Ideology of the Aesthetic* Eagleton groups Derrida and Foucault with the "libertarian pessimists."[4] This position is engaged in the performative contradiction of continuing to dream of liberty in the face of a pessimistic skepticism about resistance and emancipation.[5] In *Ideology: An Introduction* Eagleton levels this charge more explicitly against the literary critic Jonathan Culler:

In much deconstructive theory, the view that interpretation consists in an abyssal spiral of ironies, each ironizing the other to infinity, is commonly coupled with a political quietism or reformism. If political practice takes place only within a context of interpretation, and if that context is notoriously ambiguous and unstable, then action itself is likely to be problematic and unpredictable. This case is then used, implicitly or explicitly, to rule out the possibility of radical political programmes of an ambitious kind. . . . It is a case which the poststructuralist critic Jonathan Culler, among others, has several times argued. One would, then, be singularly ill advised to attempt any very "global" sort of political activity, such as trying to abolish world hunger; it would seem more prudent to stick to more local political interventions.[6]

Eagleton thinks that this strategy "plays right into the hands of Whitehall or the White House,"[7] and thus that the poststructuralist abandonment of the concept of ideology serves only to perpetuate the reality of ideology and to undermine critical resistance.

Everyone is still too afraid of the holocaust to act.

In *Theory, (Post)Modernity, Opposition*, Mas'ud Zavarzadeh and Donald Morton share Eagleton's concern that abandoning the Marxian aspirations for global critique will entail a lapse into quietism. They apply Marx's critique of Hegel once again to Culler:

Deconstruction collaborates with this program [of "reformism"] by putting forth the mode of immanent reading. . . . This desire not to impose closure on the text accounts for why, as Jonathan Culler explains in *On Deconstruction*, "deconstruction appeals to no higher logical principle or superior reason but uses the very principle it deconstructs" (87). The political and ideological consequence of such a reading strategy is that it posits as intelligible the internal ("local") economy of the system without ever subjecting that system itself to a global relational interrogation. The outcome of a purely immanent reading is a reification of the text's "own terms," as if these terms were freestanding. The immanent reading of texts of culture in a deconstructive mode finally leads to a discovery of their internal discrepancies, contradictions, aporias, and gaps. In short, such a reading is nothing more than a mere "logical" reading that obscures the "politics" of truth by positing "truth" as a matter of internal, formal coherence and not as something constructed by the social relations of production.[8]

Zavarzadeh and Morton want to go beyond deconstruction for the same reason that Marx wanted to go beyond the Hegelians. For Marxians, the reading strategy that (in Marx's words) simply "discovers contradictions everywhere" is to be superseded by the task of explaining the *genesis* and *necessity* of these contradictions. A social rather than a merely immanent reading is required to show that the text's terms are not "natural" and "universal" but instead are tied to a particular political economy that is historical and not eternal. The charge against deconstruction is not simply that it does not go far enough toward promoting critical resistance and social change, but that it refuses to envision social change and therefore actually *retards* social change: "By confining itself to an immanent reading of texts of culture, deconstructive critique remains essentially a conservative and retrograde ideological practice."[9] Deconstruction is ideological because by confining itself to the contradictions of textual analysis and refusing to envision alternatives, it "displaces" politics[10] and thus "is ultimately a device for systems-maintenance and the conservation of the status quo."[11]

Zavarzadeh and Morton think of social change as histori-cal progress toward the final goal of overcoming the class struggle. Poststructuralists such as Foucault reject this model of universal history and progress toward a classless society. Hence, the poststructuralists could not offer as the justification for such a critique of deconstruction what Zavarzadeh and Morton call "global relational interroga-tion," which I take to mean base-superstructure explana-tions or utopian post-historical speculations. Indeed, from a neo-Marxian point of view, such as Goldmann's, Derrida and Foucault will appear to be in the same boat.

The issue for poststructuralism in general and decon-struction in particular is this: If deconstruction is skeptical about one's ability to know exactly who is speaking, and from where and about what one is speaking, does that imply that one is inevitably mired in ideology? Is there no hope for escape? If not, then is not deconstruction itself also ideological? To deconstruction's Marxist critics deconstruc-tion seems necessarily reactionary and conservative because it seems to lose all grounds for criticizing and resisting social oppression. Deconstruction itself cannot claim to be free of ideology, and its critics therefore accuse it of serving to perpetuate the status quo, including all the inequalities of the present.

To counter this criticism I think that deconstruction has only one alternative. That alternative is neither to admit to the inevitability of deconstruction's serving ideology nor to claim that deconstruction is a means to attaining ideology-free consciousness. Instead, deconstruction must differenti-ate its method from that of "ideology critique." Ideology is, after all, a theoretical notion tied to other notions, such as the distinction between true and false consciousness. I do not mean to suggest that deconstruction could abandon the distinction between the true and the false. But it can abandon the idea that an entire consciousness is either true or false, and it can also go so far as to abandon the idea of such a thing as an entire group or class consciousness.

One general reason for not relying on the term 'ideology' is that it is used in so many different senses that it has become meaningless.[12] Another reason is that the term carries over too many connotations from the modern philosophy of consciousness that poststructuralism wishes to leave behind. These connotations become especially problematic for the specific sense of 'ideology' as false consciousness, which is my primary concern in this chapter. Even Pierre Bourdieu, whom I do not consider to be a poststructuralist despite his attempt to replace talk about "subjects" with talk about "agents," says in *Pascalian Meditations* that he has "little by little come to shun the word 'ideology'."[13] He decries the ambiguities produced by its polysemy, and furthermore, he thinks that it contributes to overlooking the material effects of symbolic violence. More precisely, in *Masculine Domination*, he attributes the deficiency of the use of the notion of false consciousness "from Lukács onwards" to an intellectualist and scholastic fallacy that comes from the use of the language of consciousness rather than from a dispositional theory that recognizes "the opacity and inertia that stem from the embedding of social structures in bodies."[14]

Foucault expresses most succinctly the theoretical and practical reasons for abstaining from ideology in this sense:

The notion of ideology appears to me to be difficult to make use of, for three reasons. The first is that, like it or not, it always stands in virtual opposition to something else which is supposed to count as truth. Now I believe that the problem does not consist in drawing the line between that in a discourse which falls under the category of scientificity or truth, and that which comes under some other category, but in seeing historically how effects of truth are produced within discourses which in themselves are neither true nor false. The second drawback is that the concept of ideology refers, I think necessarily, to something of the order of a subject. Third, ideology stands in a secondary position relative to something which functions as its infrastructure, as its material, economic determinant, etc. For these three reasons, I think that this is a notion that cannot be used without circumspection.[15]

Thus, both Foucault and Bourdieu find the notion of ideology problematic because of its links to a model of consciousness and subjectivity ever since Lukács interpreted it as "false consciousness."

However, even if a satisfactory case were made for the theoretical shift away from reliance on the concept of ideology, more would have to be argued. If the practical task is not simply to contemplate but to resist social oppression and to change the world, then some explanation of how deconstruction could serve the task of social criticism is required. Remembering Marx's critique of the Hegelians for being merely "critical critics," proponents of deconstruction should show that deconstructive criticism does not inhibit critical resistance and social transformation, but could well even engender it.

Critical Theory

To broach these issues I begin with the question of how deconstruction can be combined with social theory to go beyond the neo-Marxist method of ideology critique. Fortunately, this extension has already been worked out by the "post-Marxist Marxists" Ernesto Laclau and Chantal Mouffe. But because their adaptation of Derridean deconstruction for the purposes of social philosophy has been sharply attacked by Zavarzadeh and Morton, my goal is not to investigate all the details of Laclau and Mouffe's hegemony theory, but more generally to assess the deconstructive strategy for critical resistance.

To set the scene, I must explain briefly the method of ideology critique as it is developed from Lukács and the Frankfurt School through the early Habermas. For the early Lukács ideology is thought that is distorted by inequalities between classes and by oppressive power relations. The standard definition of ideology as "false consciousness" gets into epistemological difficulties when it applies itself to itself. Lukács raises the "bourgeois" objection that in a society divided by the class struggle it would be impossible to distinguish between thought that was ideological and thought that was not ideological, for all thought would be distorted by class differences and class interests. On this line of thinking, even the proletariat could not claim to have "true" as opposed to "false" consciousness because its perception of social reality would be relative to its particular circumstances.[16] Only in a classless society would there be "true consciousness," and it would no longer be the property of a specific class.

The epistemological problem with this model is that it is not clear how "false consciousness" can be identified as false in the absence (in principle) of true consciousness. More recent theorists, including the early Habermas and the sociologist Steven Lukes, try to get around this epistemological paradox by identifying some grounds in contrast to which one can speak of ideological distortion. The social theorist often finds it necessary to speak of ideology not only when subjects do not act in their own best interests, but also when they seem to want to act against their own best interests. Thus, ideology seems to be in play when one group of agents gets another group of agents to do what the first group wants by shaping the wants of the second group. In short, the oppressed seem to *desire* to do what the oppressors wish. Ideology critique thus assumes that if socially oppressive conditions had not forced the dominated social group to have certain apparent interests, that group would have seen that its real interests would have been different from these apparent interests.

A little-noticed advantage of this appeal to real interests is that it would lead to an analysis that could explain why the oppressors and not simply the oppressed would have reason to want the oppressive relations to be overcome. On the strict determinist model the oppressors would probably be able to do little about changing the oppressive relations, even if they wanted to. Moreover, there seems to be no reason why they should want to. On the model appealing to "real interests," however, real interests are postulated by the observer as what the agents would have done as rational agents if their perception of their interests had not been distorted. By implication, the observer would also have to reason that if the oppressors had been fully rational agents perceiving their real interests, they would not have acted oppressively. After all, one can rationally want to be as well off as the oppressors, but a rational agent cannot knowingly want to be an oppressor. In the final analysis, then, the real interests would be the same for all concerned, oppressed and oppressor alike.

So conceived, ideology critique would have global emancipatory potential as the paradigm of social resistance. However, a crucial difficulty with the model of real interests is in identifying what the specific *real* interests would be, and then in ascertaining that these were not simply postulates of the observer but attributable to the agents even when the agents were, by definition, unaware of them as their interests. Theorists such as Gramsci, Habermas, and Steven Lukes have different ways of addressing this problem, but rather than linger on their specific solutions, I wish to contrast this general model with poststructuralism. If I read poststructuralists such as Foucault, Derrida, and Laclau and Mouffe correctly, they are skeptical about the possibility of identifying these real interests in a substantive way. That is, either the real interests will be so universal and abstract that they will not be able to explain concrete historical cases, or they will be merely attributes of common sense, ones about which we should be historically suspicious insofar as the common sense of one age may not be the same as that of another. The poststructuralists therefore have little use for the concept of ideology, at least in the specific sense of distorted group consciousness. But at the same time, if the poststructuralists abandon ideas such as false consciousness and ideology, they run the risk of losing the normative basis from which to call for critical resistance. Before analyzing this risk, however, I should first make clear why the idea of false consciousness seems so suspect from the poststructuralist perspective.

To state the issues concisely, there are three reasons for this suspicion. First, the appeal to distorted consciousness is unhelpful if there is no consciousness that is not distorted. Second, the idea of a group consciousness is a fiction, and the idea of consciousness should be replaced with other ideas (such as "discourse," "*habitus*," or "the background") that capture the sense in which the structures of social behavior often are below the threshold of conscious decision making, perhaps at the level of the body. Third, if the ideas of distortion and consciousness are abandoned, one can live with the recognition that there is no single way in which to perceive "society" globally and no utopia in which all would describe it univocally.

I think that Zavarzadeh and Morton would acknowledge my description of the poststructuralist approach to social theory, for the term they would apply to what I have just described is 'pluralism'. Pluralism is for them a pejorative term, and is roughly equivalent to bourgeois liberalism. To be a pluralist is to prefer reform to revolution, to acquiesce to the inequalities of the status quo instead of to struggle for change, and to settle for political, "semiotic" democracy instead of true, economic democracy.[17] In short, pluralism would undercut the possibility of critical resistance. I want to defend Derrida and Laclau against this critique. But first I need to explain in more detail just how Laclau uses Derrida for the purposes of social theory. If a central critique of deconstruction is that it cannot be applied to social theory and political critique, then this critique is undermined by Laclau's ability to put it to such uses.

Hegemony Theory: Laclau and Mouffe

In *Hegemony and Socialist Strategy*,[18] Laclau and Mouffe abandon the vestiges of metaphysics still found in Marx, including the class struggle, history as motoring single-mindedly toward a classless society, and any account of the whole of society or the whole of history. Laclau goes beyond even Gramsci in rejecting the concept of the subject as a "centered social agent whose identity is constituted around a set of well delineated 'interests.'"[19] Subjects can find themselves in contradictory positions depending on the different social places they occupy: "We may ask, for example, what is the linkage between the degree of union militancy of a white worker in the workplace on the one hand, and his attitude towards racial conflicts in his neighbourhood on the other."[20] Laclau finds the notion of false consciousness unhelpful because it depends on the idea that subjects "misrecognize" their interests, as if there were a non-contradictory set of interests that each self-identical subject must have. Laclau thinks that classical Marxism incorrectly identifies "subjects" and "physically existent individuals" because it underestimates the increasing complexity of the social. Indeed, on his view there is no such thing as society. As Laclau and Mouffe say famously in *Hegemony and Socialist Strategy*, " 'society' is not a valid object of discourse."[21] They reject any ideal of grasping the social-historical totality, and they try to do social theory without any vestiges of utopian thinking (unlike Habermas, who admits that a utopian kernel is preserved in the ideal of uncoerced discourse).

Furthermore, Laclau does not see social relations as causal effects of the material base on the discursive superstructure: "Assertions such as 'society is an integrated ensemble of functions' or 'in every society it is possible to differentiate the base from the superstructure,' are neither correct nor incorrect, for they are, in the strict sense of the term, meaningless; 'society in general' is not a legitimate object of discourse."[22] Instead of seeing society as different from the discursive, as that which the discursive is about, Laclau sees all significant social practices as similar to the discursive in that they involve an "infinite play of differences."[23] Social practices are thus not on a different level than the discursive, but must be theorized with the same principles that would apply to any discourse. Laclau and Mouffe theorize social practices on the principle of difference adapted from Saussure and Derrida. The principle of difference implies, roughly, that units in a system of signification have a signifying value only through each one's contrast to all the other units in the system. One reason for rejecting the global explanations of society and history as a whole is that there is no end to such a system of differences. Just as a language is an infinite play of further substitutions where closure is never reached, the "totalization" of the social is impossible.[24]

Laclau rethinks the concept of ideology in the light of this discourse model of the social in his 1983 essay aptly titled "The Impossibility of Society." Thinking of the social as an infinite play of differences suggests that society is not a totality or an essence, but that "society" is only ever a construct that "fixates" a subset of this play into a system of frozen identities. Of course, this fixation *must* occur, for real discourse would be psychotic unless meanings were fixed. The attempt to limit the play of differences to a finite order is what Laclau means by *hegemonizing* the social. Hegemonization is necessary, because we cannot master an infinite play of differences. But the hegemonic fixation of a finite subset is always only partial because the infinity is never completely capturable. Laclau even claims that complete hegemonic fixation is finally impossible. If I read him correctly, the reason for this impossibility is that the excess that is not fixed or that is fixed in competing ways will always undo any hegemonic formation of identity. Laclau thinks that this process is repeated in the traditional conception of ideology as false consciousness. Given the notion of the social construction of subjectivity, what sense does it make, he asks, to say that social subjects misrecognize themselves? If their identity or "essence" is not fixed *a priori*, but is instead "the unstable articulation of constantly changing positionalities," then "the kaleidoscopic movement of differences," "the theoretical ground that made sense of the concept of 'false consciousness' has evidently dissolved."[25]

Laclau does not want to abandon the concept of ideology entirely, however, and this is where I think that this particular essay makes a problematic move. He thinks that to remain *critical*, social theory must hold on to the idea that it reveals places where social concepts and social beings have misrecognized their true character. "Without this premise," he maintains, "any deconstruction would be meaning-less."[26] He appears to be tempted to assert that it is true that the social is really an infinite play of difference and not a fixed totality or essence. This quasi-metaphysical commit-ment is apparently required to be able to say that a hege-monic reduction of the infinity to a fixed order is a misrecognition of the truth. Thus, he inverts the traditional concept of ideology:

> The ideological would not consist of the misrecognition of a posi-tive essence, but exactly the opposite: it would consist of the non-recognition of the precarious character of any positivity, of the impossibility of any ultimate suture. The ideological would consist of those discursive forms through which a society tries to institute itself as such on the basis of closure, of the fixation of meaning, of the non-recognition of the infinite play of differences. The ideolog-ical would be the will to "totality" of any totalizing discourse.[27]

Because the imposition of order and the fixation of meaning are necessary for us, the social will always include the ideo-logical. Moreover, there will always be a job for critical the-ory, even if there is no reconstruction of what society is that is not exceeded by the infinite play of differences.

Laclau's attempt to retain the notion of ideology, even if by inverting it, strikes me as coming dangerously close to unnecessary paradox, precisely because of the vestigial con-notations of the ideal of true consciousness. If social theory must give up any claims about the true character of the totality, then it should also not say that the totality is truly the infinite play of differences. Instead, Laclau should have said, as I just quoted him in *Hegemony and Socialist Strategy*, that such a totalizing claim would be neither correct nor incorrect, because it is meaningless. The most that should be said, and all that Laclau really wants to say, is that, if the term 'ideology' is to be used at all, it should be applied to those conceptions that take the social order to be inevitably or necessarily the way it is and that fail to recognize its malleability or its precariousness. But because the ideal of true consciousness always tempts the user of the term 'ideology' into epistemological conundrums and hasty ontologizing, even an inverted conception of ideology should be avoided.

Critical Debates

Zavarzadeh and Morton resist Laclau's "rhetoricization of the social" for opposite reasons. They resent the reduction of the social to the interplay of incommensurate language games because it eliminates the meta-narrative or the all-encompassing theoretical standpoint aspired to by traditional Marxism: there are no longer universal laws of history and economics, or necessary connections between the levels of society. For Zavarzadeh and Morton this rhetoricization of the social makes all struggle simply ideological struggle and not class or economic struggle. Zavarzadeh and Morton read Laclau and Mouffe as saying that "the social will change only when subjectivities have changed."[28] This claim is inadequate for Zavarzadeh and Morton because "such a notion of change ... leaves the economic structure intact and merely reforms its local practices: exploitation, which determines the logic of capitalism and maintains it, does not disappear but simply shifts its site."[29] The Derridean rhetoricization of the social simply serves, in their view, "to give capitalism 'a human face': to change cultural patterns of behavior, lifestyles, and modes of thinking in order to make the exploitative economic relations more tolerable."[30] The effort of Laclau and Mouffe to see the social much as Derrida sees textuality thus reproduces, for Zavarzadeh and Morton, the basic error of deconstruction, which in their view is necessarily and fatally "a rather sophisticated reproduction of dominant values."[31]

Before evaluating this critique of deconstruction, I would like to reflect briefly on a similar critique of deconstruction from an entirely different direction, that of Habermas. Habermas also sees Derrida as unable to generate social criticism with the deconstructive method. Laclau and Mouffe construct their revisionary social theory on a theory of discourse and to this extent their approach to social theory resembles Habermas's social philosophy of communication. However, they understand discourse in a markedly different way than Habermas understands communication. Whereas Habermas thinks of rational discourse as a form of communicative action, Laclau and Mouffe are distrustful of the ideal of communication. Laclau's critique of communication is that there is always a power play in the communicative exchange. While Laclau accepts the idea of language games, he maintains that subjects in the language game do not start by being transparent to themselves. Furthermore, he denies that such transparency could be attained as a result of the language game.

Laclau and Mouffe generalize this point about individual speakers to social interaction, and deny the ideal of a society with no relations of domination. Like Foucault, they think that there is no freedom without power. Antagonisms are inevitable in society, and on their account even a theorist such as Rawls is pursuing hegemonic purposes in proposing his theory of justice as the best theory of justice. They think of themselves as pluralists, but they reject the pluralism of liberals because liberals overlook the fact that new groups cannot enter democratic discourse without hegemonic conflict. Liberals allegedly fail to recognize that there is not enough to go around, and for Laclau they do not take power, conflict, and politics seriously enough. The ideal of public discussion and final agreement is illusory. Agreement, which for Habermas is the telos of language, is for Laclau and Mouffe only the triumph of a particular hegemony.

Deconstructing the Future

An apparent difficulty with Laclau and Mouffe's position is that the status of the hegemonic conception of social interaction itself becomes uncertain. If the theorists' own assessment of social antagonisms is itself hegemonic, then both the theory itself and its empirical research could not count as genuine knowledge for anyone not already sharing the view. Traditional Marxism was able to appeal to the ideal of progress in history toward a future classless society to deal with the issue of how to distinguish true from false consciousness, or legitimate resistance from co-optation. But this notion of progress through universal history is no longer acceptable to poststructuralists who abandon this meta-narrative. However, then the poststructuralists must confront the further question whether the deconstructive skepticism about progress entails not only giving up the idea of resisting oppression, but also becoming resigned to the status quo.

This is a crucial objection that critics raise against both Foucault and the early Derrida. The best short answer in the case of Foucault seems to me to be that we can still use the idea of resisting oppression without invoking the ideal of a society in which there is *no* oppression. That is, we can think that our society is less oppressive in some respects, and therefore "better" than before, at the same time that we believe that there are many different kinds of oppression still around, some of which may even have been caused by our very success in alleviating previous oppression.[32]

I see no reason to think that this response is not also available to the defenders of deconstruction. Let me first consider Eagleton's accusation that Culler's position entails abandoning global political efforts to reduce world hunger in favor of more local actions, such as changing the professoriat at a particular university. (Eagleton's ironic epigraph to *Ideology: An Introduction* suggests that he is similarly skeptical about Richard Rorty's argument that postulating solidarity with "humans in general" is empty and that we should feel more social solidarity to those closer to home.) A natural response to Eagleton's supposed counterexample to Culler is to admit that skepticism about the likelihood of one's own action successfully reducing world hunger is reasonable (especially given recent cases of failures by famine-relief efforts to distribute donations where they were needed). One could then argue that this skepticism does not entail that one not make any effort at all to reduce world hunger, but perhaps that one first make such efforts in one's own neighborhood. Of course, someone might contribute to Oxfam, or other world hunger organizations, and be applauded for doing so. However, it would be strange if that same person were then completely indifferent to the hungry at home. I see no reason to think that deconstruction rules out either global or local action, even if it does suggest that one undertake such resistance with a certain skepticism both about the likelihood of success and about the purity of one's motives.

Eagleton's concluding paragraph shows that he thinks that we need to retain the idea of ideology to explain how the experience of even "quite modest, local forms of political resistance" can change people's "political consciousness."[33] He thinks that the attempt by poststructuralist "post-Marxists" to replace the notion of ideology with the notion of discourse will fail to explain such change. I myself would think that all that happens is that such change gets explained differently. Instead of a change in political consciousness, what can be analyzed is a change in political discourse, including the terms people use and the kinds of things they say.

Eagleton thinks that substituting discourse for ideology is a mistake because discourse theory sees the subject as fragmented, and loses the degree of identity that is necessary to explain the social as the result of human agency. In *Ideology: An Introduction*, he thus launches a vehement attack on what he calls the "left-semiotic" position of "Jacques Derrida and his progeny." The *Tel Quel* group is said to equate political revolution in a "starry-eyed" Maoist fashion as "ceaseless disruption and overturning":

[It] betrays an anarchistic suspicion of institutionality as such, and ignores the extent to which a certain provisional stability of identity is essential not only for psychical well-being but for revolutionary political agency. It contains no adequate theory of such agency, since the subject would now seem no more than the decentred effect of the semiotic process; and its valuable attention to the split, precarious, pluralistic nature of all identity slides at its worst into an irresponsible hymning of the virtues of schizophrenia. Political revolution becomes, in effect, equivalent to carnivalesque delirium; and if this usefully reinstates those pleasurable, utopian, mind-shattering aspects of the process which a puritanical Marxism has too frequently suppressed, it leaves those comrades drearily enamoured of "closure" to do the committee work, photocopy the leaflets and organize the food supplies.[34]

This critique is then extended to Laclau and Mouffe because of their rejection of the idea of real or objective interests. Eagleton

agrees that if by real interests one means those interests auto-
matically supplied by the agent's economic place, that conception ought to be rejected. But he thinks that there is a more
useful sense that should be retained:

An objective interest means, among other things, a course of action
which is in fact in my interests but which I do not currently recognize as such. If this notion is unintelligible, then it would seem to
follow that I am always in perfect and absolute possession of my
interests, which is clearly nonsense. There is no need to fear that
objective interests somehow exist outside social discourse altogether; the phrase just alludes to valid, discursively framed interests which do not exist for me right now. Once I have acquired such
interests, however, I am able to look back on my previous condition and recognize that what I believe and desire now is what I
would have believed and desired then if only I had been in a position to do so. And being in a position to do so means being free of
the coercion and mystification which in fact prevented me at the
time from acknowledging what would be beneficial for me.[35]

Eagleton here is trying to salvage a notion of "false consciousness" that does not appeal to some objectionable
(because "metaphysical" or "unhistorical" or "supra-
historical") conception of true consciousness. His proposal
is a modest one, and I find it difficult to construct a knock-
down argument against it. Probably no such argument is
needed because Eagleton has purchased plausibility at the
price of loss of forcefulness. The route now seems open to
the poststructuralist simply to prefer another vocabulary,
and to give some supporting reasons for a different way of
describing such changes of social perception.

The deconstructor could point out, for instance, that
Eagleton models social development on personal development, without demonstrating that an analysis of the organic
individual could be extended to social development.
Eagleton thus might simply be extending a neo-Hegelian

fiction that could bring out some useful analogies, but that also is recognizably disanalogous to concrete social complexity. Given Laclau's critique of the subject, which I described earlier, he would also probably reply that Eagleton relies on a simplified notion of the individual subject's identity. Laclau claims that subjects are not self-identical in this way *at any given time* because they can simultaneously belong to different groups with different or even competing interests. He could also ask why we should attribute such self-identity to subjects *over time*. Contrary to Eagleton, Laclau might infer that instead of speaking of the same subject who has come to see its true interests, we should recognize the subject as becoming increasingly discontinuous with itself, not as more truly itself. Or at least, different stories are equally possible. Given this more complex perception, the model of organic individual development would lose its explanatory value. Or if the claim of discontinuity seemed too strong in particular cases, then perhaps we should say that subjects find themselves using different discourses in the present than in the past; they might then prefer the present discourse not for the reason that it is truer in general to their continuing self, but for the reason that it more usefully captures social change and increasing complexity. This same reason could then be used by the neo-Nietzschean poststructuralists to explain why they do not buy into the neo-Hegelian fiction of the self. Nietzscheans resist the assumption that the self is a self-identical substance that goes through a process both of getting in touch with its real interests over time, and of converging with all others who share these interests.

The poststructuralists would find Eagleton's view of the self to be neither correct nor incorrect, but imprecise and unhelpful. They are less interested in whether the subject

believes that it understands itself truly than in how the various discourses in which it finds itself inscribed actually
work. Furthermore, to accuse the poststructuralists of
reducing social practices to discourses, as Eagleton and others do, seems off target. Eagleton is afraid that "the category
of discourse is inflated to the point where it imperializes the
whole world, eliding the distinction between thought and
material reality," the distinction on which the whole idea of
the critique of ideology rests.[36] Eagleton's "short reply" to
the reduction of social practices to discourses is that "a practice may well be organized like a discourse, but as a matter
of fact it is a practice rather than a discourse."[37] However, to
this reply the poststructuralist can make the even shorter
rejoinder that Eagleton's distinction between discourse and
social practice cannot be cashed in. For one thing, a discourse is language in use and is thus, from the pragmatist
point of view, a social practice. For another, social practices
may contain non-discursive features in addition to discursive ones, but that does not entail that social practices are
not permeated by discursivity. I do not see discourse theory
as imperializing the whole world so much as making sure
that the notion of the world include rather than exclude the
discourses that are a central part of what makes the practices *social*.

Zavarzadeh and Morton take on deconstruction even
more archly, and accuse it of constantly "deferring" social
action by saying, "Not now; it is not practical today; maybe
later."[38] Deconstruction may regard itself as subversive
because it destabilizes rigid fixations, but these critics think
that it has really been co-opted by the dominating hegemony as a place where "the pressures of social contradictions are safely released."[39] The only effective form of social
critique and resistance, they believe, is one that shuns plu-

ralism and instead "offers a global understanding in which the dominant and the dominating, the now and the later, are all related to the underlying logic of the social division of labor."[40] Although they do not want to project a utopia somewhere in the future, they still seem to believe in progress toward a "later" time where social division is overcome.

I myself see nothing wrong with trying to destabilize present fixations or reifications just because they are there, and deconstruction seems to be an appropriate strategy for such destabilization. Deconstruction is said by its critics to lack emancipatory potential because it does not appeal to universals, or because it does not project an emancipatory trajectory in history. However, I do not see why we have to know in advance all the non-oppressive structures to put in place of the oppressive ones that we find ourselves resisting. Philosophy can no longer be expected to provide the story of how the fractured present is necessarily headed toward a perfect future. Instead, the most that philosophy can do now is to speak in the future perfect, telling how "it will have been." That is, a pragmatic and critical philosophy asks the present to imagine how the current ways of speaking, thinking, and acting would look from a situation where those ways are no longer practiced. This exercise will not necessarily show how those who share in the present practices could opt for different ones, but it might encourage the questioning of incongruity and incoherence that otherwise would be ignored.

The exercise, however, cuts both ways. On the one hand, a healthy society should welcome the efforts to question its limits. On the other hand, the destabilizers may find limits to their own endeavors. They might reasonably be expected not to want to destabilize entirely the social arrangements that tolerate and encourage the destabilizing experiments themselves. Either way, social critique is possible and social transformation is practicable without the fiction of a single path of necessary progress toward a perfect future.

Post-Critique: Slavoj Žižek

If one were to rethink all the associated concepts that go into the idea of "false consciousness," including concepts such as the subject, the self, reality, truth, and power, then the term 'ideology' would be able to be used more meaningfully. Laclau and Mouffe revised the conception of ideology significantly in their 1985 book by reworking Marxism and poststructuralism. In 1989, *The Sublime Object of Ideology*, the first major book in English by the Slovene theorist Slavoj Žižek, transcended these two traditions and changed the terrain of the debate. Žižek rethinks these crucial concepts through Lacanian psychoanalytic theory and through a unique reading of Hegel. Ernesto Laclau signals the emergence of this new approach to the critique of ideology when he praises Žižek's book for being "one of the most innovative and promising projects on the European intellectual scene."[41] In this section I focus in particular on Žižek's rethinking of ideology.

Even if Žižek is not classifiable as a poststructuralist because of the lack of influence of Nietzsche on Lacan, I want to portray Žižek as sharing poststructuralism's suspicion of the idea of false consciousness. There are moments, however, where Žižek's account of ideology appears to be mired in the standard terminology of both falsity and consciousness. For instance, in his "Postface" (written in 2000) to Lukács's 1926 defense of *History and Class Consciousness*, Žižek takes up what Lukács calls the "bourgeois" critique of the notion of class consciousness. As I pointed out at the beginning of this chapter, the issue is that if no class can claim to have a complete grasp of the society, then even the proletariat's perspective is just that, a perspective. Perspectives fall short of objectivity and complete truth because they involve only a partial picture of social reality. The analysis of the problem offered by Lukács depends on the distinction between the actual consciousness exhibited by workers, and the consciousness that could be "imputed" to the class. This solution depends on being able to say that even if the actual consciousness is incomplete and ideological, the imputed consciousness can be thought to be objective and true.

This approach depends for its success on how the conditions of objectivity are specified. Žižek sees that the description of the society that purported to be "neutral" would not be objective, but would formally be "false" because it would involve accepting the existing order. In a manner that is reminiscent of Max Horkheimer's 1937 essay "Traditional and Critical Theory," Žižek reads Lukács as maintaining that a critical theory must recognize its own situatedness and its own commitments to political action and social transformation.[42] Žižek wants to follow Lukács by showing that historicism is not sufficiently historicist because it does not give an account of itself as a social phenomenon and is thus incomplete. Žižek maintains that social theory cannot be objective in the sense of being politically "neutral," and it is incomplete unless it takes its own social embeddedness into account. An important aspect of what the critical social theory would have to explain is a question that traditional theory ignores: Why does it meet with resistance? In this respect for Žižek critical social theory is similar to psychoanalytic theory, which also has to explain why its explanations are often resisted at first by patients.

Does Žižek's interpretation of Lukács succeed in avoiding the paradox of relativism and historicism? Unfortunately, Žižek's explication founders in its attempt to steer between the shoals of a partial explanation and a complete one. Whereas Žižek insisted that a better social theory is one that is more complete if it can give a self-referential account of its own social functions and effects, he nevertheless falls back into an admission that because a social theory is engaged in bringing about social transformation, its perspective is only ever "partial." Žižek says of Lukács's imputed class consciousness that "far from 'relativizing' the truth of an insight, the awareness of its own embeddedness in a concrete constellation—and thereby of its engaged, *partial*, character—is a positive condition of its truth."[43] Saying that a theory is partial is not the same as saying that it is false insofar as partial representation is not the same as misrepresentation or distortion.

However, I would argue against relying on the distinction between partial and complete on the grounds that the idea of giving a complete account of anything is unintelligible. Furthermore, insofar as a theory that is partial would have to abandon some beliefs in order to accommodate a more complete account, and insofar as it could not know in advance which particular beliefs these would be, its epistemological status is subject to radical doubt. For these reasons I think that Žižek would have been better advised not to deploy the contrast between partial and complete. Nevertheless, he does invoke it in defending Lukács and he thereby risks the same epistemological problems that beset any theorist who frames ideology in terms of false consciousness.

When Žižek is working out his own views in books such as *The Sublime Object of Ideology* instead of defending Lukács, he does suggest a much different approach that does not get bogged down in these perennial paradoxes. To present this approach, I begin again with Marx, but this time with the Marx of *Capital* rather than the Marx of *The German Ideology*. There Marx's most famous statement about ideology is "They do not know it, but they are doing it."[44] For Žižek this definition has been misunderstood as a result of the traditional emphasis on the *wissen* rather than the *tun*, the knowing and not the doing. Focusing on knowledge rather than on the reality of what we do leads to the situation today where the classic concept of "false consciousness" is no longer convincing. Following Peter Sloterdijk's *Critique of Cynical Reason* (1983), Žižek thinks that the formula should instead be "They know very well what they are doing, but still, they are doing it."[45] Cynical reason thus undermines the traditional critique of ideology. If one thinks of ideology as false consciousness, Marx's statement is heard as implying that we misrecognize what we are really doing and what is really going on. Žižek's interpretation is a remarkably different way to hear Marx's claim. Instead of implying that *we misrecognize what is really going on*, it can suggest that *we misrecognize that nothing is really going on*. In the first locution, which is the traditional way of understanding Marx, there is a real way things are in society, including what our real interests are, and we are misunderstanding that reality because of asymmetrical relations of domination.

Does the second locution rely in the same way as the first one on a notion of what is "really" going on? One might think so, because otherwise, how could one use the term 'misrecognition'? The thought that things seem to be one way but really are another way implies that there is a level of reality that could be grasped correctly. Žižek manages to disrupt this traditional epistemological understanding of the distinction between appearance and reality. The very idea of a reality that can be known is a fantasy. In *The Sublime Object of Ideology* he insists that this assertion is not to be understood simplistically as the claim that *reality is just an illusion.*[46] To invert the claim of traditional ideology critique that ideology is an illusory grasp of the social reality by asserting that the belief in reality is illusory still construes ideology as a representational relation between consciousness and reality. In the introduction to his edited volume *Mapping Ideology*, Žižek concludes, after a review of the antinomies of other approaches to ideology, that "the theoretical lesson to be drawn from this is that the concept of ideology must be disengaged from the 'representationalist' problematic: *ideology has nothing to do with 'illusion,'* with a mistaken, distorted representation of its social content."[47] Žižek thus maintains explicitly that social theory must move not only beyond thinking of itself as seeing through illusion to the underlying reality, but also beyond seeing the belief in reality as illusory. Both of these approaches are still caught up in the epistemological problematic of false consciousness, and he wants to move beyond that way of problematizing the issue.

Thus, in *The Sublime Object of Ideology* when Žižek follows Lacan and ties reality to fantasy, he is asserting that fantasy is stronger than dreamlike illusion. The fantasy-construction contains a hard kernel that cannot be shaken off so easily. Ideology is not an illusion that is built to escape an insupportable reality, but instead it "structures our effective, real social relations and thereby masks some insupportable, real, impossible kernel."[48] Ideology does not offer us "a point of escape from our reality," but instead it offers us "the social reality itself as an escape from some traumatic, real kernel."[49]

This kernel supplies the material force of fantasy and it allows Žižek to say that what we call "social reality" is an "ethical construction."[50] Ethics is construed not in the sense of a moral code, but in the sense of the ethical substance that underlies the moral code and that makes us who we are. As such, it involves beliefs, which are not taken to be interior mental states, but which are "radically exterior, *embodied* in the practical, effective procedure of people."[51] In contrast to theoretical reason, whereby we believe "because we have found sufficient good reasons to believe," from the standpoint of action "we find reasons attesting our belief because we already believe."[52] With this insistence on embodiment and the logic of practice, Žižek can be seen as the latest development in the tradition that also includes Merleau-Ponty, Foucault, and Bourdieu.

Although Žižek thinks that to speak of a post-ideological age is too hasty, in his framework the notion of ideology changes drastically, as do related notions such as the subject, the reality, the totality, and truth. Marxism standardly defines ideology as "a partial gaze overlooking the totality of social relations."[53] Here again consciousness is "false" not because it is untrue, but because it is partial or incomplete. The Hegelian thought is that truth is the whole, and any thought that does not grasp the totality of things and relations is incomplete and inadequate as knowledge. This, at least, is the standard reading of Hegel.

In a later exchange with Judith Butler and Ernesto Laclau, however, Žižek puts a different spin on the Hegelian notion of totality and thus ends up with a different reading of the conceptual relation of ideology and the totality. Generalizing on Hegel's discussion of the "beautiful soul" in *The Phenomenology of Spirit*, Žižek maintains that the totality is encountered in its purest form when it fails, and when one tries to distance oneself from it in order to maintain one's own purity. The "beautiful soul" in Hegel attempts to abstain from any committed action in order to retain the purity of intention and not to get what Sartre calls "dirty hands." In the dialectic of the beautiful soul, Žižek says, "'totality' is encountered at its purest in the negative experience of falsity and breakdown, when the subject assumes the position of a judge exempt from what he is passing judgement on."[54] The contradiction is that in the attempt to remain pure, the beautiful soul is nevertheless involved in the system that it pretends to reject. As Žižek remarks, "purity is the most perfidious form of 'cheating.'"[55]

When Žižek defines ideology in relation to totality, it is to a "totality set on effacing the traces of its own impossibility."[56] In contrast to his reading of Lukács, it is important to notice that Žižek is here decrying not the *partiality* of any actual knowledge of the totality, but the belief in totality as such. Reality is usually thought of in terms of everything that is the case, and it is also assumed that everything coheres with everything else to form a totality, whether one can grasp this totality or not. Generally it is granted that the human mind cannot grasp the totality. If that is so, it can reasonably be asked whether this notion of the totality is not simply a product of the imagination. Žižek's statement that the totality, which is impossible, tries to cover up its own impossibility, is admittedly paradoxical. How could something that did not exist cover up its own nonexistence? The answer depends on a psychoanalytic premise that the fantasy desires to hide from itself its own inability to face up to the nonexistence and the impossibility of its fantasized object. The psychoanalytic explanation thus changes the order of inference: instead of ideology being the false consciousness of reality, for Žižek reality is a symptom of an internal contradiction that, if it were resolved, would allow the "reality" to disappear.

Given this explanation, the connection of the concepts of reality and fetish becomes pertinent. According to Žižek in *The Sublime Object of Ideology*, for traditional Marxism the fetish "conceals the positive network of social relations," whereas for Freud "fetish conceals the lack ('castration') around which the symbolic network is structured."[57] The philosophical point is that instead of thinking of reality as a given that is antecedent to experience, one must try to think of reality as a failed effect. Reality is posited as the result of a lack that must be filled in, but never is. Thus, when ideology is glossed as the misrecognition that there is nothing really going on, the philosophical point is to dismiss altogether the idea of reality as the way things are in themselves. Žižek sums up Hegel's critique of Kant's notion of the thing-in-itself in his remark that "the negative experience of the Thing must change into the experience of the Thing-in-itself as radical negativity."[58]

Can Žižek avoid the paradox of saying that *there really is no way that things really are?* He can if one distinguishes the sense of the first "really" in this formulation from that of the second "really." The second occurrence of the term 'really' covers (or quantifies over) the particular things, whether they are objects or relations. The first 'really' covers (or quantifies over) the "way" that things are. Presumably, one could deny that there is a single *way* that things are without denying that the things are real. Bourdieu would probably have insisted that the reality of the interpretation not be confused with the interpretation of reality. In any case, as I understand Žižek, his account of ideology is sufficiently distant from the language of false consciousness to be able to avoid the paradox that has troubled theorists of ideology since Lukács.

Changing the conception of the object will also change the conception of the subject, and Žižek has intriguing thoughts not only about reality, but also about consciousness. Žižek notices that Hegel's critique of Kant comes down to the claim that the transcendental object is nothing but a projection by the subject of its own nothingness. This is not an extrinsic criticism of Kant, since it was Kant who defined the transcendental object as an empty X, and then had to grant that the unity of consciousness was empty of content as well.[59] If the transcendental object is nothing determinate, then neither is the subject, and thus for Žižek consciousness (as self-awareness) becomes a mystery. As he remarks during his exchange with Butler and Laclau, "the status of consciousness is much more enigmatic than it may appear: the more its marginal and ephemeral character is emphasized, the more the question forces itself upon us: What *is* it, then?"[60] If consciousness is nothing but the consciousness of something other than it, and if that which is other-than-it is nothing in itself, then it is not surprising that consciousness is inscrutable. Given this confrontation of nothing with nothing, Žižek proposes the formula "Consciousness, in effect, equals anxiety."[61]

In light of the discussion in the previous chapter of the relation of death and finitude, this is a fascinating speculation. It makes one begin to wonder why anyone ought to worry about death if consciousness is in itself quintessentially anxious. Although this account of the relation of subjectivity and objectivity might have been enough for Žižek to complete his equation between consciousness and anxiety, in fact in the exchange with Butler and Laclau, he goes on to speculate that it is only the unconscious that disavows one's mortality. Consciousness, in contrast, is where one is aware of one's finitude and mortality. Žižek even suggests that the anxious awareness of mortality is not simply one among many aspects of conscious awareness, but its "very zero-level."[62]

This claim that anxiety is the zero-level of consciousness comes surprisingly close to the conclusions of Heidegger's fundamental ontology. In addition, there are also vestiges of anthropocentric humanism in Žižek's claim that anxiety sets humans apart from the animals, and that "only 'conscious' beings are actually finite and mortal, that is, only they *relate* to their finitude 'as such.'"[63] He wants to use this account of consciousness to set it off from the unconscious in this exemplification of the "very model of self-awareness": "'I know very well that I am mortal, but nevertheless. . . . (I do not accept it; I unconsciously believe in my immortality, since I cannot envisage my own death).'"[64] Cynicism is now built into the essential structure of self-awareness.

To sum up, moving from the perspective of Lukács in the 1920s to Žižek's perspective today involves major changes in the way that one thinks not only about ideology, but also about subjectivity and social reality. At the risk of oversimplifying complex ideas and arguments, I will condense Žižek's main points first about reality, and then about consciousness and community, as follows:

• In contrast to traditional ideology critique, which relies on the idea of seeing through illusion to reality, Žižek's model sees the 'Real' as a function of fantasy (which is not the same as illusion).

• Whereas ideology on the standard understanding of the term masks agents' real interests, for Žižek a sign of the ideological is this very belief in the uninterpreted fact of the matter or the self-evidently true state of affairs.[65]

• Whereas for the tradition we misrecognize the truth, for Žižek, following Lacan, "the Truth arises from misrecognition."[66]

Not only is the analysis of reality changed in this new approach of the Slovene School; the idea of consciousness changes in the following respects:

• Whereas humanistic Marxists influenced by Hegel and the early Marx assume that self-consciousness is essential to our being, for Žižek the ideal of self-transparency creates delusions.

• The role of misrecognition also changes. For traditional theorists, overcoming misrecognition allows us to see our true selves, and misrecognition can even destroy our true selves. For Žižek, in contrast, the misrecognition is that there is a "true Self."

• The formation of the self even depends on misrecognition, such that if there were no misrecognition, there would be no self.

• In contrast to traditional ideology critique that presupposes that emancipation from illusion promotes freedom, for Žižek the ideal of complete emancipation is itself a fantasy. One finds out retroactively that one has already chosen.[67]

Finally, there are some changes in how one understands one's relations to others as one moves from the older to the newer model.

• If the traditional model sees community as linked to ideal consensus, Žižek (and Laclau and Mouffe) are suspicious of actual consensus because of the asymmetry that may be introduced insofar as the self-interests of the powerful will carry more weight.

• Where there is a tendency in the tradition to see social practices as interfering with our ability to choose ourselves genuinely and to create community, on this new model bodies are colonized by social practices, which make us who we are.

Žižek has offered, then, an account of ideology that is consistent with the poststructuralist suspicion of the idea of "false consciousness." I should point out, however, that Žižek questions whether there is any such thing as poststructuralism in France. For him poststructuralism is a misunderstanding of French philosophy by North Americans: "In short, an entity like 'poststructuralist deconstructionism' (the term itself is not used in France) comes into existence only for a gaze that is unaware of the details of the philosophical scene in France: this gaze brings together authors (Derrida, Deleuze, Foucault, Lyotard, . . .) who are simply not perceived as part of the same *épistème* in France."[68] On his view, to consider poststructuralism as a form of critical theory is "a classification which is unthinkable in France."[69]

He is not entirely right about this last point, for Foucault on several occasions acknowledges an affinity for critical theory.[70] In the 1983 interview with Gérard Raulet, for instance, Foucault hints that the reason why the Frankfurt School theorists were not read in France after the war was some lingering bias among French academics.[71] Furthermore, Foucault's major work, *Discipline and Punish,* draws on an earlier study of the prison system by two Frankfurt School theorists. In any case, I think it is generally recognized that the works of Foucault, Derrida, and other thinkers (including, undoubtedly, those of Žižek himself) have a different life in North America than they do in their own national circles. Although the historical origins of the texts are important to their understanding, these texts also have effects beyond those origins. Those effects are significant in their own right. Hence, even if poststructuralism is not a totally genuine French import, and even if truth in marketing would require it to have a warning label specifying "Made in the USA," the term might still have some viable shelf life. For teaching purposes, for instance, it continues to be useful as the designation for a paradigm shift in the reception of Continental philosophy in Anglophone universities.

However, the signs of the times also indicate that the label 'poststructuralism' may have outlived its usefulness. Perhaps now is an appropriate moment to recognize that philosophy has moved on. If new categories for classifying philosophical movements came into use, they could well be productive of new ways of thinking about the innovations introduced into philosophy during this time. A recent suggestion has been to think of philosophy as having evolved a style of thinking called deconstructive genealogy. Less indeterminate a label than "poststructuralism," such a postcritical program could represent a promising synthesis of Foucault's genealogy and Derrida's deconstruction. I turn now to an assessment of its prospects.

Postscript: On Deconstructive Genealogy

Today Derrida believes that philosophy should be pursued as "deconstructive genealogy." He calls for a philosophical approach that recognizes the *duties* of criticizing totalitarian dogmatism and of cultivating "the virtue of such *critique, of the critical idea, the critical tradition,* but also submitting it, beyond critique and questioning, to a deconstructive genealogy that thinks and exceeds it without yet compromising it."[1] Derrida's description of a deconstructive genealogy that is "beyond critique" (or, in my terms, "post-critical") is reflected in his analysis of what he terms the "university without condition."[2] For deconstruction to admit that there is anything without condition or unconditional, or anything that cannot be deconstructed, is a surprising move. Derrida had always insisted on the necessity of context, and thus of conditions for understanding and interpretation. Now, however, he posits justice and messianicity as notions that in principle cannot be deconstructed, and he goes on to affirm the unconditional character of freedom and resistance. Thus, Derrida says that the ideal of the university is the "*unconditional* freedom to question and to assert, or even, going still further, the right to say publicly all that is required by research, knowledge, and thought concerning the *truth*."[3] This unconditional freedom is the basis for the "unconditional resistance" that the university in general and the humanities in particular should pursue. The university is thus affirmed as "an ultimate place of *critical resistance*—and more than critical—to all the powers of dogmatic and unjust appropriation."[4]

What is this critical resistance that is "more than critical"? The answer is deconstruction, defined as "an unconditional right to ask critical questions not only about the history of the concept of man, but about the history even of the notion of critique, about the form and the authority of the question, about the interrogative form of thought."[5] Post-critique is thus self-critique all the way down.

What is the relation of deconstructive genealogy to the tradition of critique, even if they are not co-extensive? Critique is the starting point, and there is a duty to criticize dogmatism. But criticism alone, Derrida suggests, is not enough. Why not? The familiar Marxian response would be to say that one must also change the world. However, if a deconstructive genealogy does not appeal to the teleological imperative of global change, does resistance thereby become directionless? Derrida's critique of critique may target only a certain form of criticism: the purely negative criticism that protects itself by not asserting any positive alternatives to what is being criticized, probably because of the fear of being criticized in turn. When resistance is coupled with this negativity, it becomes susceptible to the objection that haunts political theory. Wendy Brown expresses it aptly: "Resistance goes nowhere in particular, has no inherent attachments, and hails no particular vision."[6]

But this charge is applicable only to one form of critique. As Deleuze noted, critique is not necessarily always reactive and negative. There is, after all, constructive criticism. However, by now we have seen how other theorists respond to the accusation that resistance is directionless. In these responses, much depends on what degree of direction is expected. Foucault's view is that too much is expected of philosophy if it is supposed to specify some universal direction *a priori*. Even limited, piecemeal advice on direction might sound to Foucault too much like telling others what to do. What Foucault does say is that his own critical resistance is intended to minimize domination. Any more specific direction will depend on the particular circumstances addressed by the critique generated though a particular genealogical analysis.

Drawing on Derrida's critique of good conscience, I can imagine him taking a different tack in approaching this issue. To the charges that resistance is directionless and critique only negative, I can hear him responding with his critique of critique. He would resist the sense of direction suggested by any line of criticism proffered with the tacit implication that it knows the true picture and the best solution, even if it never fully articulates this knowledge. I take it that Derrida objects to the complete self-confidence of the critic who seems to have no doubts about where society ought to be going. I assume, therefore, that Derrida would be equally opposed to cynical reason, which is only the flip side of good conscience. I also do not believe that Derrida is calling for psychological self-doubt. That is certainly not be a move that Nietzsche would tolerate. Instead, I understand Derrida to be calling for the openness to other possibilities that can be gained through an openness to self-criticism. In short, deconstructive genealogy disrupts methodological smugness by calling into question the very grounds of critique.

This blend of Foucault's genealogy and Derrida's deconstruction holds out the promise of a program for critical resistance that would bridge the social and ethical concerns of this book. In the first three chapters I was concerned with the task of using the genealogical mode of inquiry of Nietzsche and Foucault in the construction of pluralist social theories. In chapter 4 deconstruction was the approach that was at stake in the task of explaining the possibility of ethical responsibility. Derrida confronts the paradox of ethics: to behave ethically toward the other is to behave unethically toward all the other others. This paradox calls the grounds of ethics into question, but it also serves to show how the ethical invariably relates to the social. In fact, that paradox now points toward a crucial parallel between the social and the ethical. Just as for Foucault being a social subject requires the subject to call itself and its situation into question, for Derrida being ethical involves calling the grounds of ethics into question. While this move of Derrida's might appear to be a deconstruction of ethics, I see it as targeting the foundationalism still invoked in Levinas's account of ethics. While Derrida would abandon Levinas's metaphilosophical claims for first philosophy, Derrida does not have to abandon the sense of responsibility to the other that is at the core of Levinas's substantive ethical claims. This responsibility is the motivating force of deconstructive genealogy that wants to avoid the self-certainty of good conscience. Just as ethical responsibility thus turns out to be tied to social responsibility, the deconstructive account of ethics has many of the features of a genealogical account of the social.

To underscore these parallels and to indicate the fecundity of connecting the genealogical and the deconstructive, I wish to show how this post-critical program can clarify two problems that linger in my account of critical resistance.

First, I should address the distinction between the proliferation that I resisted in Kofman's interpretation of Nietzsche and the openness to possibilities that I praised in Foucault. Then I can return to the Heidegger-Levinas debate about the source of the sense of ethical responsibility that motivates critical resistance and determines what matters.

The Limits of Pluralism

The first problem arises because of the pluralism that some of Nietzsche's French interpreters (e.g., Kofman and Foucault) find in him. The issue that concerns me is how to avoid the proliferation of possibilities such that anything goes while at the same time allowing the openness to possibilities that is essential if the genealogist is to distinguish freedom and resistance from domination. In my view, Nietzschean pluralism is a useful antidote to the monistic assertion of the "one right theory." At the same time, however, if this pluralism is to be a form of *critical* resistance, it should be neither as anarchistic as "anything goes" nor as nihilistic as "nothing matters."

Bourdieu and Levinas cannot be considered to be deconstructive genealogists, but they give answers that genealogists could well adopt. Bourdieu's appeal to social ontology and Levinas's ethical generalization are equally opposed to both methodological nihilism and methodological anarchism. Bourdieu could reject the nihilism that "nothing matters" with his argument that society (and not "God") is the source of values, and that these values are built into our bodies. Furthermore, society is a way of making certain things matter and of prohibiting certain other things. Therefore, the logic of social practice is such that neither nihilism nor anarchism would be possible in a vital social arrangement.

Levinas could respond with the more eternal claim that we cannot avoid responding to the face, and the mortality, of the other. Nihilism is wrong because the face of the other is a *summons,* an obligation that cannot be enforced but that one nevertheless has to heed. Furthermore, although Levinas is a pluralist, he could not accept methodological anarchism because of his recognition of ethical resistance and the responsibility it engenders.

These arguments suggest that even if no sharp line separates pluralism from methodological anarchism and nihilism, there is enough difference that pluralism can be kept separate from these proliferative positions and from the restrictive positions of monism and dogmatism. Proliferation is different from the openness to possibility that I argued for in chapter 2. There I interpreted Foucault as distinguishing power from domination. While power produces and structures possibilities, domination narrows and restricts possibilities. Thus, power is not necessarily oppressive, and it becomes so only when it transmogrifies into normalization and domination by becoming rigid and fixed. While Foucault prefers possibilities to be open-ended, this is not to say that anything goes. The particular social grid of intelligibility permits and delimits the range of possibilities, and it is only in terms of this grid that possibilities are determined. In sum, openness to possibilities is not the same as saying "anything goes" because possibilities are always limited and situated. Furthermore, openness is the opposite of saying "nothing matters" because possibilities are considered open only insofar as they are found to be worth pursuing.

Much the same issue came up in chapter 5 with Ernesto Laclau. Laclau astutely does not think of critique as the tool of some disengaged (and disembodied) theorist for recovering hidden, necessary truths. Instead, critique sees that any totalizing theory is trying to turn the complexity and flux of social practices into a stable, closed, and institutionalized necessity. The Nietzschean point here is that there is nothing intrinsically wrong with this attempt to impose order and to fix meaning because doing so is necessary to our survival. Our minds are finite and the complexity of all the possibilities exceeds our capacity of understanding. Derrida also affirms as much when he says that deconstructive genealogy thinks and exceeds critique; that is, deconstruction shows that even critique is exceeded by the complexity of possibilities.

Where this Nietzschean line becomes paradoxical is when it is taken to entail skepticism about the very possibility of social knowledge. For instance, Laclau's talk of social reality as "the infinite play of differences" may suggest sheer proliferation and the methodological anarchism whereby anything goes. A critic might then object to Laclau that his position founders on the following paradox: if there is such an infinity, then the mind could not in principle grasp it; and if the mind cannot grasp it, then Laclau cannot assert it to be true.

To avoid this paradox, I think that Laclau in particular and deconstructive genealogists more generally should argue that even if the social is infinitely complex, complete skepticism about our social knowledge does not follow. The set of integers is infinite, the genealogist could point out, and there are lots of them that we will never state, given that we have finite minds. Nevertheless, we still can say that we know many features not only of the integers that we do know, but also of those that we have not yet articulated. For instance, we know that they are all greater than zero, and that for every integer there is a greater one. Hence, even if society is an infinite play of differences, social knowledge should not be any more problematic in principle than our knowledge of arithmetic. Instead of dwelling on the perils of proliferation (including talk about unknowability and undecidability), the genealogist should aim at awakening the more limited but also potentially emancipatory recognition of agents' situated openness to specific possibilities.

In sum, I can offer no principle or algorithm or criterion for distinguishing what Nietzsche might have called a healthy pluralism that prizes openness to possibility from either an unhealthy dogmatism that insists on the one true view or a proliferative relativism that believes that anything goes. The main concern about proliferation is that it lacks the capacity for *critical* resistance. However, recognizing when the openness that pluralism prizes shades off into the proliferation that goes too far requires what Aristotle called *phronesis* or practical wisdom. *Phronesis* cannot be articulated into rules and principles, but without it rules and principles are useless. This Aristotelian notion is a central topic in ethical theory, so let me now turn to the question of why anything matters.

Why It Matters

I have been defending what I take to be a claim by Nietzsche, Foucault, and Derrida that critical resistance requires freedom, and freedom is tied conceptually to the openness to possibility. At the same time I have been saying that this openness is more circumscribed than sheer proliferation. Part of the argument depends on my sense that sheer proliferation does not describe human understanding correctly. Understanding is situated and finite, and could not possibly entertain an infinite play of possibilities all at once.

Heidegger therefore speaks of freedom not simply as the (ontic) capacity to make choices, but also as the (ontological) ability to tolerate the finitude that follows from the fact that making one choice excludes all the other choices that one could have made at that point. This tolerance also involves the recognition that some things matter more than others (for otherwise, there would be no basis for choice). At the same time, choices may have to be taken back at any moment since they are made contingently and fallibly.

These points lead to the debates about ethics that I portrayed in chapter 4. To sum up the debate and what I believe Derrida's position to be, the outcome of the deconstruction of death is that neither Heidegger nor Levinas carries the day. While death is central to our ethical comportment for Derrida precisely because of the finitude of human understanding, the question of whether my own death or the death of the other is more primordial is undecidable. Part of Derrida's argument for this claim is that the distinctions between perishing, demising, and dying and between humans and animals cannot be sustained. Even if one is not convinced that this analysis is entirely fair to Heidegger, one could still agree to the further point that the question of whether my death or the other's death is more *primordial* entails a philosophical project that need not be accepted. The search for primordiality could well be thought to be a vestige of first philosophy and foundationalism, which Heidegger himself wanted to leave behind. Certainly deconstructive genealogy would also want to avoid it, no matter how seductive it is even today.

A plausible alternative is to say "neither Heidegger alone nor Levinas alone" because they could both be saying something right. In other words, this neither/nor could mean *both* Heidegger *and* Levinas. Derrida himself often turns a neither/nor into a both/and statement. In this case, the deconstructive genealogy could be said to conclude that both my own death and the death of the other are ethically significant. But the death of the other has to be understood more in the fashion of Levinas than in that of Rilke and Heidegger. For Levinas the death of the other is not a small death, and is not inauthentic. Instead, it is as tragic as one's own death, even for oneself.

Giving up the question of which is more primordial could also lead to giving up on other philosophical pretensions. For instance, the Heidegger-Levinas debate may be a case study that encourages skepticism about the traditional philosophical task of keeping the descriptive statements of pure theory entirely separate from the normative language of ethics and practical philosophy. Furthermore, if the line between descriptive and normative language blurs, the debate about whether ontology precedes ethics or ethics precedes ontology falls away. In fact, Heidegger's view that *death* is what makes things matter will also be altered if we take his enterprise as interpretation and not as transcendental philosophy. Mortality may well contribute to making things matter to us, since mortality leads to my sense of having only a finite time to complete my tasks. For instance, if I had an infinite life and therefore an infinite amount of time to write this book, I would lack the urgency that compels me now to complete it. Finitude is an unavoidable feature of existence. But to claim that death is the only such feature, or the most primordial of these features, is to go beyond what is phenomenologically accessible. Only a particular quasi-foundationalist conception of philosophy forces on us such an inflation of the importance of the concept of mortality in human existence.

This conception of philosophy is no longer so seductive because philosophy today has alternative anti-foundationalist approaches such as hermeneutics, pragmatism, and now "deconstructive genealogy." These approaches are deflationary about death because they recognize that the social need for critical resistance supersedes the isolated anxiety of the single subject. If the new generation of deconstructive genealogists accepts this deflationary view, they could also reject claims about the ontological primordiality of either my death or the death of the other. At least, that is the response that my own *phronesis* suggests, for even without ontological inflation, death is problematic enough.

The accounts of critical resistance that I have presented in this book can stand on their own and they do not need to be synthesized into a single methodology of deconstructive genealogy. However, the idea of such an approach does raise two intriguing questions that I should address by way of conclusion: What would make deconstructive genealogy "deconstructive"? What would make it "genealogical"?

A brief answer to the first question is that genealogy is "deconstructive" because, as Derrida suggests, it thinks and exceeds critique without compromising it. I read this remark on the one hand as challenging the self-certainty of the critical attitude that confidently assumes that it is really in the know. On the other hand, this remark also implies that the need for criticism and change is still pressing. There may well be an urgent need to act. However, action in specific social and historical situations is less than perfect and is not well described by more idealized philosophical accounts of rationality and choice. Practical action in concrete settings thus requires *phronesis*. That is to say, action often occurs without full information, or consensus, or sufficient reflection on principles and motivations. Action without self-certainty implies that one must always remain open to taking back one's commitment to a given course of action. Hence, even if one persists in that course of action, one must remain open to other possibilities.[7] As a philosophical attitude, then, deconstructive genealogy involves a heightened sense of responsibility and of the obligation to act. At the same time, however, it recognizes the limitations of universal precepts and the value of *phronesis.* Insofar as criticism grows out of a contextual understanding of contingent circumstances, it can never be fully transparent to itself. Acting always with less than good conscience, critical resistance must inevitably be ready to be self-critical.

A brief answer is equally possible to the second question. The program of deconstructive genealogy is genealogical insofar as one inquires into the origins of one's own beliefs and reasons for acting. Genealogy, at least in the hands of Nietzsche and Foucault, has the effect of showing that what is taken as natural or as necessary is really contingent and historical. Genealogy may not change the world, but it does prepare the world for change. Genealogy contributes the initial condition for possible change by freeing agents from the fatalistic assumption that the given oppressive social arrangement is eternal. Genealogy shows that these assumptions came into being at a certain point, perhaps for rather arbitrary reasons or purposes, and thus could cease to be the case, if not immediately then at least in the foreseeable future.

Freedom, according to the quotation from Nietzsche at the outset of this book, can be measured by the exertion required in resisting the resistance to it. This passage by itself does not see all resistance as emancipatory, because emancipatory resistance will also meet with resistance. Resistance will have to be critical, then, and it will have to make an effort to understand what Bourdieu calls its own field, that is, its own standpoint and situation. Moreover, it will also have to be self-critical, and reflect on its own contingent circumstances and contextual limitations. Being critical and even self-critical does not guarantee that resistance will succeed in increasing freedom and decreasing domination. Nothing can guarantee success. However, if there is one point to which all the theorists whom I have discussed could agree, it is that resistance that was unwilling to be both critical and self-critical would not even be worth attempting in the first place.

Notes

Introduction

1. Nietzsche, *Twilight of the Idols,* in Nietzsche 1959, p. 542.
2. See Hoy 1994a.
3. Brown 1995, p. 7.
4. Hans-Georg Gadamer is also an adherent of the branch of the tradition that emphasizes the concrete situation. In *Truth and Method* (1989, p. 21) he explains that for Vico "what gives the human will its direction is not the abstract universality of reason but the concrete universality represented by the community of a group, a people, a nation, or the whole human race." I discuss this difference between abstract universality and concrete universality (or solidarity) in Hoy 1998.
5. Jameson 1984, p. 57.
6. Bensaïd 2001, p. 34. See Herman Melville, "Bartleby, the Scrivener," in *Tales, Poems, and Other Writings,* ed. J. Bryant (Modern Library, 2002).
7. Derrida 1998, p. 2. On Bartleby as Job, see Derrida 1995, pp. 74–81.
8. Slavoj Žižek, "Holding the Place," in Butler et al. 2000.
9. Proust 1997, p. 186.
10. Walzer 1986, p. 51.
11. Hoy and McCarthy 1994.
12. Foucault 2000, p. 236.

Chapter 1

1. In 1983 the Athlone Press published an English translation (by Hugh Tomlinson) of *Nietzsche and Philosophy* with a succinct and lucid preface by Deleuze. Foucault recognizes the importance of this book when he says that

we live in a Deleuzian age. West (1999, p. 283) comments: "This position—the trashing of totality, the trashing of mediation, the valorization of difference outside the subject-object opposition, the decentering of the subject—all these features that we now associate with postmodernism and poststructuralism go back to Deleuze's resurrection of Nietzsche against Hegel."

2. Deleuze 1983, p. xiii.

3. Ibid., p. 105

4. Williams 2002, pp. 12–19.

5. Deleuze 1983, p. 3.

6. Ibid., p. 185.

7. Ibid.

8. Descombes 1997, p. 90.

9. Deleuze 1983, pp. 141–142.

10. Ibid., p. 139.

11. Ibid., pp. 188–189.

12. Ibid., p. 189.

13. Ibid., p. 190.

14. Ibid.

15. Ibid., p. 61.

16. Ibid., p. 127.

17. Ibid., p. 131.

18. Ibid.

19. Ibid., p. x

20. Ibid., p. 82.

21. Ibid., p. 61.

22. Ibid., p. 58.

23. Ibid., p. 183.

24. Ibid., p. 184.

25. Ibid.

26. Deleuze 1977.

27. Ibid., p. 145.

28. Ibid., p. 148.

29. Ibid., p. 149.

30. Criticisms of the neo-Nietzschean tendencies in poststructuralism can be found in Habermas 1987 and in Ferrry and Renaut 1997. See also Hoy and McCarthy 1994.

31. For a comprehensive account of French readings of Nietzsche, see Schrift 1995. Some parts of this section and the next are excerpted with revisions from my essay "Philosophy as Rigorous Philology? Nietzsche and Poststructuralism" (Hoy 1981).

32. See Rorty 1979.

33. Foucault's "Nietzsche, Freud, Marx" is an address delivered in July 1964 and published in 1967 in *Cahiers de Royaumont, Philosophie Numéro VI:*

Nietzsche (Minuit). I cite it here (as Foucault 1998) from the English translation in volume 2 of *Essential Works of Foucault*.

34. Foucault 1998, p. 275. Gutting (1989, p. 274) maintains that in this essay Foucault is merely explicating Nietzsche and not adopting these views as his own. I read Foucault as trying Nietzsche's views on for size, even if he finds that they do not fit well. Whether the insistence on interpretation is Foucault's, Foucault is saying that these views about interpretation are "ours." Foucault states that although the hermeneutical assumptions and techniques that he is describing emerge in the nineteenth century, "we" still share these assumptions and "we" continue to apply these techniques to ourselves.

35. Foucault 1998, p. 275.

36. Ibid.

37. Ibid., p. 278.

38. Derrida 1979, pp. 131–133.

39. Sarah Kofman's review essay is titled "Genealogy, Interpretation, Text" and is published as an appendix to the English translation of her book *Nietzsche and Metaphor* (Kofman 1993).

40. Kofman 1993, pp. 135–136.

41. Ibid., p. 140.

42. Ibid., p. 141.

43. See Feyerabend 1975.

44. Kofman 1993, p. 143.

45. Ibid., p. 142.

46. For a development of the difference in Nietzsche between the relation of an interpretation and a text, on the one hand, and the relation of a perspective and its objects, on the other hand, see Cox 1999, especially pp. 109–168. On Nietzsche's interpretation of interpretation, see Murphy 2001, especially chapter 4.

47. Derrida 1979, p. 125.

48. Nietzsche, *Beyond Good and Evil,* in Nietzsche 1968a, p. 216.

49. Nietzsche 1966, pp. 34–35.

50. Nietzsche, *Beyond Good and Evil,* in Nietzsche 1968a, pp. 216, 217.

51. The idea of multiple drafts comes from p. 113 of Dennett 1991.

52. Nietzsche 1968b, p. 302 (§556).

53. Ibid., p. 267 (§481).

54. Ibid.

55. Nietzsche 1974, pp. 298–299 (§354).

56. Blondel 1991, p. 242.

57. Ibid., p. 245.

58. Nietzsche 1966, p. 34.

59. Nietzsche, *Ecce Homo,* in Nietzsche 1968a, p. 710.

60. Nietzsche, *The Genealogy of Morals,* in Nietzsche 1968a, p. 493 (Essay II, §1).

61. Blondel 1991, p. 219.

62. Ibid., p. 214.

63. Ibid., p. 216.

64. Nietzsche 1968b, §556, p. 302.

65. Blondel 1991, p. 216.

66. Ibid., p. 219.

67. Ibid., p. 214

68. Ibid., p. 213

69. Ibid.

70. Ibid.

71. Cited in ibid., p. 233.

72. Cited in ibid., p. 234.

73. Cited in ibid., p. 234.

74. Dennett 1991, p. 113.

75. "It is our needs which interpret [*auslegen*] the universe; our drives are their *pro* and *contra*. Every drive is a sort of ambition to dominate, each one has its own perspective which it tries to impose as the norm on all the other drives." (cited on p. 238 of Blondel 1991)

Chapter 2

1. Foucault, "Nietzsche, Genealogy, History," in Foucault 1984, pp. 87–88 (translation modified; emphasis added).

2. See Dennett 1991, p. 24. Taking "body" as a natural kind may be the result of the mistake of what Dennett (ibid., p. 381) calls armchair naturalism: "the assumption that whatever nature makes is a natural kind."

3. Foucault, "Nietzsche, Genealogy, History," in Foucault 1984, p. 83.

4. Dreyfus and Rabinow 1983, p. 167.

5. Ibid., p. 206 (emphasis added).

6. Ibid., p. 111.

7. Ibid., p. 166.

8. Ibid., p. 167 (emphasis added).

9. Ibid., p. 112.

10. Scarry (1985, pp. 52–56) distinguishes eight features of pain, but to my mind only the first one, its aversiveness, is universal. The other features would be characteristic only of more extreme forms of pain or would not necessarily be experienced by every individual. The other features of pain that she picks out from the case of torture include the dissolution of the boundary between inside and outside the body, a conflation of the public and the private, the destruction of language-ability in the individual, the obliteration of the contents of consciousness, the involvement of the entire body, and resistance to objectification.

11. Foucault 1984, p. 335.

12. Ibid., pp. 335–336 (emphasis added).

13. Ibid., pp. 45–46.

14. Foucault 1979, p. 303.

15. Ibid., p. 304.

16. Ibid., pp. 202–203.

17. Ibid., pp. 192–194.

18. Ibid., p. 202 (emphasis added).

19. Foucault 1980, p. 157.

20. Foucault 1980b, p. xiii.

21. Best and Kellner 1991, p. 58.

22. David M. Halperin, "Forgetting Foucault: Acts, Identities, and the History of Sexuality," in Nussbaum and Sihvola 2002; McWhorter 1999. For a discussion of Judith Butler's reading of Foucault, see n. 14 on pp. 251–252 of McWhorter's book.

23. For an explanation of the distinction between *de re* and *de dicto* intellectual historiography, see chapter 3 of Brandom 2002.

24. Foucault 1984, pp. 351–359.

25. Ibid, p. 359.

26. Foucault 2002a.

27. Foucault, "Governmentality," in Burchell et al. 1991, p. 102.

28. Foucault 2002a, p. 250.

29. Ibid., pp. 242–243.

30. For an account of Foucault's discovery of the innovations introduced by the discovery of statistical explanation, see Ian Hacking, "How Should We Do the History of Statistics?" in Burchell et al. 1991, especially pp. 183–184. See also chapters 4–7 of Hacking 2002.

31. Foucault 2002a, p. 241.

32. Foucault 1988, p. 137.

33. Ibid., p. 145.

34. Foucault, "The Ethics of the Concern for Self as a Practice of Freedom," in Foucault 1997, p. 299.

35. Ibid. p. 292.

36. See Dreyfus and Rabinow 1983, p. 147.

37. See chapter 5 below.

38. Foucault, "The Ethics of the Concern for Self as a Practice of Freedom," in Foucault 1997, p. 295.

39. Foucault 1979, p. 282.

40. Ibid., pp. 279, 282.

41. Ibid., p. 280.

42. Ibid., pp. 273–274.

43. Ibid., p. 274.

44. Foucault 1980a, p. 221.

45. Foucault 1988, p. 37.
46. Ibid., p. 39.
47. Ibid., p. 43.
48. Ibid., p. 47.
49. Ibid., p. 48.
50. Ibid., p. 49.
51. Ibid., p. 43.
52. Ibid., p. 101.
53. Foucault, "Body/Power," in Foucault 1980a, p. 56.
54. Ibid.
55. Ibid., p. 57.
56. Foucault 1988, p. 95.
57. Ibid., pp. 95–96.
58. Foucault, "On the Genealogy of Ethics," in Foucault 1997, p. 264.
59. Foucault 2002a, p. 51 (translation modified).
60. Foucault 2002a, p. 46 (translation modified).
61. Foucault, "Interview with Michel Foucault," in Foucault 2000, p. 241.
62. Foucault, "Questions of Method," in Foucault 2000, p. 235.
63. Ibid., p. 236 (emphasis added).
64. Paul Rabinow, "Introduction," in Foucault 1997, pp. xxxviii–xxxix.
65. Foucault 1990, p. 8; cited by Paul Rabinow on p. xxxix of Foucault 1997.
66. Foucault, "What Is Enlightenment?" in Foucault 1997, p. 319.
67. These pieces are now readily available in the very useful anthology, *The Political,* edited by David Ingram (2002).
68. Butler 2002a, p. 214.
69. Ibid.
70. Ibid., p. 215.
71. Ibid., p. 221.
72. Foucault 2002b, p. 194.
73. Jacqueline Rose, cited on p. 97 of Butler 1997a.
74. Butler 2002a, p. 218.
75. Ibid., p. 225.
76. Ibid., p. 226.
77. Butler 2002b, p. 18.
78. Butler 1997a, p. 13.
79. Butler 1997a, p. 9.
80. Ibid.
81. Butler 1997a, p. 104.
82. Foucault 2002b, p. 208.
83. Ibid.
84. Butler 2002a, p. 224.
85. Butler 2002a, p. 226.

Chapter 3

1. Bourdieu resists relativism and defends the objectivity of his own socio-logical studies by arguing for a different understanding of objectivity than is found in absolutist philosophy or in objectivistic approaches to sociology. See, for instance, Bourdieu and Wacquant 1992, p. 51ff. See also Pierre Bourdieu, *The Logic of Practice* (Stanford University Press, 1990) (cited as Bourdieu 1990a), pp. 30–51.

2. Merleau-Ponty 1962, p. 395.

3. Ibid., p. 407.

4. Ibid., p. 386.

5. Ibid., p. 431.

6. Ibid., p. 387.

7. Ibid., p. 388.

8. Ibid., p. 400 (emphasis added).

9. Ibid., p. 405.

10. Ibid., p. 407.

11. Ibid., p. 406.

12. Ibid., p. 404.

13. Ibid., p. 407.

14. Ibid., p. 406.

15. Ibid., p. 402.

16. Ibid., p. 389.

17. Ibid., p. 390.

18. Ibid., p. 403.

19. Ibid., p. 404.

20. Ibid., p. 452.

21. Ibid., p. 453.

22. Ibid.

23. Ibid., pp. 438–439.

24. Ibid., p. 441.

25. Ibid., p. 455.

26. Ibid., p. 443.

27. Ibid., p. 447.

28. Ibid., p. 448.

29. Bourdieu 1990a, p. 49.

30. Ibid., p. 51.

31. Ibid., pp. 59, 57.

32. Ibid., p. 57.

33. Ibid., p. 86.

34. Ibid., p. 55.

35. Ibid., p. 68.

36. Ibid., p. 53.
37. Ibid., pp. 52–53.
38. Ibid., p. 56.
39. Ibid., p. 54.
40. Ibid., p. 275.
41. Ibid., p. 71.
42. Ibid., p. 293, n. 5.
43. Ibid., p. 71.
44. Ibid., p. 78.
45. Ibid., p. 79.
46. Ibid., p. 69.
47. Ibid.
48. Ibid.
49. Ibid., p. 75.
50. Bourdieu 2000, p. 147.
51. Ibid., p. 152.
52. Ibid., p. 151.
53. Bourdieu 1990a, p. 67.
54. Bourdieu 2000, p. 154.
55. Ibid. (emphasis added).
56. Ibid, p. 7.
57. Bourdieu 1996, p. 340.
58. Ibid., p. 344.
59. Bourdieu 2000, p. 153.
60. Ibid.
61. Ibid., p. 151.
62. Bourdieu 1990a, p. 68.
63. Bourdieu 2000, p. 141.
64. See Calhoun, "Habitus, Field, and Capital," in Calhoun et al. 1993, p. 72.
65. Bourdieu 1990b, p. 9.
66. Bourdieu 1990a, pp. 89–90.
67. Ibid., p. 103.
68. Ibid.
69. Ibid., pp. 91–92.
70. Ibid., p. 91.
71. Ibid.
72. Foucault 1990, p. 11.
73. Bourdieu 2000, p. 118.
74. Bourdieu 1990b, p. 11.
75. Bourdieu 1990a, pp. 60–61.
76. Ibid., p. 62.
77. Ibid., p. 60.

78. Ibid., p. 59.

79. Ibid., p. 64.

80. Ibid.

81. Bourdieu and Wacquant 1992, p. 51ff.

82. Ibid., p. 200.

83. Ibid., p. 197.

84. Ibid., p. 171.

85. Ibid., p. 172 (emphasis added).

86. Ibid., p. 173.

87. Bourdieu 2001, p. 69. In Bourdieu and Wacquant 1992, Bourdieu speaks more concisely of this effort to live up to society's ideal of what it is to be a man as "desperate and somewhat pathetic."

88. Bourdieu 2001, p. 75.

89. Bourdieu 1990b, p. 116.

90. Bourdieu 2001, p. 40.

91. Bourdieu 1991, p. 158.

92. Bourdieu 1990a, p. 57.

93. Ibid., p. 59.

94. Bourdieu 2001, p. 12.

95. Bourdieu 1990a, p. 39.

96. Bourdieu 2001, p. 244.

97. Ibid., p. 108.

98. Ibid., p. 2.

99. Bourdieu 1991, p. 109.

100. Ibid.

101. Butler 1997b, p. 147.

102. Jacques Derrida, "Force of Law: The 'Mystical Foundations of Authority,'" in Cornell et al. 1992, p. 25 (emphasis added).

103. Ibid., p. 24.

104. Ibid., p. 28.

105. Bourdieu 1990b, p. 196.

106. Ibid.

107. Ibid.

108. Ibid., p. 33.

109. Ibid.

110. Ibid., p. 32.

111. Bourdieu and Wacquant 1992, pp. 23–24.

112. See Bourdieu 1990b, p. 155, or Bourdieu and Wacquant 1992, p. 24 (cited by Wacquant).

113. Grosz 1994, p. 144. Bourdieu discusses Sandra Lee Bartky's article in *Masculine Domination* (2001, p. 68).

114. On the "double bind" that women with power face, see Bourdieu 2001, p. 68.

115. Bourdieu and Wacquant 1992, p. 24 (cited by Wacquant).

116. See Bourdieu 1990b, p. 183; Bourdieu and Wacquant 1992, p. 49.

117. Bourdieu 1990b, p. 15.

118. For the further details of a compelling reconstruction of Bourdieu that reads him as offering a theory of the intelligibility of action in contrast to a theory of the causal generation of action, see Schatzki 1987.

119. Bourdieu 2000, p. 154.

120. Goldberg 1993, p. 7.

121. Ibid., p. 6.

122. Bourdieu 2000, pp. 70–71.

123. Ibid., p. 71.

124. Ibid.

125. Ibid., p. 100.

126. West 1999, p. 311.

127. Ibid.

128. Ibid., p. 313.

129. Ibid., p. 312.

130. Ibid., p. 314.

131. Ibid., p. 161.

132. Ibid., p. 164.

133. Ibid.

134. Ibid.

Chapter 4

1. See Maurice Merleau-Ponty, "The Philosopher and His Shadow," in Merleau-Ponty 1964, pp. 166–168, discussed by Levinas in "On Intersubjectivity: Notes on Merleau-Ponty," in Levinas 1993.

2. Merleau-Ponty 1964, p. 166.

3. Ibid., p. 168.

4. Ibid., p. 169.

5. Levinas 1993, p. 101

6. Emmanuel Levinas, "Beyond Intentionality," in Montefiore 1983, p. 109.

7. Ibid., p. 110.

8. Levinas 1993, p. 102.

9. Ibid., p. 103.

10. See Levinas 1989, p. 51.

11. Levinas 1969, p. 80.

12. Ibid., pp. 305–306.

13. Ibid., p. 80.

14. For an explicit reference to and discussion of the Hegelian master-slave dialectic by Levinas, see Levinas 1989, p. 50.

15. Levinas 1969, p. 81.
16. Ibid., p. 197.
17. Ibid., p. 199.
18. Levinas 1989, p. 43.
19. See Levinas 1969, p. 229.
20. Levinas, "The Paradox of Morality: An Interview with Emmanuel Levinas," in Bernasconi and Wood 1988, p. 176.
21. See Levinas 1969, p. 189ff.
22. Ibid., p. 191.
23. Ibid., p. 194.
24. Ibid.
25. Ibid., p. 195.
26. See ibid., pp. 205–207.
27. Ibid., p. 212.
28. Ibid., p. 209.
29. Ibid., p. 200.
30. Ibid.
31. Ibid., p. 134.
32. Ibid., p. 188.
33. Ibid., p. 300.
34. Levinas 1989, p. 83.
35. Levinas 1969, p. 199.
36. Emmanuel Levinas, "Ethics as First Philosophy," in Levinas 1989, p. 82.
37. Ibid., p. 83.
38. Levinas, "The Paradox of Morality," in Bernasconi and Wood 1988, p. 179.
39. Levinas 1989, p. 291.
40. Levinas, "Beyond Intentionality," in Montefiore 1983, p. 110.
41. Levinas 1989, p. 290; see also p. 86.
42. Ibid., p. 84.
43. Derrida 1993, p. 61.
44. See Derrida 1992, p. 41.
45. Derrida 1993, p. 42.
46. Ibid., p. 24.
47. Ibid., p. 43.
48. Ibid., p. 22.
49. Ibid., p. 19 (emphasis added).
50. Derrida 1992, p. 10.
51. See Jorge Luis Borges, "The Immortal," in Borges 1964.
52. See Derrida 1993, pp. 39–40.
53. Heidegger 1962, p. 289.
54. Ibid., p. 295.
55. Ibid., p. 237.

56. Ibid., p. 232.
57. Ibid., pp. 331, 334.
58. See Levinas 1987, pp. 70–71.
59. Levinas 1969, p. 241.
60. In "Donner la mort" (Rabaté and Wetzel 1992, p. 50), Derrida cites Levinas's line "La mort de l'autre, c'est la mort première"; he then raises some critical questions about Levinas's account.
61. Derrida 1993, p. 76.
62. Ibid., p. 39.
63. Ibid., p. 80.
64. Ibid., pp. 80–81.
65. Levinas 1987, p. 74.
66. Derrida 1993, p. 76.
67. Ibid.
68. Derrida 1993, p. 79.
69. Ibid.
70. Ibid., p. 45.
71. Ibid., p. 32.
72. Ibid., p. 80.
73. Ibid., p. 18. Here Derrida is quoting himself (*The Other Heading*, pp. 76–78).
74. Derrida 1993, p. 19.
75. Derrida 1995, p. 85.
76. Ibid., p. 86.
77. Derrida 1992, p. 81.
78. Ibid., p. 73.
79. Derrida 1993, p. 19; Derrida 1992, p. 78.
80. Derrida 1995, p. 44.
81. Ibid., p. 45.
82. Ibid., p. 68.
83. Ibid., p. 67.
84. Ibid., p. 78.
85. Ibid., p. 84.
86. Ibid., p. 87.
87. Levinas 1989, p. 43.
88. Levinas 1969, p. 213.
89. Ibid.
90. Jacques Derrida, "Marx & Sons," in Sprinker 1999, p. 248.
91. Ibid., p. 249.
92. Ibid., p. 253.
93. Ibid., p. 242.
94. Ibid., p. 249.
95. Ibid., p. 251.

96. Ibid.
97. Ibid., p. 229.
98. Ibid., p. 257.
99. Sprinker 1999, p. 113.
100. See Derrida, "Marx & Sons," in Sprinker 1999, p. 257.

Chapter 5

1. Goldmann 1977, p. 93. See my discussion of this work (Hoy 1979). Parts of chapter 5 are revised from Hoy 1994b.
2. Marx and Engels 1959, p. 247.
3. Cited in Michel Foucault, "What Is an Author?" in Foucault 1984, p. 101.
4. Eagleton 1990, p. 387.
5. Ibid.
6. Eagleton 1991, pp. 40–41.
7. Ibid., p. 41.
8. Zavarzadeh and Morton 1991, p. 196.
9. Ibid., p. 203.
10. Ibid., p. 193.
11. Ibid., p. 194.
12. For the many senses of 'ideology', see chapter 1 of Geuss 1981.
13. Bourdieu 2000, p. 181.
14. Bourdieu 2001, p. 40.
15. Foucault, "Truth and Power," in Foucault 1984, p. 60.
16. See Lukács 1971, p. 228.
17. Zavarzadeh and Morton 1991, p. 127.
18. Laclau and Mouffe 1985.
19. Ernesto Laclau, "Transformations of Advanced Industrial Societies and the Theory of the Subject," in Hanninen and Paldan 1983, p. 43.
20. Ibid.
21. Laclau and Mouffe 1985, p. 111.
22. Laclau, "Transformations," in Hanninen and Paldan 1983, p. 40.
23. Ibid., p. 39.
24. See Derrida 1978, pp. 280, 289, cited by Laclau ("Transformations," p. 41) and by Zavarzadeh and Morton (1991, p. 122).
25. Laclau 1990, p. 92.
26. Ibid.
27. Ibid.
28. Zavarzadeh and Morton 1991, p. 124.
29. Ibid., p. 125.
30. Ibid., p. 126.
31. Ibid., p. 219.

32. For further discussion see my introduction to *Foucault: A Critical Reader* (Hoy 1986).

33. Eagleton 1991, p. 224.

34. Ibid., pp. 197–198.

35. Ibid., p. 217.

36. Ibid., p. 219.

37. Ibid.

38. Zavarzadeh and Morton 1991, p. 227.

39. Ibid., p. 228.

40. Ibid.

41. Ernesto Laclau, "Preface," in Žižek 1989, p. xii.

42. For a discussion of this issue in Horkheimer, see pp. 103–114 of Hoy and McCarthy 1994.

43. Slavoj Žižek, "Postface" to Lukács 2000, p. 175 (emphasis added).

44. Marx, *Capital*: "Sie wissen das nicht, aber sie tun es" (cited on p. 28 of Žižek 1989).

45. Žižek 1989, p. 29.

46. Ibid., p. 47.

47. Žižek 1999, p. 60.

48. Žižek 1989, p. 45.

49. Ibid.

50. Ibid., p. 36.

51. Ibid., p. 34 (emphasis added).

52. Ibid., p. 37.

53. Ibid., p. 49.

54. Žižek, "Da Capo senza Fine," in Butler et al. 2000, p. 228.

55. Ibid.

56. Žižek 1989, p. 49.

57. Ibid.

58. Ibid., p. 206.

59. Kant 1963, p. 137 (German page A109).

60. Žižek, in Butler et al. 2000, p. 256.

61. Ibid., p. 257.

62. Ibid., p. 256.

63. Ibid.

64. Ibid.

65. See Žižek 1999, p. 64: "One of the fundamental stratagems of ideology is the reference to some self-evidence—'Look, you can see for yourself how things are!' 'Let the facts speak for themselves' is perhaps the arch-statement of ideology—the point being precisely, that facts *never* 'speak for themselves', but are always *made to speak* by a network of discursive devices."

66. Žižek 1989, p. 57.

67. Ibid., p. 166.

68. Butler et al. 2000, p. 243.

69. Ibid., p. 260, n. 25.

70. See my esssay "Foucault and Critical Theory" in Moss 1998.

71. Foucault 1998, pp. 433–458. On p. 440 Foucault remarks: "It is common knowledge that many representatives of the Frankfurt School came to Paris in 1935, seeking refuge, and left very hastily, sickened presumably—some even said as much—but saddened anyhow not to have found more of an echo."

Postscript

1. Derrida 1993, p. 18; Derrida 1992, p. 77.

2. Derrida, "The University without Condition," in Derrida 2002.

3. Ibid., p. 202.

4. Ibid., p. 204 (emphasis added).

5. Ibid.

6. Brown 1995, p. 49.

7. See Heidegger 1962, §62, p. 355.

Bibliography

Bensaïd, Daniel. 2001. *Résistances: Essai de taupologie générale.* Librairie Arthème Fayard.

Bernasconi, Robert, and David Wood, eds. 1988. *The Provocation of Levinas: Rethinking the Other.* Routledge.

Best, Steven, and Douglas Kellner. 1991. *Postmodern Theory: Critical Interrogations.* Guilford.

Blondel, Eric. 1991. *Nietzsche: The Body and Culture. Philosophy as a Philological Genealogy.* Stanford University Press.

Borges, Jorge Luis. 1964. *Labyrinths.* New Directions.

Bourdieu, Pierre. 1990a. *The Logic of Practice.* Stanford University Press.

Bourdieu, Pierre. 1990b. *In Other Words: Essays Towards a Reflexive Sociology.* Stanford University Press.

Bourdieu, Pierre. 1991. *Language and Symbolic Power,* ed. J. Thompson. Harvard University Press.

Bourdieu, Pierre. 1996. *The Rules of Art: Genesis and Structure of the Literary Field.* Stanford University Press.

Bourdieu, Pierre. 2000. *Pascalian Meditations.* Stanford University Press.

Bourdieu, Pierre. 2001. *Masculine Domination.* Stanford University Press.

Bourdieu, Pierre, and Loïc J. D. Wacquant. 1992. *An Invitation to Reflexive Sociology.* University of Chicago Press.

Brandom, Robert B. 2002. *Tales of the Mighty Dead: Historical Essays in the Metaphysics of Internationality.* Harvard University Press.

Brown, Wendy. 1995. *States of Injury: Power and Freedom in Late Modernity.* Princeton University Press.

Burchell, Graham, Colin Gordon, and Peter Miller, eds. 1991. *The Foucault Effect: Studies in Governmentality.* University of Chicago Press.

Butler, Judith. 1997a. *The Psychic Life of Power: Theories in Subjection.* Stanford University Press.

Butler, Judith. 1997b. *Excitable Speech: A Politics of the Performative.* Routledge.

Butler, Judith. 2002a. "What is Critique? An Essay on Foucault's Virtue." In *The Political,* ed. D. Ingram. Blackwell.

Butler, Judith. 2002b. "Bodies and Power, Revisited." *Radical Philosophy* 114: 13–19.

Butler, Judith, Ernesto Laclau, and Slavoj Žižek. 2000. *Contingency, Hegemony, Universality: Contemporary Dialogues on the Left.* Verso.

Calhoun, Craig, Edward LiPuma, and Moishe Postone, eds. 1993. *Bourdieu: Critical Perspectives.* University of Chicago Press.

Cornell, Drucilla, Michel Rosenfeld, and David Gray Carlson, eds. 1992. *Deconstruction and the Possibility of Justice.* Routledge.

Cox, Christoph. 1999. *Nietzsche: Naturalism and Interpretation.* University of California Press.

Deleuze, Gilles. 1977. "Nomad Thought." In *The New Nietzsche,* ed. D. Allison. Dell.

Deleuze, Gilles. 1983. *Nietzsche and Philosophy.* Athlone.

Dennett, Daniel C. 1991. *Consciousness Explained.* Little, Brown.

Derrida, Jacques. 1978. *Writing and Difference.* University of Chicago Press.

Derrida, Jacques. 1979. *Spurs: Nietzsche's Styles.* University of Chicago Press.

Derrida, Jacques. 1992. *The Other Heading: Reflections on Today's Europe.* Indiana University Press.

Derrida, Jacques. 1993. *Aporias.* Stanford University Press.

Derrida, Jacques. 1995. *The Gift of Death.* University of Chicago Press.

Derrida, Jacques. 1998. *Resistances of Psychoanalysis.* Stanford University Press.

Derrida, Jacques. 2002. *Without Alibi.* Stanford University Press.

Descombes, Vincent. 1997. "Nietzsche's French Moment." In *Why We Are Not Nietzscheans,* ed. L. Ferry and A. Renaut. University of Chicago Press.

Dreyfus, Hubert L., and Paul Rabinow. 1983. *Michel Foucault: Beyond Structuralism and Hermeneutics,* second edition. University of Chicago Press.

Eagleton, Terry. 1990. *The Ideology of the Aesthetic.* Blackwell.

Eagleton, Terry. 1991. *Ideology: An Introduction.* Verso.

Ferry, Luc, and Alain Renaut, eds. 1997. *Why We Are Not Nietzscheans.* University of Chicago Press.

Feyerabend, P. K. 1975. *Against Method.* New Left Books.

Foucault, Michel. 1979. *Discipline and Punish: The Birth of the Prison.* Vintage.

Foucault, Michel. 1980a. *Power/Knowledge.* Pantheon.

Foucault, Michel. 1980b. *Herculine Barbin.* Pantheon.

Foucault, Michel. 1984. *The Foucault Reader,* ed. P. Rabinow. Pantheon.

Foucault, Michel. 1988. *The History of Sexuality,* Volume I: *Introduction.* Vintage.

Foucault, Michel. 1990. *The Use of Pleasure.* Vintage.

Foucault, Michel. 1997. *Ethics: Subjectivity and Truth.* New Press.

Foucault, Michel. 1998. *Essential Works of Foucault: Aesthetics, Method, and Epistemology,* ed. J. Faubion. New Press.

Foucault, Michel. 2000. *Power,* ed. J. Faubion. New Press.

Foucault, Michel. 2002a. *"Society Must Be Defended:" Lectures at the Collège de France, 1975–76.* Picador.

Foucault, Michel. 2002b. "What Is Critique?" In *The Political.* Edited by David Ingram. Blackwell.

Gadamer, Hans-Georg. 1989. *Truth and Method,* second edition. Crossroad.

Geuss, Raymond. 1981. *The Idea of a Critical Theory: Habermas and the Frankfurt School.* Cambridge University Press.

Goldberg, David Theo. 1993. *Racist Culture: Philosophy and the Politics of Meaning.* Blackwell.

Goldmann, Lucien. 1977. *Lukács and Heidegger: Towards a New Philosophy.* Routledge and Kegan Paul.

Grosz, Elizabeth. 1994. *Volatile Bodies: Toward a Corporeal Feminism.* Indiana University Press.

Gutting, Gary. 1989. *Michel Foucault's Archaeology of Scientific Reason.* Cambridge University Press.

Habermas, Jürgen. 1987. *The Philosophical Discourse of Modernity: Twelve Lectures.* MIT Press.

Hacking, Ian. 2002. *Historical Ontology.* Harvard University Press.

Hanninen, Sakari, and Leena Paldan, eds. 1983. *Rethinking Ideology: A Marxist Debate.* Argument-Verlag.

Heidegger, Martin. 1962. *Being and Time.* Harper & Row.

Hoy, David Couzens. 1979. "Critical Discussion: Lucien Goldmann, *Lukács and Heidegger: Towards a New Philosophy.*" *Philosophy and Literature* 3: 107–118.

Hoy, David Couzens. 1981. "Philosophy as Rigorous Philology? Nietzsche and Poststructuralism." *New York Literary Forum* 8/9: 171–185.

Hoy, David Couzens, ed. 1986. *Foucault: A Critical Reader.* Blackwell.

Hoy, David Couzens. 1994a. "Nietzsche, Hume, and the Genealogical Method." In *Nietsche, Genealogy, Morality,* ed. R. Schacht. University of California Press.

Hoy, David Couzens. 1994b. "Deconstructing 'Ideology,' " *Philosophy and Literature* 18: 1–17

Hoy, David Couzens. 1998a. "Solidarité ou universalité?" In *La modernité en question,* ed. F. Gaillard, J. Poulain, and R. Schusterman. Cerf.

Hoy, David Couzens, and Thomas McCarthy. 1994. *Critical Theory.* Blackwell.

Ingram, David, ed. 2002. *The Political.* Blackwell.

Jameson, Fredric. 1984. "Postmodernism, or, the Cultural Logic of Late Capitalism." *New Left Review* 146: 53–92.

Kant, Immanuel. 1963. *Critique of Pure Reason.* Macmillan.

Kofman, Sarah. 1993. *Nietzsche and Metaphor.* Stanford University Press.

Laclau, Ernesto. 1990. *New Reflections on the Revolution of Our Time.* Verso.

Laclau, Ernesto, and Chantal Mouffe. 1985. *Hegemony and Socialist Strategy*. Verso.

Levinas, Emmanuel. 1969. *Totality and Infinity: An Essay on Exteriority*. Duquesne University Press.

Levinas, Emmanuel. 1987. *Time and the Other*. Duquesne University Press.

Levinas, Emmanuel. 1989. *The Levinas Reader*, ed. S. Hand. Blackwell.

Levinas, Emmanuel. 1993. *Outside the Subject*. Stanford University Press.

Lukács, Georg. 1971. *History and Class Consciousness: Studies in Marxist Dialectics*. MIT Press.

Lukács, Georg. 2000. *A Defence of History and Class Consciousness: Tailism and the Dialectic*. Verso.

Marx, Karl, and Friedrich Engels. 1959. *Basic Writings on Politics and Philosophy.*, ed. L. Feuer. Doubleday.

McWhorter, Ladelle. 1999. *Bodies and Pleasures: Foucault and the Politics of Sexual Normalization*. Indiana University Press.

Merleau-Ponty, Maurice. 1962. *The Phenomenology of Perception*. Routledge.

Merleau-Ponty, Maurice. 1964. *Signs*. Northwestern University Press.

Montefiore, Alan, ed. 1983. *Philosophy in France Today*. Cambridge University Press.

Moss, Jeremy, ed. 1998. *The Later Foucault*. Sage.

Murphy, Tim. 2001. *Nietzsche, Metaphor, Religion*. State University of New York Press.

Nietzsche, Friedrich. 1959. *The Portable Nietzsche*. Penguin.

Nietzsche, Friedrich. 1966. *Thus Spoke Zarathustra*. Penguin.

Nietzsche, Friedrich. 1968a. *Basic Writings of Nietzsche*. Modern Library.

Nietzsche, Friedrich. 1968b. *The Will to Power*. Vintage.

Nietzsche, Friedrich. 1974. *The Gay Science*. Vintage.

Nussbaum, Martha, and Juha Shivola, eds. 2002. *The Sleep of Reason: Erotic Experience and Sexual Ethics in Ancient Greece and Rome*. University of Chicago Press.

Proust, Françoise. 1997. *De la résistance*. Cerf.

Rabaté, Jean-Michel, and Michael Wetzel, eds. 1992. *L'éthique du don: Jacques Derrida and la pensée du don.* Transition.

Rorty, Richard. 1979. *Philosophy and the Mirror of Nature.* Princeton University Press.

Scarry, Elaine. 1985. *The Body in Pain: The Making and Unmaking of the World.* Oxford University Press.

Schatzki, Theodore Richard. 1987. "Overdue Analysis of Bourdieu's Theory of Practice." *Inquiry* 30: 113–135.

Schrift, Alan D. 1995. *Nietzsche's French Legacy: A Genealogy of Poststructuralism.* Routledge.

Sprinker, Michael, ed. 1999. *Ghostly Demarcations: A Symposium on Jacques Derrida's "Specters of Marx."* Verso.

Walzer, Michael. 1986. "The Politics of Michel Foucault." In *Foucault,* ed. D. Hoy. Blackwell.

West, Cornel. 1999. *The Cornel West Reader.* Basic Civitas Books.

Williams, Bernard. 2002. *Truth and Truthfulness: An Essay in Genealogy.* Princeton University Press.

Zavarzadeh, Mas'ud, and Donald Morton. 1991. *Theory, (Post)Modernity, Opposition.* Maisonneuve.

Žižek, Slavoj. 1989. *The Sublime Object of Ideology.* Verso.

Žižek, Slavoj. 1999. *The Žižek Reader,* ed. E. Wright and E. Wright. Blackwell.

Index

Abstraction, 4, 56
Academic fields, 141, 144
Academy, bourgeois, 147
Acceptance, 24, 28
Acculturation, 168
Action
  impenetrability of, 52
  political, 5, 6, 11, 118, 147, 164, 193, 208
  practical, 187, 237
Aesthetic resistance, 129, 130
Affect, 48, 51
Affirmation, 24–28, 189
African-Americans, 146, 147
Agency, 3, 30, 52, 65, 82, 98, 105, 106, 114, 116, 117, 119, 120, 147, 164, 209
Agents, 13, 15, 20, 59, 103, 108, 113, 116, 118, 120, 127, 128, 133, 162–165, 196–199, 210, 211, 234
Algeria, 145
Alienation, 192
Alterity, 150, 156, 172, 179
Althusser, Louis, 115
Anarchism, 20, 209, 231–233
Animals, 175, 176, 223, 235
Anthropology, 67, 140, 174
Anti-Semitism, 145

Anxiety, 140, 172, 175, 222, 223
Apartheid, 145
Aphorism, 22, 35
Aphoristic style, 14, 30, 36
Aphrodisia, 71
Apocalypse, 188, 189
Arbitrariness, 15, 66, 72, 119, 127, 130, 136, 143, 238
Aristotle, 4, 234
Asceticism, 26, 66
Asia, 6
Assujettissement, 88
Atomic bomb, 79
Augenblick, 172
Augustine, 71
Austin, J. L., 15, 124
Authenticity, 168, 175, 176, 183
Authority, 96, 112, 116, 126, 127, 228
Authorization, 143
Autonomy, 3, 13, 15, 19, 24, 73, 94, 99, 155, 165

Background practices, 13, 116–118, 127
Bartky, Sandra Lee, 135
Bartleby, 9, 10
Base-superstructure explanations, 195, 197, 202

Bataille, Georges, 89
Beautiful existence, 88
Beautiful soul, 219, 220
Beckett, Samuel, 192
Becoming, 26, 51
Being, 37–41
Being-toward-death, 168–172, 175,
    176, 183, 188
Benjamin, Walter, 188
Bensaïd, Daniel, 9, 10
Bentham, Jeremy, 65, 66
Best, Steven, 67
Binary oppositions, 122, 166
Biological individual, 132
Biology, 107
Bio-politics, 74
Blanchot, Maurice, 89
Blondel, Eric, 14, 49–53
Bodily difference, 142
Bodily hexis, 109
Bodily invariant, 57–64, 131, 132
Body, 12–14, 19–21, 26, 31, 46–53,
    56–63, 66, 67, 70, 77–80, 89,
    101–105, 108, 109, 114, 115,
    123, 127, 131, 132, 136, 140, 142,
    151–158, 162, 165, 196, 200, 219,
    225, 231
  biological, 20, 49–51, 58, 63, 101,
    107, 108, 132, 165
  docile, 25, 63
  generic, 72, 76, 78
  individual, 72, 76–78
  lived, 61–63, 68, 156
  mechanical, 67
  natural, 63, 66–69
  organic, 67
  pluralist understanding of, 14, 21,
    26, 48–53, 72
  unhistorical conception of, 60, 67,
    68
Bourdieu, Pierre, 9, 13, 15, 16, 20,
    25, 57, 77, 101–149, 163, 186, 196,
    219, 221, 231, 239

Brown, Wendy, 3, 228
Butler, Judith, 10, 15–18, 93–100,
    127, 219, 222

Capital, 113
Capitalism, 10, 75, 205
Cartesianism, 20, 154
Cartesian theater, 54
Categorical imperative, 19
Chance, 26
Chaos, 39
Choice, 8, 48, 104, 117–120, 129, 172,
    184, 235, 237
  radical, 118, 119
  rational, 118, 119
Circularity, 32, 33
Class, 7, 84, 120, 121, 139, 144, 189,
    190, 195, 196, 198, 201, 205, 215,
    216
Classless society, 7, 195, 198, 201,
    207
Class struggle, 7, 189, 195, 198, 201,
    205
Clearing, 129
Cogito, 19, 31, 102, 104, 140, 163
  Cartesian, 31, 102, 140, 163
  tacit, 104
Cognition, 152, 153, 167
Common sense, 200
Communication, 49, 206, 207
Communitarianism, 31
Community, 30, 223–225
Complexity, 55, 56
Compliance, 3, 25, 83, 136, 139
Conceptual scheme, 36
Concreteness, 4, 5, 56, 70, 71, 96,
    118, 179, 237
Conformism, 3, 25, 100, 136, 165,
    168, 172
Conscience, 26, 27, 111, 129, 179,
    180, 181, 229, 230, 238
  bad, 26, 27, 111, 180
  good, 179–181, 229, 230, 238

Consciousness, 2, 3, 7, 12–16, 20, 21,
    26, 27, 47–54, 57, 62, 73, 80, 88, 89,
    94, 102, 103, 106, 123, 124, 147,
    151, 153, 159, 162, 191, 192, 195–
    201, 204, 205, 209, 210, 214–219,
    222–225
  false, 16, 83, 195–198, 200–203,
    207, 210, 214, 216–221, 225
  history of, 222
  stream of, 52, 54
  true, 195, 196, 204, 205, 210
  unhappy, 26
  unity of, 20, 48, 53
Consensus, 179, 224, 237
Constraints, 1, 3, 4, 9, 15, 65, 82, 88,
    94, 97, 100, 117, 137, 143
Construction, 9, 44, 45, 47, 48, 58,
    59, 63–68, 76, 106, 122, 144, 167,
    203
Context, 3, 22, 29, 32, 44, 58, 92, 118,
    128, 132, 166, 227, 238, 239
Continental philosophy, 16, 17,
    139–141, 145, 148, 226
Contradictions, 194
Co-optation, 2, 30, 83–87, 126, 135,
    143, 144, 207, 212
Corporeal intentionality, 157
Counterculture, 24, 29
Critical theory, 16, 197, 204, 215,
    225
Criticism, 64, 123, 132, 197, 229
  constructive, 229
  deconstructive, 194, 197
Critique, 2, 6, 14, 23, 32, 33, 38, 41,
    61, 64, 87–92, 95, 99, 127, 147,
    148, 178–181, 190, 201, 212,
    227–229, 232, 233, 237
Culler, Jonathan, 193, 194, 208
Cultural studies, 140, 145
Culture, 13, 14, 25, 29, 50, 51, 57, 58,
    60–63, 71, 103, 118, 122, 165–170,
    178, 194, 205
Cynicism, 143, 148, 217, 223, 229

Darwinism, 80
Dasein, 140, 158–160, 168–172,
    176
Davidson, Donald, 158
Death, 8, 10, 16, 21, 73, 77–80, 104,
    113, 132, 133, 140, 156, 161–184,
    222, 223, 232, 235–237
De Beauvoir, Simone, 140
Debt, 24, 25
Deconstruction, 15, 17, 35, 36, 44,
    45, 73, 80, 129–131, 164, 167,
    175–181, 186–198, 204–213,
    226–230, 235, 237
De dicto, 68, 69
Deleuze, Gilles, 2, 9, 10, 14, 20–32,
    38, 73, 225, 228
Demise, 170, 171, 175–177, 236
Democracy, 147, 148, 201
Dennett, Daniel, 53, 54
De re, 68, 69
Derrida, Jacques, 2, 8, 10, 13, 14, 16,
    20, 25, 31–38, 43, 44, 123–131, 145,
    149, 150, 163–168, 173–195,
    200–202, 205–209, 225–230,
    234–237
Désassujettissement, 89, 92
Descartes, René, 151
Descombes, Vincent, 24
Desire, 29, 71, 97, 98, 133, 199, 210
Destruction, 44, 59, 60, 63
Desubjectivation, 14, 88, 89, 92, 97,
    98
Desubjugation, 88, 96
Determinism, 81, 104, 115, 121–123,
    199
Development, 210, 211
Dialectics, 21, 27, 29, 73, 80, 150,
    155, 158, 220
Différance, 129, 150, 174, 192
Difference, 150, 153, 154, 164, 179,
    202, 203
Disciplinary regime, 65, 136
Discontinuity, 35, 98, 211

Discourse, 69, 106, 147, 187, 196–212
   biological, 78–80, 146
   democratic, 207
   medicalizing, 79
Disease, 77, 78, 140
Dispositions, 9, 107, 109, 115, 123,
   137, 144
Disseminated system, 45, 46
Dissymmetry, 160
Dogmatism, 40, 46, 178, 227, 228,
   232, 234
Domination, 2–5, 14, 15, 26, 27, 53,
   38, 39, 66, 70, 82, 83, 88, 89, 92, 93,
   122, 131, 135–138, 143, 147, 148,
   159, 160, 199, 206, 213, 217, 229,
   231, 232, 239
Dostoevsky, Fyodor, 161
Dreyfus, Hubert L., 60, 63
Durkheim, Émile, 133
Duty, 179, 181, 227
Dying, 177–179, 181, 235
Dystopia, 188

Eagleton, Terry, 193, 207–211
Ecology movement, 84
Economics, 86, 205
Effective resistance, 7, 17, 18, 41, 63,
   72, 81, 83, 118, 135, 137, 138, 147,
   178, 191, 212
Ego, 47, 102, 155, 173, 174
Emancipation, 2, 131, 135, 137, 193,
   199, 231, 224, 234, 238
Emancipatory resistance, 83, 138,
   182
Embodiment, 13–15, 48, 56, 58, 59,
   62, 63, 66, 70, 78, 80, 101, 102, 105,
   108, 109, 115, 127, 136, 140, 152,
   165, 219
End of inquiry, 50, 56
Engels, Friedrich, 191
Epistemic break, 98
Epistemological, 19, 32, 43, 138,
   154, 198, 205, 216, 218

Epistemology, 32, 45
Equality, 147
Eschatology, 189
Essence, 58, 71, 164, 203, 204
Essentialism, 67, 144
Ethical affirmation, 34
Ethical principles, 19, 163, 164, 179,
   180
Ethical relation to other, 152–154
Ethical resistance, 8, 10, 15, 16, 129,
   155, 156, 159, 160, 168, 181, 182,
   184
Ethical substance, 69–71, 219
Ethical, the, 130, 149, 163, 165, 166,
   185
Ethical turn, 16, 163, 164, 182, 185
Ethics, 15, 30, 69, 144, 149, 150–162,
   171, 175, 178–184, 219, 230, 231,
   235, 236
   genealogy of, 63, 69, 70, 88
   history of, 70, 71, 98, 150, 162
Ethnic differences, 79
Ethnography, 63
Ethos, 8, 69, 70, 162
Eurocentrism, 174, 175
Europe, 145, 174, 175, 179, 214
Evaluation, 23
Everydayness, 168, 169
Evolutionary model, 71
Existential analysis, 174, 176
Existentialism, 140
Experience, 47, 48, 62, 63, 103, 104,
   107, 119, 132, 167, 170, 174, 187,
   208, 221

Face, 16, 150–156, 159–163, 174,
   182–187, 232
Falling, 168, 175
Fanon, Franz, 145
Fantasy, 218–224
Faulkner, William, 145
Fetish, 221
Feyerabend, Paul, 40

Fiction, 27, 28, 53
Field, 15, 101–104, 109–119, 124,
    136, 139, 141, 143, 144, 186, 239
Finitude, 55, 169, 171, 172, 177, 184,
    222, 223, 234–236
First philosophy, 149, 162, 164, 182,
    184, 230, 235
Fleeing, 168, 169
Flesh, 71
Forces, active and reactive, 26, 27, 53
Foreclosure, 97, 98
Foucault, Michel, 2, 7–20, 25, 27,
    31–35, 56–101, 106, 112, 117, 118,
    125, 126, 131, 132, 135–138,
    146–150, 155, 162–164, 186,
    191–197, 200, 206, 207, 219, 225,
    226, 229–234, 238
Foundationalism, 12, 20, 47, 48, 51,
    52, 132, 150, 164, 175, 177–182,
    185, 230, 235
Fragmentation, 53, 209
Frankfurt School, 17, 198, 225
Fraser, Nancy, 67, 93
Freedom, 1–5, 13, 15, 82, 92, 98–100,
    104, 105, 112, 114, 117, 119, 134,
    147, 158, 162, 163, 170–173, 180,
    188, 198–200, 206, 209, 224, 227,
    228, 231, 234, 235, 238, 239
  individual, 163
  originary, 98–100
  radical, 15, 114, 117, 119, 172
  situated, 15, 104, 114, 172
  unconditional, 227, 228
Freud, Sigmund, 29, 174, 178
Freudianism, 21, 29
Functionalism, 121, 122
Future, 8, 120, 147, 148, 161, 188,
    189, 207, 213, 214

Gelassenheit, 39
Gender, 18, 88, 122, 123, 135, 139,
    140, 143
Genealogical method, 4, 14, 23, 24,

26, 29, 36, 39, 42, 51, 63, 59, 60,
    68–70, 81–85, 88, 130, 147, 163,
    229, 230, 233, 237
Genealogy, 2, 3, 14–17, 23–25, 29,
    38, 40, 41, 46, 50, 57, 59, 60, 63, 64,
    69–73, 80, 83, 88, 92, 130, 131, 138,
    146, 179, 226–238
Genocide, 146
Global critique, 193, 194, 195, 199,
    202, 208, 209, 213, 228
Globalization, 6, 10
Goldberg, David Theo, 142
Goldmann, Lucien, 191, 192, 195
Goodness, 158, 159
Governmentality, 14, 74
Governmentalization, 88, 96, 98, 99
Gramsci, Antonio, 200, 201
Granier, Jean, 37–40
Greece, 70, 71, 88, 126
Grosz, Elizabeth, 135, 136
Grund, 52
Guattari, Félix, 21
Guilt, 24, 25, 159, 161

Habermas, Jürgen, 5, 15, 93, 112,
    132–134, 198, 200, 206, 207
Habitus, 9, 15, 25, 101, 105–115,
    118–124, 138, 139, 141, 143, 144,
    186, 200
Halperin, David, 67
Handshake, 151–154
Hatred, 27, 145, 160
Health, 30, 46, 81, 86
Hegel, G. W. F., 19, 21, 26–29,
    70–73, 80, 91, 155, 160, 169, 173,
    183, 193, 214, 219–224
Hegelians, 13, 191–194, 197
Hegemony, 198, 201–207, 212
Heidegger, Martin, 21, 23, 28, 37,
    38, 115, 116, 120, 124, 125, 129,
    132, 140, 149, 153–161, 164–178,
    180–183, 188, 191, 192, 223, 231,
    234–236

Hermeneutic circle, 32, 45
Hermeneutics, 17, 31–33, 36, 42, 44, 51, 237
Historical approaches, 14, 15, 57–71, 85, 91, 92, 96, 98, 109, 113, 131, 133–135, 138, 146, 150, 162, 166, 174, 178, 183, 194, 197, 200, 215, 216, 228, 237, 238
Historicism, methodological, 134, 135
History
  critical, 64, 70
  effective, 57, 58, 64, 92
  end of, 5, 188
  universal, 188, 195, 207
Hobbes, Thomas, 155
Homer, 126
Homme-espèce, 73
Hope, 3, 10, 11, 148, 188, 195
Horkheimer, Max, 215
Humanism, 67, 146, 223, 224
Humanities, 148, 228
Human nature, 30
Hume, David, 2, 103, 142
Hunger, 140, 158, 159, 179, 193, 208
Husserl, Edmund, 19, 21, 29, 40, 109, 115, 151

Idealism, 28, 44, 105, 172,
Identity, 3, 4, 56, 95, 108, 119, 156, 165, 168, 180, 201, 203, 209, 211
Ideologiekritik, 16
Ideology, 7, 16, 80, 146, 190–205, 208, 209, 214, 216–225
Ideology-critique, 195–199, 212, 218, 223, 224
Ignorance, 5, 115
Illusion, 218, 223, 224
Immortality, 223
Incommensurability, 35–37
Individuality, 148
Individualization, 65, 165, 170
Innovation, 56

Institution, 7, 8, 64, 65, 74, 147, 173, 233
Insubordination, 96
Integrity, 20, 165, 169, 172
Intellectual climate, 37, 38
Intellectualist fallacy, 196
Intelligibility, 3, 20, 35, 44, 46, 68, 74, 108, 117, 127, 139, 143, 232
Intention, 220
Intentionality, 102, 106, 129, 157
Intercorporeality, 153
Interests
  objective, 209, 210
  real, 199, 200, 209–211, 217
Interpellation, 97, 98
Interpretandum, 33
Interpretans, 33
Interpretation, 13, 14, 20–23, 31–34, 37–56, 193, 221, 227
  conservative dimension of, 56
  death of, 34
  first-order, 39, 40, 46
  higher-order, 39, 40, 46
  life of, 34, 46
  primacy of, 33, 34
  and text, 42
Interpretations, multiple, 46, 53, 54
Intersubjectivity, 105, 149, 150, 152, 174
Intertextuality, 37, 45
Irony, 79, 141, 193, 208

Jameson, Fredric, 9, 188
Jemeinigkeit, 153, 154, 173, 174
Juridical regime, 65
Justice, 4, 39, 58, 129–131, 159, 160, 186, 187, 189, 206, 227
Justification, 130, 133

Kafka, Franz, 30
Kant, Immanuel, 4–6, 19, 21, 28, 90, 95, 103, 104, 128, 132, 142, 147, 159, 184, 186, 221, 222

Kellner, Douglas, 67
Kierkegaard, Søren, 180, 181
Kingdom of Ends, 5
Knowledge, 31, 90, 91, 104, 108,
    115, 121, 133, 137, 138, 152, 153,
    157, 187, 207, 217–220, 227, 229,
    233, 234
  absolute, 91, 103, 134
  empirical, 90, 91
  practical, 4, 108, 234
  tacit, 104
Kofman, Sarah, 14, 32, 39, 40, 42,
    44, 231
Kojève, Alexandre, 22, 27
Kuhn, Thomas, 35, 40

Lacan, Jacques, 218, 224
Laclau, Ernesto, 10, 16–18, 129, 197,
    198, 200–211, 219, 222, 224, 232,
    233
Language, 15, 45, 103, 104, 123–127,
    131, 157–159, 163, 166, 175, 176,
    192, 196, 203–207, 212, 221
Law, 85, 87, 130, 160, 180, 186
Laws, 57, 58, 205
Legal right, 160
Letting Being be, 39
Levinas, Emmanuel, 8, 16, 20, 129,
    140, 149–187, 230–232, 235, 236
Lévi-Strauss, Claude, 115
Liberalism, bourgeois, 201
Liberating effect, 26
Liberation, 26, 146
Lies, 28
Life, 8, 39, 40, 53, 66, 73, 76–81,
    94–96, 104, 105, 169–172, 176, 192
  generic, 80
  prolonging, 77, 78
  promoting, 80
Limit experience, 90, 91
Limit situations, 8
Linguistic turn, 164
Love, 154, 170

Lukács, Georg, 191, 192, 196–198,
    214–216, 220, 221, 223
Lukes, Steven, 198, 200
Lyotard, Jean François, 225

Marxism, 21, 23, 29, 146, 186–190,
    193, 202–209, 212, 214, 219, 221,
    224, 228
Marx, Karl, 29, 75, 101, 187–194,
    197, 201, 217, 224
Masochism, 140
Master, 27, 55, 73
Master-slave dialectic, 22, 27, 73,
    150, 155, 158
Materiality, 64, 77, 78, 80, 212
McCarthy, Thomas, 12
McWhorter, Ladelle, 67
Meaning, 33, 36, 42, 48, 53, 55, 203,
    204
Medicine, 7, 72, 77, 85, 170
Melville, Herman, 9, 10
Merleau-Ponty, Maurice, 15, 60–62,
    101–106, 109, 114, 115, 132, 140,
    141, 149–152, 156, 157, 219
Messianicity, 186–190, 227
Meta-narrative, 207
Metaphysics, 32, 41, 185, 187, 201
Middle East, 6
Mill, John Stuart, 142
Mineness, 153, 173
Misrecognition, 25, 134, 141, 179,
    202–204, 217, 223
Misrepresentation, 216
Mode d'assujettissement, 70, 88
Mode of subjectivation, 70
Močnik, Rastko, 190
Monism, 232
Mortality, 77, 161, 169, 174,
    180–184, 222, 223, 232, 236
Morton, Donald, 193–197, 201, 205,
    206, 212, 213
Mouffe, Chantal, 16, 197–209, 224
Mourning, 174

Mozart, Wolfgang Amadeus, 43
Multiplicity, 20, 21, 25–27, 31, 38,
    41, 46, 53, 55, 76, 87
Mystery, 183, 222
Mystification, 210

Nationalism, 145
Naturalization, 25, 58, 60, 63, 66–72,
    109, 194, 238
Natural-kind terms, 58, 71
Needs, 55
Negation, 25
Neutrality, 88
Nicholas of Cusa, 115
Nietzsche, Friedrich, 1–3, 6, 13, 14,
    19–60, 64, 66, 70, 72, 89, 91, 94,
    101, 102, 116, 129, 214, 229–231,
    234, 238
Nihilism, 34, 163, 179, 231, 232
Nomadism, 29, 30
Normalization, 27, 63–69, 81, 83,
    93, 232
Normative engagement, 5, 13, 16,
    58, 65, 69, 89, 92, 118, 129, 144,
    164, 171, 179, 200, 236
Nothingness, 222

Objectivity, 106, 117, 118, 137, 190,
    215, 222
Ontology, 21, 91, 171, 185, 186, 189,
    223, 236
Onto-theology, 174, 175
Oppression, 2, 3, 92, 144, 195, 197,
    198, 207, 208, 213, 232
Organic individual, 210, 211
Organizing significances, 129
Otherness, 142, 156, 161, 164, 189
Oxfam, 208

Pain, 61, 62, 77, 78
Panopticon, 65, 66
Paracelsus, 35
Parks, Rosa, 127

Partial perspective, 129, 203, 215,
    216
Partial representation, 216
Part-whole relation, 32, 45, 147, 154
Pascal, Blaise, 160
Patriarchy, 135, 136
Penser autrement, 93
Perception, 42, 101, 102, 107, 108,
    113, 115, 118, 120, 121, 139, 141,
    143, 150, 151, 157, 198–200, 210
Performativity, 124, 127, 129, 130
Perishing, 170, 171, 175–178, 235
Perpetual decodification, 30
Perspective, 20, 38–44, 49, 50, 56,
    91, 103, 215, 216, 223
Perspectivism, 38, 42, 44, 49, 91, 117
Pessimism, 136, 188, 193
Phenomenological introspection, 57
Phenomenology, 15, 17, 57, 60, 89,
    162
Philology, 33–44
Philosophical ground, 52
Phronesis, 4, 44, 132, 234, 237, 238
Physical disability, 140
Physical resistance, 160
Plasticity, 26, 56, 106, 115, 123, 138
Plato, 4, 5, 157
Platonic tradition, 23, 31
Play of difference, 16, 25, 26, 42, 46,
    129, 202–204, 233, 234
Pleasure, 67, 71, 86
Pluralism, 13–15, 21, 26, 31, 40, 41,
    48–55, 72, 143, 150, 155, 156, 197,
    201, 206, 213, 230–234
Political economy, 75, 194
Political interventions, 193, 205,
    208, 209
Political mythology, 109, 122
Political resistance, 6, 8, 9, 129, 208,
    209
Political theory, 1, 64, 75, 228
Politics, 130, 144, 164, 165, 175, 193,
    194, 207

Popular illegalities, 84, 85
Population, 7, 8, 75, 76, 78, 80
Possibilities, 10, 15, 55, 56, 66, 82,
    92, 93, 104, 117, 120, 122, 136, 139,
    152, 163, 166, 229–
    234, 238
Possibility of impossibility, 175
Post-critique, 17, 18, 53–56, 93–100,
    139–148, 185–190, 227, 228, 230
Post-historical speculations, 195
Post-ideological age, 219
Postmodernism, 17, 134, 147, 189,
    190
Poststructuralism, 4–22, 30–35, 38,
    41, 45, 46, 49, 145–150, 163, 179,
    182, 189–196, 200,
    201, 207–211, 214, 225, 226
Power, 3–11, 14–16, 25–29, 53, 60,
    64–66, 72, 78, 74, 81, 82, 85, 87,
    92–100, 155, 160, 163, 182–186,
    198, 206, 207, 214, 232
  bio-, 7, 14, 15, 60, 61, 63, 72–81, 86,
    94, 98, 146
  biological, 78–80, 146
  democratic, 207
  disciplinary, 7, 9, 14, 15, 63, 66, 67,
    72–78, 81, 94
  invisible, 15, 137
  medicalizing, 79
  psychic dimension of, 95, 98
  of sovereign, 73–75
  technologies of, 74, 80, 81
  will to, 14, 26, 29, 38, 41, 46, 48,
    51–55, 129
Powerlessness, 8, 10, 16
Power-over, 78, 82
Power-to, 78, 82
Practical sense, 15, 115
Practice, 25, 96, 115, 119, 127, 128,
    202, 212, 219, 231, 233
Pragmatism, 32, 147, 148, 212, 213,
    237
Praxis, 187, 189

Principles, abstract, 4, 5, 11, 12, 15,
    19, 64, 70, 83, 88, 92, 132, 134, 138,
    163–165, 179, 180, 235
Prison, 65, 66, 84, 225
Progress, 8, 146, 188, 189, 195, 207,
    213, 214
Proletariat, 198, 215
Proliferation, 15, 40, 41, 46, 231–234
Proust, Françoise, 10
Proust, Marcel, 109
Psyche, 95
Psychoanalysis, 21, 29, 121
Psychoanalytic theory, 29, 214, 215,
    220
Psychology, moral, 19, 168, 180, 182
Punishment, 64, 66
Purpose, 147

Quotation marks, 36, 43

Rabinow, Paul, 60, 63, 90
Race, 18, 139–148, 201
Racism, 72, 78–80, 127, 139,
    142–146, 180, 201
Radicalism, 143, 193
Rationalist approach, 5, 11, 13
Rationality, 30, 60, 61, 134, 237
Rawls, John, 5, 206
Reality, 10, 16, 27, 28, 41, 42, 52,
    66–71, 76–82, 112, 114, 122, 125,
    128, 146, 166, 167, 185, 192, 193,
    212, 214, 217–223
Reason, 134, 137, 217, 229
Reasons, 238
Recodification, 29–31
Reductionism, 20, 49, 50
Reflected intractability, 94, 96
Reform, 201, 205
Reformism, 189, 193
Refusal, 9, 11
Regency council, 53
Regulative ideal, 186, 187
Reigning collectivity, 53

Relations of production, 194, 213
Relativism, 33, 34, 39, 40, 117, 133,
    143, 179, 216, 234
Religion, 174, 181, 187
Repetition, 128
Representationalism, 16, 218
Repression, 45, 87, 148
Responsibility, 24, 25, 28, 30, 65, 79,
    129, 153, 154, 158–164, 171,
    178–184, 189, 230–232, 238, 255
Ressentiment, 2, 3, 23, 26, 27, 51
Revolution, 7, 30, 188–190, 200, 209,
    210
Rhetoric, 7, 125, 126, 146, 147
Rhetorical strategies, 138
Rhetoricization of the social, 205
Rights, 81
Rilke, Rainer Maria, 167, 169, 171,
    236
Rorty, Richard, 118, 208
Rose, Jacqueline, 95
Ruin, 52
Rules, 62, 63, 88, 110, 115, 129, 130,
    143, 165, 234

Sadism, 140
Sartre, Jean-Paul, 8, 15, 19, 104–106,
    111, 114, 117, 140, 145, 149, 155,
    158, 160, 166–173, 220
Saussure, Ferdinand de, 202
Schizophrenia, 209
Schizophrenic laughter, 30
Scholastic fallacy, 196
Schutz, A., 109
Science, 35–41, 134, 146
Searle, John, 177
Second nature, 107
Security, 75
Se déprendre de soi-même, 90
Seduction, 140
Self, 19, 20, 50–53, 63, 89, 94, 96, 99,
    150–155, 158–161, 164, 173, 174,
    179, 180, 211, 214, 224
  Kantian, 20, 89, 102

noumenal, 19
  unity of, 52, 53
Self-awareness, 150, 151, 154, 174,
    222, 223
Self-consciousness, 2, 3, 12, 13, 115,
    160, 224
Self-critical resistance, 191, 238–
    239
Self-critique, 228, 229
Self-transparency, 13, 224
Self-understanding, 50, 68, 70, 71,
    88, 91, 94, 95, 134, 137, 138, 154,
    137, 138, 153, 154, 180
Semiotic process, 209
Senses, 157
Seriousness, 22, 30
Sexuality, 70, 71, 84, 86, 98, 108
Sin, 27
Singularity, 50–54, 55, 62, 63, 86,
    132, 179–181
Sittlichkeit, 70
Situatedness, 20, 59–62, 131, 142,
    215, 232, 234
Skepticism, 44, 134, 137, 164, 179,
    193, 195, 200, 207, 208, 233, 236
Skill, 102, 111, 113, 118, 127
Slave morality, 41
Slaves, 27, 28, 42, 73
Sloterdijk, Peter, 217
Slovene School, 224
Social change, 6, 7, 9, 11, 63, 114,
    120, 121, 123, 134, 147, 148, 179,
    194, 195, 197, 201, 205, 208, 211,
    215, 216, 228
Social construction, 9, 47, 48, 58, 59,
    63, 65, 67, 68, 76, 106, 122, 144,
    167, 203
Social critique, 114, 121, 131, 206,
    212
Social dimension, 57, 98, 101, 108,
    137, 183, 185, 202–205, 209, 230
Social ontology, 9, 12–14, 75, 76, 81,
    82, 98, 99, 131, 132, 136, 168, 185,
    186, 231

Social philosophy of communica-
    tion, 206
Social reality, 16, 114,131, 132, 148,
    215, 219, 223, 233
Social science, 148
Social solidarity, 208
Social structure, 1, 3, 5, 16, 47, 108,
    138, 198
Social theory, 1, 2, 7, 11, 18, 146,
    197, 198, 201, 202, 204, 206,
    215–218, 230
Socialism, 79
Sociality, 152–154
Society, 9, 11, 16, 30, 48, 76, 106, 129,
    132, 133, 133, 168, 175, 185, 186,
    200–113, 121, 207, 213, 126, 231,
    234
Socio-analysis, 15, 113, 121–125,
    135–138
Sociology, 101, 118–123, 131–134,
    137, 139, 141
Soul, 47, 86
Sovereignty, 72–76, 81, 88, 146
Soviet Union, 7
Space, 102, 103, 109
Species being, 75
Speculative metaphysics, 163
Speech act theory, 124, 126
Speech situation, ideal, 5, 15
State, 29, 72, 78, 79
Statistics, 74, 76, 77
Stoics, 71, 88
Strangeness of text, 44
Structuralism, 17, 115
Stupidity, 23
Subject, 9, 15, 19, 21, 29, 49, 53, 55,
    88, 89, 94, 97, 98, 115–118, 123,
    128, 159, 172, 192, 196–198, 201,
    202, 206, 209, 211, 214, 219, 220,
    222, 230
    decentering, 47
    dissolution of, 90, 92
    formation of, 9, 65, 88, 94, 95, 147,
        229

intentionality without, 106
    knowing, 165
    neutral, 88
    practical, 165
    single, 52, 53, 237
Subjectification, 88
Subjection, 66, 68, 69, 88, 97
Subjectivity, 15, 29, 47, 51, 52, 57,
    65, 101, 103, 119, 155, 159, 163,
    164, 170, 172, 174, 197, 203, 222,
    223
Subjugation, 88
Submission, 135
Subordination, 97, 98
Suicide, 73, 79, 98

Teleology, 189
Telos, 45, 147
Tel Quel, 209
Temporality 177, 188, 189
Text, 22, 23, 32, 37–39, 42–46, 51, 55,
    124, 194, 206
Thinking otherwise, 93
Third party, 186, 187
Thought, history of, 62, 63
Time, 14, 37, 38, 54, 55, 61, 75, 93,
    109, 119, 171, 177, 188, 189
Torture, 173
Totality, 36, 44, 147, 155, 202–204,
    219, 220
Totalization, 203, 204, 233
Transcendental object, 222
Transcendental philosophy, 132
Transcendental unity of appercep-
    tion, 20, 53, 103, 104
Transposability, 56
Truth, 22, 23, 27, 28, 38, 41, 63, 118,
    133, 134, 137, 147, 129, 130, 184,
    194–197, 204, 211, 214–216, 219,
    223, 228

Uncertainty, 45
Unconditional resistance, 228
Unconscious, historical, 112, 113

Unconsciousness, 29, 49, 95, 106,
     112, 113, 222, 223
Undecidability, 36, 167, 177, 234
Underdetermination, 129
Understanding, 7, 13, 14, 20, 24, 31,
     32, 42, 43, 45, 51, 56, 58, 59, 62, 66,
     94, 98, 109, 111, 117, 185, 213, 217,
     226, 227, 233–235, 238
Unhistorical accounts, 60, 67, 68,
     149, 162–164, 174, 210
United States, 6, 145, 225, 226
Universal, false, 70, 138
Universalities, 112
Universal principles, 4, 5, 11, 12, 15,
     19, 64, 70, 83, 88, 92, 132, 138,
     163–165, 179, 180
Universalism, 4, 5, 11, 12, 15, 19, 20,
     30, 56, 64, 66, 70, 71, 83, 88, 92,
     132–135, 138, 140, 143, 159,
     163–165, 174, 175, 179, 180, 187,
     188, 194, 195, 200, 205, 207
Universality, 4, 5, 62, 63, 112, 179,
     181
Utopia, 3, 121, 147, 160, 188, 189,
     195, 200, 202, 209, 213

Values, 163, 231
Vico, Giambattista, 4
Victorian period, 86
Violence, 33, 121, 130, 155, 156, 160,
     196
Virtue, 95–97, 100
Vision, 156, 157, 159, 172
Voluntarism, 48, 90, 94, 106, 136

Wacquant, Loïc, 135
Walzer, Michael, 11
War, 50, 140, 155, 156
West, Cornel, 146, 147, 148
Will, 54
Williams, Bernard, 23, 105
Winner-loses logic, 9
Woolf, Virginia, 122

Xenophobia, 145

Zarathustra, 47, 50
Zavarzadeh, Mas'ud, 193–197, 201,
     205, 206, 212, 213
Žižek, Slavoj, 10, 16, 17, 18, 214–
     226